Legal Aspects of Globalization

Legal Aspects of Globalization

Conflict of Laws, Internet, Capital Markets and Insolvency in a Global Economy

Edited by
Jürgen Basedow and Toshiyuki Kono

KLUWER LAW INTERNATIONAL
THE HAGUE – LONDON – BOSTON

Published by Kluwer Law International
P.O. Box 85889
2508 CN The Hague, The Netherlands
sales@kli.wkap.nl
http://www.kluwerlaw.com

Sold and Distributed in North, Central and South America by:
Kluwer Law International
657 Massachusetts Avenue
Cambridge, MA 02139, USA

Sold and Distributed in all other countries by:
Kluwer Law International
Distribution Centre
P.O. Box 322
3300 AH Dordrecht, The Netherlands

Printed on acid-free paper

Cover design and typesetting: The Bears Communications, Amsterdam

ISBN 90 411 1332 0

© 2000 Kluwer Law International

Kluwer Law International incorporates the publishing programmes of Graham & Trotman Ltd,
Kluwer Law and Taxation Publishers and Martinus Nijhoff Publishers

PREFACE

As economic and social developments all over the world are getting increasingly interconnected the social sciences are being confronted with new issues. They are reflected in a growing body of literature in economics, sociology and political science. So far, legal scholarship has taken little notice of the changes brought about by globalisation. These changes may be summarised by the observation that law still is to a large extent rooted in national sovereignty, whereas its object, i. e. social and economic conflicts, is more and more characterised by a transnational dimension.

When the editors of this volume met in Berlin in early 1997 we decided that the scholarly debate on the repercussions of globalisation on law should be fostered by a German-Japanese conference which would not focus on differences in legal culture as reflected by comparative law, but on the common experience of legal developments under the impact of globalisation. This conference took place at the university of Kyushu at Fukuoka on March 28th and 29th, 1999. Scholars from both countries have scrutinised the effect of globalisation on various aspects of the legal framework of international commerce: on the conflict of laws, on the laws of internet and capital markets, and on international insolvencies. The collected papers of that conference are published in this book which is met to inspire further discussions about globalisation and law.

The editors are debted to Dr. Mark Dalton Fenwick, Ms. Sumi Sakata and Ms. Monick T. Paul for the linguistic revision of the papers, to Moritz Bälz and to Frau Ingeborg Stahl for the preparation of the manuscript.

Hamburg and Fukuoka, October 1999

Jürgen Basedow   Toshiyuki Kono

TABLE OF CONTENTS

CONTRIBUTORS

Prof. Dr. Jürgen Basedow, Max-Planck-Institute for Foreign and International Private Law, Hamburg

Dr. Harald Baum, Max-Planck-Institute for Foreign and International Private Law, Hamburg

Prof. Dr. Masato Dogauchi, Tokyo University

Prof. Shinichiro Hayakawa, Tohoku University, Sendai

Associate Prof. Yoshihisa Hayakawa, Rikkyo University, Tokyo

Prof. Dr. Thomas Hoeren, Münster University

Prof. Mitsuru Iwamura, Waseda University, Tokyo

Prof. Hideki Kanda, Tokyo University

Prof. Toshiyuki Kono, Kyushu Fukuoka

Prof. Junichi Matsushita, Gakushuin University, Tokyo

Prof. Yoshiaki Nomura, Ôsaka University

Prof. Dr. Alexander Trunk, Kiel University

Prof. Dr. Peter von Wilmowsky, Hannover University

ABBREVIATIONS

AASCO	Inter American Association of Securities Commissions
ADR	Alternative Dispute Resolution
art.	article
Art.	Article
B.C.	Bankruptcy Code (US)
B.R.	Bankruptcy Reports (US)
BGB	Bürgerliches Gesetzbuch (Germany)
BGBl.	Bundesgesetzblatt (Germany)
BGHZ	Entscheidungen des Bundesgerichtshofes in Zivilsachen (Germany)
BMJ	Bundesministerium der Justiz (Germany)
BVerfG	Bundesverfassungsgericht (Germany)
cf.	confer
Cir.	Circuit
CMR	Convention on the Contract for the International Carriage of Goods by Road
Columbia-VLA J. Int'l L. & Arts	Columbia – VLA Journal of International Law & the Arts (US)
D.L.R.	Dominion Law Reports (Canada)
DJT	Deutscher Juristentag
e.g.	for example
EC	European Community
EEC	European Economic Community
EFT	Electronic Fund Transfer
EGBGB	Einführungsgesetz zum Bürgerlichen Gesetzbuch (Germany)
EGInsO	Einführungsgesetz zur Insolvenzordnung (Germany)
e-money	electronic money
Ent. L. R.	Entertainment Law Reporter (US)
et seq.	et sequens
EU	European Union
EWiR	Europäisches Wirtschaftsrecht (Germany)
FESCO	Forum of European Securities Commissions
fin.	finis
FRC	Financial Reconstruction Commission (Japan)

FSA	Financial Supervisory Agency (Japan)
Fschr.	Festschrift
GDP	General Domestic Product
GesO	Gesamtvollstreckungsordnung (former East Germany)
Hrsg.	Herausgeber (editor)
I.L.M.	International Legal Materials (US)
IA	Insolvency Act (Great Britain)
IC card	integrated circuit card
Id.	idem
InVo	Insolvenz & Vollstreckung (Germany)
IOSCO	International Organisation of Securities Commissions
IP adress	Internet Protocol address
IPrax	Praxis des Internationalen Privat- und Verfahrensrechts (Germany)
ISD	Investment Services Directive
Jb. f. OstR	Jahrbuch für Ostrecht (Germany)
JCP	Juris-Classeur Périodique (France)
KEPCO	Korean Electric Power Company
KG	Kammergericht (Germany)
KO	Konkursordnung (Germany)
KTS	Zeitschrift für Insolvenzrecht (Germany)
LG	Landgericht (Germany)
LSE	London Stock Exchange
MLAT	Mutual Legal Assistance Treaties
MOU	Memorandum of Understanding/Memoranda of Understanding
Nat'l L.J.	National Law Journal (US)
NBL	New Business Law (Japan)
No.	number
NYSE	New York Stock Exchange
NZG	Neue Zeitschrift für Gesellschaftsrecht (Germany)
NZI	Neue Zeitschrift für das Recht der Insolvenz und Sanierung (Germany)
O.J.	Official Journal (of the EC)
OLG	Oberlandesgericht (Germany)
ÖSGRUM	Österreichische Schriftenreihe zum gewerblichen Rechtsschutz, Urheber- und Medienrecht
p.	page
para.	paragraph
paras.	paragraphs
RabelsZ	Rabels Zeitschrift für ausländisches und internationales Privatrecht (Germany)
RIW	Recht der internationalen Wirtschaft (Germany)
SEC	Securities and Exchange Commission (US)

sec.	section
SPC	Special Purpose Company
SPV	Special Purpose Vehicle
subs.	subsection
TRIPs Agreement	Agreement on Trade-Related Aspects of Intellectual Property Rights
U. Chicago Legal Forum	University of Chicago Legal Forum (US)
U. Pittsburgh L. Rev.	University of Pittsburgh Law Review (US)
U.K.	United Kingdom
U.S.	United States (of America)
U.S.C.	United States Code
UN	United Nations
UNCITRAL	United Nations Commission on International Trade Law
UNIDROIT	International Institute for the Unification of Private Law
URL	Uniform Resource Locator
US	United States (of America)
USA	United States of America
Vanderbilt J. of Transnat'l L.	Vanderbilt Journal of Transnational Law (US)
var.	variant
VglO	Vergleichsordnung (Germany)
vol.	volume
vs.	versus
WIPO	World Intellectual Property Organisation
WW I	World War I
WW II	World War II
ZinsO	Zeitschrift für das gesamte Insolvenzrecht (Germany)
ZIP	Zeitschrift für Wirtschaftsrecht (Germany)

THE EFFECTS OF GLOBALIZATION ON PRIVATE INTERNATIONAL LAW

by Jürgen Basedow, Hamburg

Contents

A. Introduction

One of the most conspicuous features in the world-wide development of modern society is what people usually refer to as globalization. Its very name indicates that it must have some bearing on international affairs and their legal framework. In the field of public international law this aspect is very clearly witnessed by the acceleration of world-wide treaty making activities and by the creation of new international tribunals. Despite this there does not seem to be much discussion upon the influence produced by globalization on private international law. This may be due to the fact that scholars in this field are very often seduced by the intellectual niceties of an ever increasing number of cases bearing transnational elements, and by the flood of legislation which usually responds to national problems without taking into account the international dimension. Thus, discussions are devoted more to a refined criticism of legal

1

practice than to an assessment of the long-term developments of the whole discipline.

While private international law, by its very nature, is much more closely connected with the every day problems of the courts we can safely assume that general changes in international relations also have some repercussions on this discipline. The following remarks are meant to be an initial glimpse at the interrelation of globalization and private international law. Part II contains a general description of globalization. In Part III, I will focus on the effect that globalization produces on the role of states and the characteristics of legislation in the field of private law. In Parts IV and V, there will be a general analysis of these observations and I will detail some consequences for the adjudication of private law in transnational cases.

B.   Globalization: Concept and Origins

Globalization has become a very popular word in the social sciences in recent history. It is generally used to describe the fact that an increasing number of social problems have a global dimension today and can no longer be solved by national solutions. For example, John Baylis and Steve Smith, two British political scientists, define globalization as 'the process of increasing inter-connectedness between societies such that events in one part of the world more and more have effect on people and societies far away. A globalised world is one in which political, economic, cultural, and social events become more and more interconnected . . . In each case, the world seems to be "shrinking", and people are increasingly aware of this.'[1]

As described in this definition, globalization refers rather to the economic, cultural, political, and social effects of the process than to its origin and reasons. Those origins are due to technical changes, in particular to the tremendous acceleration and cost reduction of the transport of passengers, goods and data. The construction of the first wide-body passenger aircraft thirty years ago led to considerable overcapacity in civil aviation which paved the way for deregulation and intense competition in that sector. As a consequence the cheapest return tickets on the North Atlantic market today cost only half as much as the lowest airfares that were available twenty years ago. Over the same period of time the per capita income has at least quadrupled in industrialised nations.[2] This means that today, large portions of the population can afford long

---

[1]   *John Baylis/Steve Smith* (eds.) The globalization of world politics, Oxford 1997, p. 7. Various similar definitions are cited at p. 15.

[2]   See for example the data reported in *Gustav Fochler-Hauke* (ed.), Der Fischer Weltalmanach 1976, Frankfurt am Main 1975, p. 279 and *Mario von Baratta* (ed.), Der Fischer Weltalmanach 1996, Frankfurt am Main 1995 col. 955; the per capita
cont. ...

distance travel, and the soaring growth rates of international civil aviation tell us that many people make effectively use of that opportunity.

A similar development is going on in the world-wide transport of goods. This is mainly due to the so called container revolution and to the new organization of shipping and of multimodal transport. Traditionally the handling of cargo depended heavily on human labour for the loading, trimming, stowing and discharge of goods. Today, the use of standardised boxes has considerably reduced labour costs and at the same time contributed to an unprecedented acceleration of terminal operations, which used to account for a very important part of the overall transportation time. Huge vessels carrying thousands of containers on intercontinental shipping routes now call only at major ports around the world where only a few hours are needed for the transshipment of containers, which are then distributed by smaller feeder vessels or by land transport to destinations in that region of the world. These changes have brought about a continuous and extraordinary decrease in the rate index of container shipping.[3] The reduction in freight rates means that traders can reach out for more distant markets without incurring additional transportation costs. In other words, this is tantamount to an extension of the geographical scope of the relevant markets.[4]

Not everyone is aware of the changes reported so far. These changes are creeping along gradually. The situation is quite different with regard to the transport of data. The enormous progress of the communication sector as evidenced by the World Wide Web and the transmission of television and telephone signals by satellite is a striking feature of contemporary society. The transfer, within seconds, of large quantities of electronic data to remote parts of the world has brought about a qualitative change in economic, social, and political thinking. Capital markets have become practically interconnected, and share values can hardly differ in different parts of the world. As news spreads all over the world within moments, distance loses its importance in the formation of political judgements. The violation of human rights or the destruction of the environment are of equal importance, whether they occur in a neighbouring country or at the other end of the world.

This outline of the technological background of globalization should make it clear that the true motive behind these developments is the eternal desire of mankind for mobility. History tells us that mobility has always been one of the driving forces of economic and social development. From this point of view

---

income in the USA has soared from 6600,-- US-$ to 24.750 US-$, that of Switzerland from 5.780,-- US-$ to 36.410,-- US-$.

[3] Cf. *Der Bundesminister für Verkehr* (ed.), Verkehr in Zahlen 1994, 1994, p. 265: the rate index calculated by the Federal Ministry of Transport and fixed at 100 for the year 1985 moved up to 179 in 1993 for tanker shipping, to 125 for trampshipping, but dropped to 74 for general goods and even to 64 for containers.

[4] Cf. *Gerd Aberle*, Transportwirtschaft, München 1996 p. 1 seq.

globalization is much more than a fashionable concept used by social scientists at the end of 20th century, it rather appears to be another decisive step in the irreversible development of human society.

C. The Impact on Governance

For several hundred years the European, and later the world order, has been characterised by the central role of the sovereign nation state.[5] The world is divided into territorial units housing permanent populations each of which is subject to the exclusive and comprehensive rule of an apparatus consisting of various agencies – including those responsible for legislation, adjudication and administration – which is called a sovereign state.[6]

This model of the world order turning upon the nation state as the supreme source of an all-embracing governance is reflected in many legal concepts and rules. Take the very name of public international law and private international law – although the number of non-state organisations which are recognised as subjects of international law is increasing from year to year the discipline is still called inter-*national* law. This name assumes that nations are the only persons addressed by its rules. The confusion is even greater in private international law. Here again, the name suggests that the nation state is the cornerstone of private law. While it is true that nationalism had some impact on the development of private law throughout the 19th century,[7] it appears somehow contradictory that the term private international law in Germany replaced the former denomination 'conflict of laws' (*conflictus legum*) at a time when there was neither a nation state nor a uniform private law in Germany.[8] Another strange consequence of the nation-centred approach to the world legal order is that a small country like the Principality of Liechtenstein which has a population of not more than 30,000 inhabitants and never claimed to be a nation, recently has enacted a statute on

---

[5] Cf. for example *Ian Brownlie,* Principles of Public International Law, 4th ed. Oxford 1990, p. 60 who regards this category as 'the most important'.

[6] Cf. *Brownlie*, supra n. 5, pp. 72–73 and 287 seq.

[7] See *Erik Jayme,* Nation und Staat im Internationalen Privatrecht—Einführung, in: *Erik Jayme/Heinz-Peter Mansel* (eds.), Nation und Staat im Internationalen Privatrecht, Heidelberg 1990, p. 3, 6 with further references, in particular to Mancini.

[8] See *Wilhelm Schaeffner*, Entwicklung des Internationalen Privatrechts, Frankfurt am Main 1841, p. 1 who writes in note 1 that the term private international law needs no justification. Some years later, *Carl Ludwig von Bar,* Theorie und Praxis des Internationalen Privatrechts vol. 1, reprint of the 2nd ed. Hannover 1889, Aalen 1966, p. 1, n. 1 explicitly points out that the basic issues of private international law equally come up when the laws of different 'legal communities' get into conflict.

private international law.[9] The focus on the nation state also emerges within the content of various conflict rules which refer to a national law although the respective state does not have a uniform private law system and perhaps not even the legislative jurisdiction to enact such a uniform private law. In many cases such choice of law rules are highly unsatisfactory and have to be supplemented by additional conflict rules which allow the identification of the relevant sub-system of private law.[10]

It is safe to assume that the structures of governance will change in the course of globalization.[11] The general quest for more mobility and efficiency will put pressure on nation states to open up their borders and allow globalization to expand. But nations will not limit themselves to the simple permission of the free movement of goods, services, information, capital and persons. They still want to maintain a certain grip upon the economic and social conditions in their respective countries. If this is no longer possible at a national level they will therefore try to enact supra-national regulations, either at a global or at a regional level. Many international regulations are conceived as international conventions which require the ratification of the contracting states. Since these conventions may be terminated at a later stage they appear to maintain the formal quality of national law. In reality, however, nations make very little use of the right of termination because the fallback position of a purely national law is no viable alternative. In practice the difference between international conventions and the binding supranational law of regional organisations such as the European Community is less important than it may appear at first sight.

The new world order which is to emerge from globalization will thus be characterised by four groups of regulations:
(1) world regulations which in most cases will be contained in international conventions;

---

[9] Gesetz vom 19.9.1996 über das internationale Privatrecht, Liechtensteinisches Landesgesetz 1996 Nr. 194 vom 28.11.1996, also printed in RabelsZ 61 (1997) 545 with an introductory article by *Alexander Appel*, Reform und Kodifikation des Liechtensteinischen Internationalen Privatrechts: RabelsZ 61 (1967) 510; see also the contributions by *Jürgen Basedow, Monique Jametti Greiner*, and *Axel Flessner* in *Benedikt Marxer/Fritz Reichert-Facilides/Anton K. Schnyder* (eds.), Gegenwartsfragen des Liechtensteinischen Privat- und Wirtschaftsrechts, Tübingen 1998.

[10] See for exemple art. 4 section 3 of the introductory law of the German Civil Code (Einführungsgesetz zum Bürgerlichen Gesetzbuch, EGBGB) and art. 18 of the Italian Act of 31.5.1995 no. 218 for the reform of the Italian Private International Law, suppl. ord. n. 68 of the Gazzetta Ufficiale no. 128 of 32.6.1995, German translation in *Wolfgang Riering* (ed.), IPR-Gesetze in Europa, Bern and München 1997, p. 43.

[11] For the following see *Jan Aart Scholte*, The globalization of world politics, in *Baylis/Smith*, supra n. 1, pp. 13, 21 seq.

(2) regional regulations, such as those of the European Union, which may go
     beyond the model of the international convention and produce a binding
     effect on the member states and their respective populations;
(3) traditional national regulations, and
(4) regulations at a sub-state level, such as the laws of states within a
     federation.

Private international law, or rather the conflict of laws, will have to cope with
these different categories of legislation.

D. Consequences for Private International Law in General

I. New Problems

The new problems created by globalization, and which private international law
will have to accommodate in the future, are twofold. In the first place, the
increased interconnectedness of individuals, societies and economies will
produce a sharp rise in the number of legal conflicts bearing transborder
elements. The share of such transborder operations has grown ever since World
War II. For example, a foreign spouse is involved in one out of ten marriages
celebrated in Germany, requiring the application of foreign marriage laws under
the nationality principle. Due to modern communication and the introduction of
the EURO as a transnational currency we can expect a similar growth of cross-
border operations in other fields such as capital investment, insurance, or consumer transactions. It should be clear that this development may pose serious
problems to the whole judicial system, if it entails a corresponding increase of
the number of cases decided on the basis of foreign law. Neither lawyers nor the
courts are prepared to apply foreign law as speedily and easily as they give
advice on and enforce their national laws; thus the mass application of foreign
law may eventually threaten the functioning of the whole court system. It will
therefore be necessary to think about conflict rules which restrict the application
of foreign law to the degree required by the protection of vested rights.

The second problem posed by globalization is that of the dislocation of
legislative powers which has been described in the preceding section. If private
law legislation no longer hinges upon the nation state, but is distributed among
several levels, it is difficult to understand why conflict rules always should refer
to the private law of a certain nation. Moreover, the denomination as private
international law itself is loosing its justification. We should sooner or later
return to the former denomination of the 'conflict of laws'. This is not
equivalent to a return to unilateral conflict rules, but it implies the formulation
of conflict rules which may refer to a foreign supranational law, to a foreign
national law, or to a foreign sub-national law, as the case may be. Some more
recent conventions in the field of private international law in fact contain
general provisions which directly refer to the private law of a sub-national unit

in the respective field.[12] Similar conflict rules should provide for the application of foreign supra-national private law.

II.   Uniform Law and Principles

The solutions to problems described above have many aspects and can only be outlined here. In the first place it is safe to assume that we will witness increased activities in the field of unification and harmonisation of laws in those areas where transactions are inherently world-wide and have little or no connection with a particular legal system. In particular, some transactions related to the internet call for a progressive unification since their roots in a given national system are purely casual.[13]

Uniform law is never comprehensive. Gaps and exceptions from its scope of application cannot be avoided altogether. Courts have traditionally filled these gaps by having recourse to a national law, either the *lex fori*, or more correctly, the *lex causae*. In practice this method of composing the applicable law from two sources, i. e. the convention and the national law, has turned out to be overly complicated and to threaten the uniform enforcement of the convention. More recent conventions have therefore introduced an intermediate level of rules between the convention and the national law: the general principles of law. The best known example is that of Art. 7 of the UN Sales Convention which mandates the filling of gaps 'in conformity with the general principles on which [the convention] is based'. Recourse to the applicable national law can only be had where such principles are absent.

There is a broad discussion on the question of how to find such principles. It should be recalled that UNIDROIT, the Rome based Institute for the Unification of Private Law has adopted, in 1994, so-called principles of international commercial contracts which purport to set forth general rules to be used as an aid to interpret or supplement international uniform law instruments.[14] It is submitted that the UNIDROIT Principles can effectively help to clarify the meaning of uniform law conventions and moreover fill in gaps at least in so far as the relevant questions in principle are covered by the scope of the convention (so called 'internal gaps'). The gap filling role should not be limited to

---

[12]   See for example art. 19 of the Hague Convention on the Law applicable to agency of 14.3.1978; art. 19 of the Rome Convention on the Law applicable to contractual obligations of 19.6.1980.

[13]   Cf. *Herbert Kronke*, Electronic Commerce und Europäisches Verbrauchervertrags-IPR: RIW 1996, 985.

[14]   See the preamble; the UNIDROIT Principles are reproduced and commented upon by *Michael Joachim Bonell*, an international restatement of contract law, 2nd ed. Irvington-on-Hudson, New York, 1997.

conventions which explicitly refer to such general principles.[15] The formulation
of such general principles and their application by courts and arbitration panels
can bring about what has been called the 'creeping' codification of transnational
business law.[16]

III. Party Autonomy and lex fori

A third recommendation for the future development of the conflict of laws
would consist in the broad recognition of party autonomy. The traditional
counterargument that the free choice of the applicable law can only exist within
and not above that legal order, cannot be maintained as the legislative powers
are being redistributed among several levels. This process which has been
described in the preceding section clearly demonstrates that the nation state is
not the only and natural cornerstone of legislation. It would rather appear that
the individual, being invested with inalienable human rights is the more stable
factor in a future world order and that the free determination of the applicable
law by the individuals should therefore be respected as long as it is not imposed
by overwhelming economic or social power and as long as it does not intrude
upon the rights of third parties.

The broad admission of party autonomy would justify the restrictions to
which the application of foreign law has to be subjected in the absence of a
choice of law. In the long run such a reduction appears inevitable in order to
safeguard the workability of the national court systems. If interested private
parties have the possibility of planning their own affairs by choosing the
applicable law, they can hardly complain at a later stage of the *lex fori* being
applied in the absence of such a choice.

E. Consequences for Specific Areas of Private International Law

I.   Personal Status and the Nationality Principle

In the light of what has been said, the central role of the nationality principle in
many civil law systems for questions regarding personal status, family relations

---

[15] For a thorough treatment and further references cf. *Jürgen Basedow*, Die
      UNIDROIT-Prinzipien der internationalen Handelsverträge und die Übereinkommen
      des einheitlichen Privatrechts—eine theoretische Studie zur praktischen Anwendung
      des internationalen Transportrechts, besonders der CMR in: *Jürgen Basedow/Klaus
      J. Hopt/Hein Kötz* (eds.), Festschrift für Ulrich Drobnig, Tübingen 1997, p. 19, 23
      seq.

[16] *Klaus Peter Berger*, Formalisierte oder 'schleichende' Kodifizierung des transnatio-
      nalen Wirtschaftsrechts, 1996.

and succession should be reconsidered. To take the example of succession, it would appear sufficient to give effect to choice of law clauses contained in wills and to subject intestate successions to the law of the last domicile or habitual residence instead of applying the national law to the estate of millions and millions of foreign decedents.[17]

It is true that globalization may also reinforce the need of many people for strengthened ties with their own cultural environment, a countermovement which sometimes is described as a particular aspect of post-modernity.[18] This cannot result, however, in an unqualified adherence to the nationality principle. In the first place, cultural identity very often is not connected with the nation state but rather with sub-national units, and in the second place the administrative costs caused by the adherence to the nationality principle, i. e. by the application of foreign law will get unreasonably high in a globalised society which hosts more and more foreign citizens who are living and litigating in that country. In the third place, the overall justice in a society can hardly be furthered by the mass application of foreign laws which are outside the expertise of judge and counsel.

To reduce the application of foreign law does not amount to an outright recognition of the *lex fori* principle. This target can equally be served by a change of the relevant conflict rules relating to personal status from nationality to habitual residence, at least after a person has resided in the host state for a certain period, for example three years. The preservation of the nationality principle for short term visitors would safeguard a certain stability of legal relations of those people who do not effectively settle down in a foreign country for long. On the other hand, the change to domicile or habitual residence for long-term residents would take account of their closer social integration in the host state.

While these solutions are entirely rooted in private international law it should be pointed out that the same effect can be achieved by more liberal rules relating to the acquisition of the citizenship of the host state. Where residents of foreign nationality are made citizens of the host state after a certain lapse of time they will usually be treated, by the courts of that country, as citizens of that state for the purposes of private international law even though they may have kept their original nationality.

---

[17] For a thorough discussion, see *Jürgen Basedow/Barbara Diehl-Leistner*, Das Staatsangehörigkeitsprinzip im Einwanderungsland—zu den soziologischen und ausländerpolitischen Grundlagen der Nationalitätsanknüpfung im internationalen Privatrecht, in: *Jayme/Mansel*, supra n. 7, p. 13, 37 seq.

[18] *Scholte*, supra n. 11, p. 20 and 21 seq.; see also *Erik Jayme*, Identité culturelle et intégration: le droit international privé postmoderne: Recueil des Cours 251 (1995) p. 9, 56 seq.

II. Economic Regulation

While the trend towards the application of the court's own law can be explained, in the field of personal status, by the need to contain the costs of the administration of justice a different motivation applies when it comes to the enforcement of the *lex fori* in matters relating to the public order, in particular with regard to economic law. In this field globalization is threatening the implementation of the regulatory policies of the forum state. If foreigners acting abroad can affect the national economic order by means of the inter-connectedness of the world economy the possibility of nation states to form their own economic order by means of regulation is severely curtailed. There is for example no doubt that the merger of two of the world's remaining three manufacturers of wide body aircraft in the USA must hamper the competitive environment on that market world-wide.

While the appropriate solution would certainly be the enactment of a world competition law,[19] this perspective is not very realistic, at least not in the case of mergers. Depending on national laws and national enforcement the protection of competition requires a very large scope of application of the national competition statutes, i.e., the so-called effects doctrine which does not appear to be contested as contrary to international law any more.[20] Although primarily discussed in connection with the antitrust laws, the effects doctrine is of equal importance for other sectors of economic regulation. It is the necessary and perhaps the last tool available to the nation state in order to maintain the influence of national politics in a globalised economy.

The interrelation of globalization and the conflict of laws certainly merits a much more comprehensive and systematic treatment which should also include the growing role of issues of international civil procedure such as jurisdiction and the enforcement of foreign judgements. But that treatment is not possible in this context. The preceding remarks must suffice and they hopefully can initiate a necessary and also fertile debate on the changing theoretical bases of the conflict of laws.

---

[19] See *Jürgen Basedow*, Weltkartellrecht, Tübingen 1998.

[20] Cf. *Ivo Schwartz/Jürgen Basedow*, Restrictions on competition, in: International Encyclopedia of Comparative Law vol. III, ch. 35, Tübingen and Dordrecht 1995, in particular sect. 60–73; see also the decision of the US Supreme Court in *Hartford Fire Insurance Co. v. California*, 125 L. Ed. 2d 612, 640 (1993).

Part 1: The Internet, Private Law and
International Private Law

ELECTRONIC MONEY AND INFORMATION SOCIETY

by Mitsuru Iwamura, Tokyo

Contents

A. Introduction

Electronic money has been receiving a lot of attention lately. However, when the discussion comes to whether or not electronic money will really bring drastic change to our society, most people can't answer with confindence.

It is not difficult to see why. If electronic money was simply defined as a transformation from money made of paper or metal to data recorded in the memory of an IC card, it would not bring any extensive change to our society in any way. Instead of paper or metal cash, people would insert plastic cards to buy a ticket or candy from a vending machine. It might change the medium of payment and the form of currency that people carry, but it would not change the way we take a train, or say, the way a person tastes a candy. Then, the question comes: how would electronic money change our society?

Take contactless IC cards for example. The general IC card must be inserted to the device (called reader writer) in order to be read, while contactless IC cards use wireless technology to complete actions without physical contact. By using this technology, it becomes possible to establish non-stop tollgate on

13

highways. From this point of view, electronic money might be able to change the world in some ways.

How much would it cost to build a non-stop toll collecting system? It will take around 10 or 20 million yen. While not extremely expensive, it is definitely not a cheap solution to traffic congestion. Nonetheless, the price-performance ratio of electronic machines tends to double after one or one and half years of use. Calculated by this cost decreasing speed, a machine costs 10 million yen today might be reduced to 10 thousand yen after 10 or 15 years, which will make the non-stop tollgate system much cheaper and make it possible to apply more broadly. It would be economically possible to apply this system to general roads, which have shorter intervals between 100 meter to 200 meter. Consequently, it is possible to collect smaller amounts such as one-tenth of one yen or even one over hundred yen from drivers using contactless IC cards. This technology will make some of the originally defined public goods become applicable to the market mechanism in which the optimum balance between the frequency of usage and the bearing of building cost can be achieved. In this sense, electronic money will play a significant role.

Simply applied as described above, the technological development in payment systems should not have a big social impact. After all, payment systems are merely the means of settlement for economic transactions. However, if technological developments in payment systems contributes to providing a new era, which was not formed due to the prior absence of efficient payment systems, then the story will be different. In other words, providing that the new market or transaction forms from the development of new business brought by contactless IC card, there is no doubt that electronic money will bring a dramatic impact to our economic society.

In the following paragraph, I would like to state how electronic money may affect our society from the above mentioned point of view.

B.   The Position of Payment Instruments and Electronic Money

Please refer to Figure 1. The figure provides a general idea of how payment instruments have been used in our present economy. It also shows that as amounts become larger, the payment instrument changes from cash to credit card, or relatively more electronic instrument. We are not incidentally using varied kinds of cash or credit cards, instead, we tend to use more physical payment instruments such as cash to pay smaller amounts and we tend to use digital ones to settle larger amounts. This situation is similar to the phenomenon of so-called 'segregation', in which the living beings individually chose the best biosphere of their own to survive. Then, there comes the question in what kind of fields will electronic money be most acceptable?

Figure 1

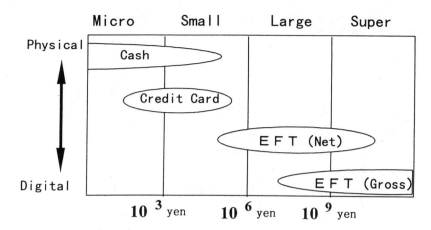

Figure 2

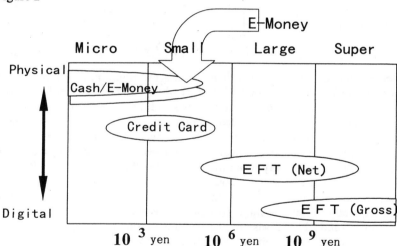

Figure 2 shows the simplest scenario, in which electronic money replaces the position of cash. In other words, electronic money becomes the substitute of banknotes made of paper or coins made of metal. In Japan and in the rest of the world, most of the electronic money experiments and projects carried out are actually based on this premise. Many demonstration videos of electronic money experiments show how people take trains and use vending machines with electronic money. It makes people associate electronic money with plastic card loaded IC and take it as a substitute for paper or metal money. Based on this premise, from the viewpoint of law, the main issue has been put in how to protect the user, for example how to respond if the electronic money issuing institute went bankrupt.

Figure 3

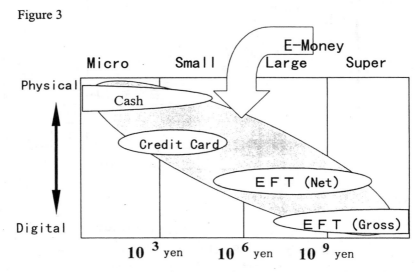

Please refer to Figure 3. This demonstrates electronic money replacing credit card and EFT (Electronic Fund Transfer) which has been generally practiced as a settlement system among banks. In this definition, electronic money means digital data which are protected from counterfeit or copying by the latest information technology. The reason we associate electronic money with plastic cards is that one of the practical forms created by information technology is nothing more than IC. By using the type of distributed computing, IC card and personal computer would be possible to reach the same security level with mainframes which are used in the center of many banking-online systems. Consequently, electronic money would be possible to be applied to the area of credit card and EFT. It was not possible to enter the field without the computer center clustered with mainframe. Despite of that, industrial barriers still exist. People originally in the field of payment system for credit card and EFT would not easily allow electronic money to be substituted for their services. Many people are concerned about electronic money will cross industry borders.

Instead of replacement of already existing payment businesses or payment instruments, electronic money should be placed into new field. It should be placed in a new category to make transactions that have up till now been impossible and to create new markets. Figure 4 demonstrates this possibility. As the figure shows, without depending on network of EFT, electronic money would make large amount transfers possible.

Some people might think that cash could be used to perform transaction amounts in the range of billions or trillions of yen. This is not correct. The reason is that cash made of paper is definitely not a convenient medium to deal with for large transactions.

Figure 4

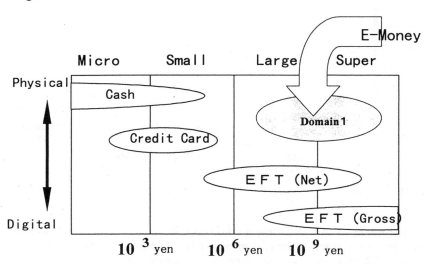

The paper 10 thousand yen note is used in daily life in Japan. From a global perspective, this is a large bill for everyday use. The 10 thousand yen note weighs around one gram. It may sound light, but take larger amount into consideration, it is neither light nor a convenient medium at all. 100 million yen of paper money weighs 10 kilograms, and 10 billion yen of paper money weighs 1 ton. Thus we generally use bank account transfer, in short, EFT, to complete this kind of large transaction. It makes people associate carrying billions of yen with some crime. In other words, the inconvenience of carrying cash makes paper money become a safety instrument to prevent crime. Accordingly, some people are concerned that electronic money might cause crime and tax evasion to increase, or some other money laundering.

Needless to say that electronic money was not created to meet this suspicious demand, but to create more efficient economic transactions. As figure 5 shows, such new territory is expected to be developed in terms of data communication to settle smaller amounts. In the beginning of this paper, what I mentioned about the possibility of toll collecting system by using IC card is based on the capacity of electronic money to develop new payment fields.

Figure 5

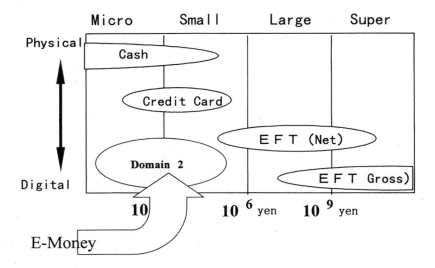

Doubt might be expressed that it could take 10 or 20 years to see new markets appear for electronic money. However, with the rapid progress of internet and related information communication infrastructure, electronic money may be used as a vehicle to bring on new commerce opportunities and new management possibilities. The expansion of internet finance offers us a hint.

C.   Internet Finance

The title of pioneer of internet finance should belong to Spring Street Brewing Company located in New York. Spring Street Brewing was, up until recently, a small unknown local beer established in New York by a Harvard Law School graduate, Andrew Klein, in 1993.

However, the company turned out to be famous later on. The credit should be given to internet finance. The venture company suffered from poor sales performance and accumulated losses. Nevertheless, the problem was solved by an initial public offer through the internet. Being indebted to the utilizing internet, the story was broadly reported by the media which made the company very well known and its stock rise considerably. Moreover, Andrew Klein, the founder of this company, become famous for making the first internet finance successful and later established Wit Capital Corporation, which is one of the leading 'investment banks' on the internet. This could be categorized as one of the successful stories.

It sounds not easy utilize internet finance, but actually it is very simple the way Spring Street Brewing Company did. First, the company established its homepage and advertises its own stock on the web. The interested investors download the Offering Circular and the other necessary application documents to purchase the stock. Then investors print the downloaded application contract from their personal computer, sign it, and mail it to Spring Street Brewing Company with an enclosed personal check. The procedure from internet then is finished and left the remaining procedure the same as general way of stock direct issuing. A question remains whether the case could be called true internet finance because of mixture usage of the traditional way of paper based trans-action. Setting aside the question, Spring Street Brewing Company did demon-strate a successful case by collecting 840 thousand stocks for a total amount of 1.6 million dollars from 3,500 investors.

However, many people think that the impact of internet finance to the business management in reality should not be overemphasized.

For example, Even Spring Street Brewing Company collected 1.6 million dollars from 3,500 investors in around one year, the respective amount was only limited to 400 dollars, which is no more than the scale of mail order selling for books or cosmetics.

So far, it is not doubtful that insufficient technology is an obstacle for their way of doing internet finance. The mission of communication networks ended at providing investment information, and then the mailing process is followed as the Spring Street Brewing Company did. In order to accurately confirm the will of investors, the documents must be signed on paper base. In order to accurately get the capital, the check must be received. As long as the dependence on paper and analog world still exists, the so-called successful internet finance is still technologically immature.

However, things always have both sides. It could be commented that small amount such as 400 dollars collected by Spring Street Brewing Company per investor would not be any possible to be a big deal. On the other hand, it could mean a lot because it creates a new way of selling stocks just as selling books and cosmetics. For successful entrepreneurs, it is very difficult to image that their stocks totally amount to only hundreds of thousand yen is owned by millions of personal shareholders. We should be aware of the possibility that a company owned by many shareholders could become a competitor to the indus-try. Therefore, it is meaningful to have a company like Spring Street Brewing Company.

The way that Spring Street Brewing Company went public and the mixture of digital network world with analog paper world should be changed in the future.

It is often said that the openness of internet network makes false contracts possible. It increases the risk of encountering frauds who earn the customer's trust and then run embezzles the received monies. It is still too early to draw a conclusion that the internet is too dangerous to deal with for finance or capital transactions.

Along with the prevalence of internet, the technology of certification authority attracts broad attention. Certification authority is the technology in which mathematics cryptography theory was applied and it can recognize real sender for certain digital data, and, therefore, it has the same effect as paper signature does. If an institute providing the same function as registry or notary public is established in the communication network by utilizing certification authority technology, internet fraud should decrease. For establishing a system providing legal effect to digital signature, related law has been enacted by more than 40 states in the United States, and Germany already has legalized the effect of digital signature. In Japan, the digitalization of commercial registration is also in the process of planning by the Ministry of Justice. Provided that the project is realized functionally, the exchange data in the communication network would be treated as the same as contracts with signature in the near future.

Absolutely, certification authority is not the only requirement for internet finance. Take advertisements of initial public offerings for instance, e-mail from domestic and overseas market could swarm to show interests on buying stock. There is no assurance about the payment ability of those investors. Providing the fund payment was undoubted, it would be still complicated to dealing with the dividend payment afterward. Spring Street Brewing Company asked investors to mail signed contract and check which is not a very efficient solution. Technically, there is a more efficient method to deal with the problem, which is electronic money. The reason is that by using electronic money through communication network, as if paper cash has been used, the data money could be sent and received. Figure 5 shows how it can be used in new fields in reality.

D. Borderless Enterprise

Hereafter, I would like to describe about how progress in computer networks change the business management. Without further mention, the key word would be 'borderless enterprise'. If we could purchase the stock from overseas company through the internet display, the meaning of nationality for enterprises would certainly be changed largely. If Japanese investors collect company information by internet instead of newspaper, the trust or not trust toward a company in America or Hong Kong would have no difference toward a company in Japan. For company in Japan, comparing a company pays no consciousness to overseas investors to a company does, the cost of capital should surely be different.

Borderless production and selling activities could be characteristic of the business in 20th century accompanying the development of multinational enterprise. However, without the development of telephone and telex, the emerging of multinational enterprise would not have been possible.

Nevertheless, the activities are bound in a closed network which limits the communication partner such as telephone or telex does. Even the production and selling activities are multinationalized, the multinationalization of capital activities is fundamentally difficult. A closed network such as telephone and telex is suitable for internal contact and adjustment, but not for capital appeal toward the uncertain public majority. Such appeal can only depend on printing type media such as newspaper or magazine. However, the dependence of printing type media would limit the scope of activity of capital raise to the space covered in the media. The sphere where the capital transaction such as stock raise progress is called the capital market. Mass media, for example Wall Street Journal in New York, provide the information for the capital markets in the world. This is evidence for the indivisibility in the activity of media and the formation of market.

Nowadays, big multinational enterprises are raising capital from several capital markets, but only limited to raise capital from several regional markets at the same time. Capital raise by crossing region in global market is not yet in the progress. Those biggest capital markets in the world, New York, London or Tokyo, are just limited big regional markets from the viewpoint of informational media, and can not be described as global markets.

Contrary to this, computer networks, especially the internet, could communicate with the masses. Provided that such 'open network' are being used for raising capital, the situation would be totally different. If capital, the basis of an enterprise, could be raised beyond the local market, like New York or London, the concept of the organization would be changed. The playground of raising capital for the so far 'multinational' enterprises is generally strongly connected with the capital market located in the same place as the enterprises. However, along with the progress of computer network, instead of multinational enterprises, the borderless enterprise should be emerged in terms of disburdening from the regional limitation of raising capital, the last resort of circumscribing an enterprise in the system of a nation or a culture. In fact, borderless venture enterprises are emerging in the United States, while taking away the privilege from so far owned only by big multinational enterprises.

Certainly, whether employer or employee welcomes this kind of borderless enterprise is a matter of individual choice. The development of communication networks provides a possible environment to create a borderless enterprise, however, it does not mean every enterprise should be borderless. However, if a company intends to maintain its identity, the external condition such as being a listing company in Tokyo Stock Exchange or being established basing on the law of Japan will no longer be a persuasive reason of being a 'Japanese' company. In stead, one must demonstrate a new identity in a more abstract way, such as enterprise culture, to be Japanese.

Speaking of 'enterprise culture', there is another invisible impact brought by the internet. This impact will be directly connected to an old question: What does an enterprise mean?

E.   Capital or Information?

Along with the development of the internet, 'virtual company' became one of a popular expression. A virtual company is not necessary to be established by general procedure such as a corporation does, but it is grouped by comrades with specialty running business together and sharing the profit.

In a virtual company, the 'employees' use the internet as a tool for information exchange, for decision making, who to and how much to sell. In other words, it could be said that the virtual company is a developed concept from companions who know each other through internet and decide to do some business together. It is not necessary to think how big the impact that virtual company might bring to the Japanese economy. There are numbers of cases about how those companies made of companions, and later became large before they could build up a responsibility and management system, then consequently collapse.

However, we could not make light of the movement of emerging virtual company. Even virtual company is somewhat slightly suspicious-looking, it offers us an axis of union which forms by people who first know each other in the information society or cyber society. This is, without further saying, the axis of information network.

Furthermore, the question of what does enterprise mean is a traditional quiz in the field of economics. In the theory of economics, the market mechanism seems to be a key word for everything, in which, enterprise, the main player in the production activity, inputs materials based on the market price and output are the product. However, there seems to be a sort of paradox in this kind of description. Provided that the hypothesis in theory of economics is sufficiently correct, in the real market, the enterprise is supposed to contribute to the production activities leading by the market price. However, if the enterprise activities are incorporated in the price of goods from input to output, then who will create an enterprise? If the enterprise is restricted as a device that just change input to output as seen in the production function, it should not be the subject in the economic activity of possessing goods.

Indeed, economists are not too naive to stand paralyzed in front of the quiz addressed above. For example, economists would rearrange the explanation from the intuition that an enterprise owned by entrepreneurs is an organic combination by people to the asymmetric structure of information between inside and outside of an enterprise. In an economic society that various uncertainty exists, members of enterprise know the strength and weakness of each other, tremendous value would come out by trust and honesty among partners. Without the framework of enterprise, one must evaluate and check the technique and personality of collaborators all by oneself, which is very inefficient. Therefore, enterprise is a device in which cost of looking for partners, or cost of information production could be saved. This would be the explanation economists would reply to question of the meaning of enterprise.

However, that doesn't answer the whole question. What is the real meaning of capital for enterprise? Have we been taught by this way: the owner of an enterprise is shareholder despite economists say that the information itself is an enterprise? Doesn't it imply that stock is only a tool of raising fund just like borrowing money from bank or issuing bonds?

Economists already prepared the answer to this question also. From the viewpoint of business management, making that the shareholders, the investors who take the residual risk, are the owners of the enterprise as a rule, it is reasonable that the shareholders would supervise the managers and employees. If this viewpoint stands, a framework of joint-stock company, composed by union of people in the axis of capital, should be positioned as a social wisdom of utilizing this kind of reasoning.

By rethinking business management in the above way, we are drawn to understand that the enterprise, or joint-stock company, is the product of history, especially the industrial capitalism history emerged after the industrial revolution. The industrial revolution, begun in 19th century in England, brought up gigantic production equipment and powerful engine, however, the information exchange among people using this kind of equipment relatively only brought on small improvement. Joint-stock company is a device developed and functioned to fill up the gap between physical goods production and information production. Therefore, if what happen in 21st century would ever impact enough to be called revolution of information technology, it will not be improbable to see that the axis of backing up an enterprise turns from capital or stock to network which represents the essence of an enterprise better.

As a result, the formation of virtual company, though only small movement has been seen, could symbolize the emerging new business model, which formed by information instead of by capital. Putting the case of virtual companies aside, how about the emerging companies that congregate through internet and raise fund as selling cosmetics or books? Comparing to the generally accepted meaning of capital and stock, the meaning of capital and stock to this kind of company is nearly diminutive. Either in the case of virtual company or internet finance, the movement in common about forming enterprise is not from the searching of capital but of information network. Accompany with the disappearance of borders from the information technology revolution, different from the 'borderlesslization' concerning the nationality of enterprise, another kind of 'borderlesslization' which means the vanishing borderline between 'inside' and 'outside' of a company should come out as a new phenomenon.

F.   The Conflict of Development of Information Communication Technology and Law

In the following section, I would like to discuss the legal issue brought by development of information communication technology. Without further mention, the main issue is the inevitable conflict of legal system among countries. The reason is that the development of information communication network makes the idea of regional 'market' disappear, and produces a global unity market.

In fact, the relationship of market and information is just like the inside and outside of a coin. What we called 'market' is actually a place where people sharing information and doing transaction. A place without information can not be called a market. Economists call the things providing possible economic value as 'goods', and the place where people share the information of that 'goods' and, exchange goods according to their preference as 'market'. Therefore, the size of market depends on the scope of possible information sharing. In a time when information exchange was difficult between distance places, people cluster to a city or a transaction center in order to get information. Naturally, there were several markets in one country, and each market has its own price.

However, goes with the development of information communication technology, this situation was changed slowly from the first beginning, and then changes dramatically. The first biggest change happened after the mailing system which was initialed in 19th century. New era began along with the prevalence of telegram and telephone in 20th century. Then, the legal framework in the modern market is generally thought that it is build under the premise of one market in one country. From the middle ages till now, market has been bounded inside the domain of a country. The market then became bigger along with the development of information communication technology which enlarges the possible scope of information sharing. In the beginning of the 20th century, there is nearly only one market in one country. The legal framework concerning modern market is build based on the premise of one market in one country. For example, the systematic framework of forbidding differentiation of information providence in a market , a basic legal system attitude in order to maintain the efficiency of market, is constructed inside one country as a unit.

However, the premise of one market in one country is challenged by the development of information communication network after 1980. The big improvement of information exchange and sharing cross border through information communication network enlarges the market space, which existed in one system in one country unit. It brings out a big global market across the country unit. This trend is especially obvious in finance, electronic communication field in which fewer physical goods movement is concerned. The reason is, usually, that this kind of field would not function without taking the movement of overseas market into consider. Providing a law or a regulation is made without integration with overseas system, that will cause a lot of fortune flowing out to the overseas market.

Generally known, the prototype of Japanese Big Bang was executed in London, or British security market, as an overall revolution and open policy. British Big Bang policy was proposed to cease transactions of London flowing to the United States where financial deregulation began in 1970's. When investors could in real time access every market in the world through the information communication network, overseas regulation should no longer be of concern for each government legislative authority. In the past, the market was enlarged by competing with other markets inside the country, then the pattern was succeed to global market by competing with other countries. The continuous magnification of markets with the development of information communication network finally gets over the border and challenges the superiority of respective authority to the market.

How, therewith, should our legal system to be applied to this kind of global market? Most of the people search for the answer in the keyword of 'international'. However, 'international' implies negotiation and cooperation between each government that stands for the benefit of their own citizen. The word 'international', therefore, is not sufficient. In the era of one market in one country, government represents the market which composed by people sharing information and transaction. It is meaningful and necessary that government stands out as a representative to negotiate with other government who represents other market. However, in the global market, the standpoint of government becomes more touchy and complicated. The government in the global market must be cautious to be neither too strict, risking of causing capital flight, nor too loose, risking of arising chaos to the market. Moreover, the government plays a role as a rule maker, who gives the standard and legality to complete the market contract, and at the same time as a rule executor, who punishes the rule avoider and compulsorily expropriates assets. Such duplicative roles playing makes the situation even more complicated.

These days, there are various issues concerning cross border problems of electronic money and electronic commerce. Some assertion is based on that the electronic commerce through the internet is practiced in new cyber space which does not exist in physical space, therefore it is necessary to establish a transaction law and an international regulation for cyber space. Generally speaking, this kind of assertion deserves attention. Legal correspondence to the problem in electronic commerce is necessary, and it also must be internationally adaptive. However, whether the law should be made according to the idiosyncrasy of electronic commerce or to the superior phenomenon over other market by development of information communication network should be tested at least. Moreover, the necessity of adaptable international vision does not imply that the agreement in government conferences or recognition in private international forums should be unconditionally approved simply because that the agreement or recognition is made through international discussion.

Bearing years of experience in the finance field, I have observed many failures in the time of fast progressing market globalization. It is for sure that more impact the development of information communication network, through the emergence of new electronic commerce method and market development, will bring to the finance field and the others. In order to diminish mistakes in this new field, more discussion should be held about the impact of new technologies, meanwhile, easy compromise and impression should be prevented.

PRIVATE LAW IN THE ERA OF INTERNET

by Shinichiro Hayakawa, Sendai

Contents

A. Introduction

Along with its recent explosive developments, Internet has become one of the most beloved topics of the town. Everybody talks about Internet: artists, biologists, chefs, dancers, economists, firemen, ... and jurists. A great number of books and articles on Internet have been published by people from all walks of life. Jurists have of course written a lot about Internet.

Having read some of the literature, legal and non-legal, I found a peculiar characteristic common to what jurists (especially in the field of private law) felt about the Internet—optimism. We can observe that their optimism is working in two totally opposite directions.

Some jurists do not worry much about the Internet. They think that they can easily cope with the developments of Internet by using the traditional framework of private law (including the system of private international law). Although some adaptations would be necessary to keep up with the possible changes of legal environments to be brought about by Internet, there would be no need to fundamentally change the traditional system.

27

Others claim that there will emerge 'Cyberspace Law' which is distinct and independent from the traditional nation-based private law system. While the idea of Cyberspace Law assumes a touch of pessimism about the traditional framework of private law, we could sense fairly strong optimism in the belief that the Cyberspace Law will be a passe-partout for the problems arising on the Net.

Optimism makes our life easier and happier—that is why I prefer, in principle, optimism to pessimism—, but it sometimes makes our life dangerous as well. I do not claim at all that these two trends of 'optimistic' prospects are ridiculous: they are, on the contrary, well thought out and well grounded. However, considering the magnitude of the problems at stake, I believe that it might be of some use to make some observations and reservations about the optimistic pictures of the private law in the era of Internet.

B. Impacts of Internet on States, Communities and People

In order to examine the problems that the private law might face in the era of Internet, we need to know how the developments of Internet will affect our current society in the long run. We need to imagine what kind of society we will be living in in the future.

Will the States, the communities and the people remain more or less the same, for example in the year 2020, as they are now? Everybody would probably respond in negative but nobody knows for certain how our society will look like in twenty years. It is far beyond the scope of this paper to describe the whole picture of our future society. There are so many complicated elements to be taken into consideration (including international politics, environmental problems, genetic engineering, etc.) that it is simply impossible for a simple-minded humble lawyer to act or even pretend to act as a clairvoyant. But just for the sake of discussion, let's take a look into the crystal ball focusing on 'Cyber-space.'

In Cyberspace virtual communities based on the network are growing rapidly as the Internet develops and as more and more people throughout the world get to participate in this computer communication network. We cannot think about the private law of the future without weighing the gravity and influences of Cyberspace.

In Cyberspace, as is often said, the frontiers dividing the surface of the globe into States has virtually no meaning. It is extremely rapid and easy to effectuate cross-border communications among computers on the Net. With a small computer, everybody on the earth (and, probably in the near future, everybody above the earth as well) can send his or her messages in a second to enormous number of people throughout the world without being checked or controlled by his or her government or any other States. As the activities in Cyberspace multiply in quantity and in complexity, States will have less and less control over what is happening in Cyberspace. The power of a State to control the ideas, sentiments and behaviors of its citizens (for example, by manipulating mass media or by using physical power and so on) will considerably diminish in Cyberspace.

In lieu of sovereign States, that (still) have dominant power in Realspace (as opposed to Cyberspace), who or what will have controlling power in Cyberspace?

'Each individual will!' might be a possible answer by some prophets. There is certainly a hope for prosperity of individuals in a sort of grass-roots democracy cherished on the liberal open universal network. Looking back at the birth of Internet and its growth in initial stages, one might be tempted to take this hopeful and comfortable view. Internet used to be a convivial forum full of volunteer spirits, full of solidarity (though we should not forget that Internet has had military implications from the very beginning). After the arrival of commercialism, however, Internet could not be what it used to be, as is the case of Olympic Games. Commercialism (or the capitals) will seek all sorts of lucrative opportunities on the Net. It is not likely that individuals will enjoy controlling the peaceful Cyberspace.

People might face, in Cyberspace, another kind of difficulties that they do not usually experience in Realspace. In Cyberspace things are processed rapidly and automatically, which means the Will (and Act upon reflection) of individuals would lose significance considerably. A click of the mouse is too easy and too fast to give you time for reflection as compared to the signature with pen and ink. With the aid of sophisticated software and program, you can also place series of commands quasi-automatically even without touching the mouse or watching the screen. The Will and Act of person will thus be replaced to a large extent by technology in Cyberspace.

It is important to note that all these characteristics of Cyberspace will not be confined to Cyberspace itself but will affect the real world as well. In the next century, computers and Internet will, with no doubt, play one of the central roles in the political and economic landscape of our society. In other words, Cyberspace will become an essential part of the real world. Juxtaposing Cyberspace and Real World, as is often done by authors, is thus somewhat misleading. The real world will be covered more and more with computers and the Internet, and thus with the power of capitals and technology born and bred in Cyberspace.

C.   Optimism of Revolutionists and Optimism of Conservatives

Getting back to the two opposite prospects about the future of private law system (Revolutionists as I call the 'Cyberspace Law' school referred to in the Introduction, and Conservatives who oppose the Revolutionists), let me explain what seems to be optimistic about these views.

I.   Revolutionists

Generally speaking, once a new community is created and people begin to frequent there, rules applicable within the community will emerge by one way or another. It is thus most natural that, in Cyberspace as well, some rules will be formed in the course of its evolution. What is conspicuous about the Revolutionists is that they contend that the rules formed in Cyberspace will be more or less independent from the laws of the sovereign States on the earth. Cyberspace will be recognized, according to them, as a sort of independent jurisdiction.

It is true that, as a matter of fact, trying to regulate things in Cyberspace through the traditional legal framework would cause quite a few serious difficulties. But that could not lead, as a matter of law, to the quasi-sovereignty of Cyberspace. As several lawyers have already pointed out, the arguments of the Revolutionist are not convincing in this respect. It can be said that the Revolutionists are a little bit too optimistic as to the flexibility of ordinary lawyers.

But to my eyes, optimism of the Revolutionists seems to lie somewhere else as well. They expect that there will emerge a Cyberspace Law system and that such a system will give satisfactory self-regulation regarding the problems arising in Cyberspace. We can see a dilemma here. If Cyberspace Law system is not effective enough to give sufficiently powerful solution to problems, the system does not deserve the name of law. If it is effective enough, there will still be a serious question as to the legitimacy of that system both in its contents and in its formation process.

As the technology advances, self-regulation in Cyberspace is likely to become more effective and more powerful. For example, an Internet service provider could, with a few lines of code written in the relevant software, strike out automatically the e-mail address of a client if the client does not pay fees or has done something wrong listed in the agreement. Cyberspace Law will be formed principally on an agreement-basis. But existence of agreements among the participants will not guarantee the legitimacy of the rules with respect to its contents and its formation process. While the self-regulation rules in good old days of Internet might have had certain legitimacy thanks to the grass-roots democracy and the volunteer spirits filling then the Net, things will be totally different on the Internet where commercialism and technology govern.

II.   Conservatives

The Conservatives seem somewhat optimistic to me in that they tend to underestimate the repercussions of the proliferation of self-regulatory rules in Cyberspace.

I agree with Conservatives when they claim that there is nothing new in applying the traditional framework (of private law and private international law) to what is happening on Internet. The traditional framework has successfully managed letters, telephones, fax, broadcasts,.... Why not Internet?

By using the traditional framework, we could certainly come to a beautiful conclusion. It is so, however, only if we ever have an opportunity to use that framework.

The traditional framework, as a dispute resolution system, is meant to be used by courts of the State. In Cyberspace, however, a great number of self-regulation and self-dispute-resolution tools will appear and develop as the technology and commercialism advance. It is probable that, for the problems in Cyberspace, these self-regulatory systems will be much more frequently used than the national court system. As for transnational transactions there is already a strong tendency, at least in Japan, that national courts are not so welcome and trusted by people engaged in that sector. They would avoid using courts probably because it takes too long and because it is hard to predict for certain the outcome of the trial. This tendency will gain much more strength when it comes to Internet: in Cyberspace time super-flies or hyper-flies; and it is all the more difficult to predict the result of a trial on problems in Cyberspace, because there have been, and will be, few cases.

The traditional framework might be substantially undermined by the prosperity of self-regulations in Cyberspace also via the principle of party autonomy. Suppose that State A has substantive private law that allows party autonomy so generously that relevant self-regulations of Cyberspace can be incorporated by the parties and qualified as authorized law as it were. Suppose that State B has conflicts-of-law rules that permits party autonomy, which is normal with respect to contracts. If the parties, under the conflicts of law of State B, choose the law of State A as the applicable law, self-regulation system will be virtually applied through the traditional framework. If I were one of the kings of Cyberspace with plenty of money and technology, I would look for a Cyberspace-haven like State A above and try to make my clients click on 'yes' to the choice of law clause in the agreement.

In short, Conservatives might be vulnerable to the intrusion of efficient and powerful self-regulatory rules that will emerge and prosper in any event in Cyberspace.

D. How to Cope with the Problems

As a starting point, I would like to take the view of Conservatives rather than that of Revolutionists. To establish an independent jurisdiction of Cyberspace Law would be too romantic and too dangerous. And I believe that this impression will be shared among most lawyers in Japan and probably among many lawyers in other countries except for the United States.

What should we do then with the problems that will arise in the course of effectuating the traditional legal framework?

The possible unpopularity of national court systems, the first problem I referred to above, may be dealt with in either of the two following ways. The one is an orthodox solution of trying to invite as many cases as possible into the court by making the court system more attractive in one way or another. The other solution is to save the power and capacity of national courts just for important cases and let the self-dispute-resolution systems in Cyberspace function for ordinary cases; with, of course, necessary public control imposed on the systems.

Two solutions are possible also for the problem caused by the intrusion of self-regulations into the traditional framework. An orthodox way is to exclude the application of inappropriate self-regulations by making use of traditional tools at the level of private international law, such as l'ordre public, die Sonderanknüpfung des zwingendes Recht, etc. The other solution lies in trying to change the self-regulations in Cyberspace into acceptable ones, or rather to help appropriate self-regulations evolve in Cyberspace.

In my opinion, the orthodox solutions, for each of the two problems, will be less practical than the others. It is very likely that the system of self-regulation and self-dispute-solution will rapidly evolve and expand in Cyberspace. Chances are that the orthodox solutions will fail under pressure on the part of Cyberspace. The traditional legal framework needs to adapt flexibly to new environments of the Internet era. Controlling the self-regulatory system in Cyberspace and incorporating it into the legal framework will be one of the practical ways of such adaptation.

How could we possibly control the self-regulatory system in Cyberspace? This question requires in-depth analyses of self-regulatory system as a whole, which I could not accomplish in the course of preparation of this paper. Let me just say a few words in this regard. There will be various routes for controlling the self-regulatory system—for example using administrative measures, creating supernational law, modifying national substantive law, etc. For any of these routes, international cooperation is absolutely indispensable.

E.   Conclusion

Starting from a rather pessimistic view about the future Internet—a sort of anarchic Cyberspace where commercialism speaks loud, technology evolves dynamically, and justice might be silent—, I have tried to give a rough sketch of possible future developments of the private law system. The key phrase was self-regulatory system in Cyberspace. We need to check and control it so that our private law system can adapt, without jeopardizing the goal of attaining justice, to the new era of the Internet.

In the course of preparation of this paper, I was inspired especially by the following books and articles.

M.R. Burnstein 1996: Conflicts on the Net: Choice of Law in Transnational Cyberspace, 29 Vanderbilt J. of Transnat'l L., 3, 116.

K. Boele-Woelki and C. Kessedjian (ed.) 1998: Internet : Which Court Decides? Which Law Applies? Quel tribunal decide? Quel droit s'applique?

E.A. Cprioli/R.Sorieul 1997: Le commerce international electronique: ver l'emergence de regles juridiques transnationales, Clunet 1997.323.

J. Huet 1998: Quelle culture dans le 'cyber-espace' et quels droits intellectuels pour cette 'cyber-espace' ?, Dalloz Chronique 1998, 18 cahier.

D.R. Johnson/D. Post 1996: Law and Borders—The Rise of Law in Cyberspace, 48 Stanford Law Review 1367.

L. Lessing 1996: The Zones of Cyberspace, 48 Stanford Law Review 1403.

Vivant 1996: Cybermonde: Droit et droits des reseaux, JCP 1996, 401

[Literature in Japanese]

Akagi (A.) 1996: *Internet Shakai Ron*
Dogauchi (M.) 1997: *Cyberspace to Kokusai Shihô*, Juristo no.1117
Furuse (Y.)/Hirose (K.) 1996: *Internet ga kaeru Shakai*
Internet Bengoshi Kyôgikai/Murai (J.) (ed.) 1998: *Internet Hôgaku Annai.*
Ishiguro (K.) 1998: *Kokusai Chiteki Zaisanken:Cyberspace vs. Real World.*
Makino (J.) 1998: *Shiminryoku toshite no Internet.*
Murai (J.)1998: *Internet II.*
Natsui (T.) 1997: *Network Shakai no Bunka to Hô.*
Nishigaki (T.) 1994: *Multimedia.*
Nishigaki (T.) 1995: *Sei naru Virtual Reality.*
Ohsawa (M.) 1995: *Denshi Media Ron.*
Okamura (H.)/Kondo (T.) 1997: *Internet no Hôritu Jitsumu.*
Uchida (H.)/Yokoyama (T.) (ed) 1997: *Internet Hô.*

ELECTRONIC COMMERCE AND LAW— SOME FRAGMENTARY THOUGHTS ON THE FUTURE OF INTERNET REGULATION FROM A GERMAN PERSPECTIVE

by Thomas Hoeren, Münster[*]

Contents

[*] The following considerations only reflect some ideas which I presented at the German-Japanese Conference on 'Trade, Law and Enterprises in the Era of Globalization' Spring 1999 in Fukuoka (Japan). The footnotes only hint at some references which are necessary to understand my concept. The text is based upon the situation in Europe in May 1999; further changes could not be considered. I would like to thank Prof. Dr. Jürgen Basedow (Hamburg) and Dr. Prof. Dr. Toshiyuki Kono (Fukuoka) for their help in organizing the conference and this publication.

A. Introduction

Unlike the internet community had expected electronic commerce does not lead
to an anarchic dissolution of law. In the context of electronic trade, problems
arising between users and providers can be solved, for instance by applying
traditional principles of contract law. And yet, the legal dispute of internet
related facts and circumstances gives rise to a number of interesting topoi. Even
though these subjects have already been considered in the past (for instance in
the context of satellite technology), they only now show their specific explosive
effect and diversity in the face of the electronic commerce.

B. Dematerialization, Deterritorialization and Detemporalization of Law

I. The Phenomenon of Dematerialization and the New Property Rights

The first striking topos of the internet law is the net-inherent dematerialization,
which leads to a situation where material assets lose their significance in favor
of new intangible assets.[1] Traditionally, the European civil codifications such as
the Code Napoleon and the German Civil Act are based upon the dichotomy of
goods and services.[2] Assets which could be worthy of protection but do not
show the characteristics of neither goods nor services do not gain protection
under present private law. This phenomenon is rooted in the logic of the 19th
century. At the threshold from a farming to an industrialized society the old civil
law codes had to reflect the primacy of the production of goods. Even in view of
the needs of a modern service society it could only refer to rudimental legal
regulations in relation to service contracts. However, in a so called information
society a number of legal interests exist which do not fall within the logic of
goods versus services. In that respect we are dealing with new property rights,
assets worthy of protection, for which traditional instruments of the civil law
cannot provide security.

---

[1] See *Bercovitz*, Gewerblicher Rechtsschutz und Urheberrecht. Internationaler Teil
1996, 1010 (1011).

[2] Compare considerations in *Hoeren*, Gewerblicher Rechtsschutz und Urheberrecht
1997, pp. 866.

1. The Information

First of all, it is a question of information as such.[3] Traditionally, the protection of information is confined to the protection of know-how as it is firmly established in the traditional regulations on trade secrets. These provisions are puzzling in a number of ways. They secure a high level protection without sufficiently defining the term of 'trade secrets'. However, modern efforts to re-define the legal protection of 'information' are facing very much the same problem. Intellectual property law is based upon the idea of a protection of works of art, literature and music and has not been adjusted to the needs of a modern information society.[4] Although the European Commission is trying to initiate such a convergence by establishing a new property right for collections of information[5] in the European Database Directive[6], the outlines of this new system of protection have not been clearly defined. Nobody knows, for example, what is meant by a qualitative or quantitative substantial investment, a necessary qualification for the *sui generis* protection of databases. This symbolizes the basic dilemma of information law: definite criteria for the assignment of access to information and exclusive information rights do not exist.[7] The idea of an international system of information regulation ('Wissensordnung')[8] remains a mere utopia.[9]

---

[3]   Compare with *Hoeren*, Information als Gegenstand des Rechts, Addendum to Multimedia und Recht 1998, No. 6, 6*.

[4]   Justified in so far the fundamental criticism by *Barlow*, The Economy of Ideas: a Framework for Rethinking Patents and Copyrights, in: WIRED 2.03, 1994, pp. 84; for reformatory propositions see *Zweiter Zwischenbericht der Enquete-Kommission Zukunft der Medien, Neue Medien und Urheberrecht*, 1997, and *Schricker*, Urheberrecht auf dem Weg zur Informationsgesellschaft, 1997.

[5]   See i.e. *Bechtold*, Zeitschrift für Urheber- und Medienrecht 1997, p. 427; *Berger*, Gewerblicher Rechtsschutz und Urheberrecht 1997, p. 169; *Dreier*, Gewerblicher Rechtsschutz und Urheberrecht. Internationaler Teil 1992, pp. 739; *Wiebe*, Computer und Recht 1996, pp. 198.

[6]   Directive *96/9/EC of. 11.3.1996, OJ No. L 77 of. 27.3.1996, 20* . See articles by *Gaster*, Ent.LR. 1995, pp. 258, *Gaster*, ÖSGRUM 19 (1996), pp. 15; *Gaster*, Revue du Marché Unique Européen 4/1996, pp. 55.

[7]   Compare with the thesis by *Druey*, Information als Gegenstand des Rechts, 1995, pp. 441.

[8]   Fundamental *Spinner*, Die Wissensordnung, 1994, especially at pp. 111.

[9]   In so far the innovative considerations concerning the reformation of the data protection law by *Kloepfer* are not convincing. In his expert opinion for the next *DJT*, *Kloepfer* demands the passing of a Federal Data Act (Bundesdatengesetz) respectively of an Information Code/Statute Book (Informationsgesetzbuch), even though the particulars of such an information order would not be identifiable.

2. The Domain

But other new property rights exist besides the information as such. Their legal fate is unclear. One of these new rights is the domain.[10] The domain represents the virtual identity of the provider and his products. Today, in the internet a person is mainly present via such a clearly assigned domain. The domain is the *conditio sine qua non* for any internet appearance and therefore also features as part of the trade name, on visiting-cards, brochures and in advertising copies. Typically, property rights are being granted by public administration working as guarantors for distributive justice. In the case of domains however the state only takes repressive actions. This can be seen as a novelty. Following the principle of 'first come first served', domains are being granted by institutions under private law. A third person can only subsequently take action against such an award, drawing attention to the fact that the assigned identification could infringe the right to his own name. The state will then prohibit any further use of the domain by the domain-holder.[11] Yet, the state refuses to change the system of marketing domains.[12]

But indeed, the identifying power of a domain is diminishing. First, search engines are becoming more and more important as a means for defining the virtual identity of the provider.[13] Taking into account the tremendous speed with which the world wide web is growing, the question of investigation for information is a pressing one. Lost in cyberspace—the feeling of getting lost in the www whilst searching for a specific homepage can no longer be taken under control simply by referring to the existing domain of a provider. An efficient supply of information is to an increasing extent guaranteed by search engines. In the future, intelligent robots will assist the user when searching in the net; the

---

[10]   Compare from recent literature *Bettinger*, Gewerblicher Rechtsschutz und Urheberrecht 1997, p. 402; *Omsels*, Gewerblicher Rechtsschutz und Urheberrecht 1997, p. 328; *Stratmann*, Betriebs-Berater 1997, p. 689; *Ubber*, Wettbewerb in Recht und Praxis 1997, p. 497; *Völker/Weidert*, Wettewerb in Recht und Praxis 1997, p. 652; *Wilmer*, Computer und Recht 1997, pp. 562.

[11]   Related questions of 'identification law' (names/marks etc.) will not be reduced by the fact that a number of top-level-domains will be available in the future; this new way of conferring domains will only multiply the problem of an exact/accurate assignment of domain names. See *Bettinger*, Gewerblicher Rechtsschutz und Urheberrecht Internationaler Teil 1997, 404 (at p. 420); *Kur*, Computer und Recht 1997, pp. 325.

[12]   So at least the *Krupp*-decision OLG Hamm, Multimedia und Recht 1998, 214 with comment by *Berlit*, Neue Juristische Wochenschrift-Rechtsprechungsreport 1998, 909 = Computer und Recht 1998, 241 with comment by *Bettinger*. Of a different opinion for example *LG München I*, Computer und Recht 1997, p. 479; *LG Frankfurt a.M.*, Multimedia und Recht 1998, 151; *LG Düsseldorf*, Computer und Recht 1998, 174.

[13]   See *Wilmer*, Computer und Recht 1997, pp. 562.

user simply defines the topic for which he seeks information in general terms and receives this information periodically in easy to digest portions from the www-robot. This upheaval gives reason to reflect the identifying power of domains. In the end, a user will hardly make use of a domain in order to find a provider. It is more likely that he will act through search-engines and robots without the domain being of any importance.

II. Electronic Commerce and the Deterritorialization of the Law

In the internet, all provisions referring to the place, the territory or the seat are losing sense. The electronic speed deterritorializes the law.[14]

1. Problem Areas

The diminishing relevance of territory-based rules is primarily demonstrated in the area of international civil procedure law and of private international law. Due to their origin in the 19th century idea of sovereignty these provisions very often refer to local connections. This is for example the case when the defendant's domicile appears as the connecting factor. Something similar applies to connecting factors such as the place where the damaging act has been committed and the place where the damaging act takes effect when dealing with questions of the law of torts or the place of contract of consumer contracts. But other areas of law are also affected by connecting factors which are determined by a locality. Reference has to be made to the tax law term of the permanent establishment,[15] which creates difficult questions especially in relation to the internet.

But also in the area of online contracts, territorial criteria are very often misleading. Above all, attention has to be drawn to contracts which provide for regional restrictions of the right of exploitation, as it is for example typically in the case for television licenses or distribution agreements. Such categories of contracts lead to unforeseeable difficulties when dealing with the question of use of film material or product advertising over the internet.

Furthermore, territoriality as a connecting factor causes problem in relation to injunctions. These claims are traditionally limited to the prohibition of a specific act in the territory of a specific state; an injunction which takes effect beyond the borders of the territory of a state would not be enforceable for

---

[14] See *Vief*, Digitales Geld, in : Rötzer (Hrsg.), Digitaler Schein, 1991, p. 117, 130.
[15] For a general overview see *Vink, Albarda and others*, in: Caught in the Web, 1998, pp. 58; *Lejeune and others*, European taxation 1998, pp.2.

reasons of public international law.[16] However, in relation to internet infringe-
ments this would result in a situation where injunctions become unenforceable
because of technical reasons. A provider cannot exclude the on-line access of a
homepage by a user situated in a specific state territory. In the internet it is
impossible to define user groups on a territorial basis; no one knows whether the
user of the address hoeren@aol.com is situated in Germany, the USA, or
Malaysia. This forces courts to define the extension of injunctive relieves in
broader terms than legally permissible. The prohibition does not only extent to
the possibility of having access to a server from Germany. It has to prohibit the
whole use of a particular homepage throughout the world.[17]

2.   Possible Solutions

The question is indeed how the law should respond to its deterritorialization.
The problem of territoriality might be solved by creating a virtual space. All
actors in this 'Cyberspace' have their own net-identity which only shows a
minimal connection with the domicile or the place of business.[18] Within this
space, providers have to reveal their identity as it is in fact intended by the EU
Draft Directive on Electronic Commerce.

   This proposal however does not solve the questions of private international
law which still considers the seat, the place of business or the domicile of the
person affected. Here, the principle of territoriality should be replaced by the
concept of purported use. This concept has mayor roots in competition law[19] and
defines the applicability of national statutes according to the place where the
deliberate intervention in the market takes place. Someone who uses the internet
for advertising has to do so according to German law only to the extent to which
it is intended for the German market. This rule is now also being discussed in
relation to criminal law.[20] Furthermore, it shows similarities with the American
'minimum contacts principle'. However, the copyright lawyers have always
rejected to apply this principle to intellectual property law by arguing that these
rights are based upon territorial a jurisdiction could only confer copyrights and

---

[16]   For a short period of time, a different view has been adopted in the Netherlands in the
       De Corte Geding-decisions; see in this context *Brinkhof*, European Intellectual
       Property Review 1994, 360; *Gielen/Ebbink*, European Intellectual Property Review
       1994, 243.
[17]   *KG*, Neue Juristische Wochenschrift 1997, p. 3321–concept concept.
[18]   See *Turkle*, Leben im Netz, 1998, p. 9.
[19]   See the decision of the Federal Supreme Court *BGHZ* 113, 11 (15) = Neue Juristische
       Wochenschrift 1991, 1054—Kauf im Ausland; similar *OLG Karlsruhe*, Gewerblicher
       Rechtsschutz und Urheberrecht 1985, 556 (557); *Kotthoff*, Computer und Recht
       1997, pp. 676.
[20]   *Hilgendorf*, Neue Juristische Wochenschrift 1997, pp. 1873.

trademarks within its territory. But this gives rise to the inevitable dilemma that a provider—due to the global possibility of on-line retrieval—has to be familiar with and comply with the industrial property law of every jurisdiction.[21]

III. The Internet and the Detemporalization of the Law

But even the element of time is becoming more and more absurd in the internet.

1. Problem Areas

First aspects of the increasing digital detemporalization can be found in the law of copyright. Traditionally, European legislators distinguish in copyright law between the material and immaterial exploitation of works. Immaterial exploitation refers to broadcasting and TV where an unlimited audience can see and/or listen to works simultaneously. In the internet, services are however done successively. They are not distributed to users; the users themselves are getting access to a server at a time of their own choice. Generally, the internet is characterized as a huge collection of services on demand. In this situation one could try to apply rules for public display by analogy to services on demand. However, this (typical German) way has lost significance in the face of the decision of the international community of states to introduce a new right of 'making available to the public' into copyright.[22] This solves the problem of the categorization of services on demand; storing information for demand already constitutes an infringement of the exploitation rights of the owners of copyright and neighboring rights.[23] Yet, this new right will cause follow-up problems such as the distinction between public and non-public in the so called *intra*net and the integration of the new right into the system of statutory exceptions.

The phenomenon of detemporalization also influences consumer protection law. Consumer protection can be done by giving the user time to reconsider and withdraw contractual decisions. This protection is predominantly guaranteed by the introduction of the revocation right and the compulsory requirement of a written form for contracts. To that extent, the EU Distance Selling Directive is of great importance. This directive shows the dilemma of consumer protection in the digital context. Following the directive, a right of withdrawal from electronic orders will be introduced throughout Europe (Art. 6 I 1 and II), as well as

---

[21] The different possibilities of solution are discussed in *Hoeren/Thum*, ÖSGRUM 20 (1997), pp. 78. See also *BGH*, Multimedia und Recht 1998, 35 with comments by *Schricker*—Spielbankaffaire.

[22] See Art. 8 WIPO Copyright Treaty.

[23] See *Lewinski*, Multimedia und Recht 1998, pp. 115.

the obligation to inform the consumer in that respect (Art. 4 I lit. F). But for a number of services this right of withdrawal will be denied even though substitutes have not been developed (Art. 3 I and II). In that respect, the directive leaves a number of gaps in the protection of electronic consumers.

The problem of time is also dealt with in the discussion concerning the electronic form.[24] It is already a kind of religious belief within the European internet law community that the digital signature will be the functional equivalent to the hand-written form.[25] When complying with the rather high security standards, a digital signature does indeed fulfil most functions of the hand-written signature. However, at the same time the warning function of handwriting has been ignored. The process of signing something in hand-written form draws the signatory's attention to the fact that he is about to act in a legally relevant manner. This warning lapses when digital signatures are being automatically generated and sent within fractions of a second. Asymmetric encrypting techniques deconstruct the temporal context; the factor of time will only subsequently be recorded in the mailing protocol.

2.   Possible Solutions

The digital loss of time has to be compensated; there should be a substitute for legal rules which make reference to time. For example, when substituting the written form for electronic equivalents, the user closing a contract should be granted a pause during which it is possible for him to reflect whether he actually wants to give an expression of will with such a content. This might lead to a revocation right which allows the declaring party to revoke electronic orders after the expression of will has been received. The Distance Selling Directive introduces such a right of withdrawal for consumers. Facing the speed of communication in the net, this provision should be extended to all declaring parties, irrespective of their consumer characteristic, in order to allow everybody time to reflect.

---

[24]   Compare *Bizer/Hammer*, Datenschutz und Datensicherheit 1993, pp. 619; *Ebbing*, Computer und Recht 1996, pp.271; *Heun*, Computer und Recht 1995, p. 2; *Kilian*, Datenschutz und Datensicherheit 1993, pp. 607; *Pordesch/Nissen*, Computer und Recht 1995, pp. 562.

[25]   Of a different opinion: *Erber-Faller*, Computer und Recht 1996, 375 (pp. 378). The attempt by the *Bundesjustizministerium* to solve the problem of the written form by introducing an electronic text form has failed: see the *Entwurf eines Gesetzes zur Änderung des Bürgerlichen Gesetzbuches und anderer Gesetze vom 31.1.1997*-BMJ 3414/2 (unpublished). A further draft shall be distributed in May/June 1999.

C. Self-Regulation instead of State Regulation

The amount of problems surrounding the enforcement of the law result in a growing number of voices calling for self-control and self-regulation in the net. In the present discussion, there is strong emphasis on the so called Netiquette and other methods of voluntary self-regulation by providers. However, only little attention has been to the fact that 'the' netiquette does not exist.[26] Different services have their own rules of conduct. Such texts in that position may stretch out from ten lines to up to 40 pages. The same applies to the idea of voluntary self-control. The different self-control institutions use various sets of rules of specific content. The efficiency of self-control is unclear as well as its sanction mechanisms cannot be supported by state regulations of enforcement. Beyond contractual obligations, there is no chance to enforce codes of conduct.

In addition, it is still unclear whether the netiquette is conform with law. The rules might conflict with existing regulations on unfair contract terms and antitrust law. Art. 81 of the Treaty of Amsterdam permit rules of conduct with anti-competitive effects only in so far as such rules repeat and specify existing, EU-conform regulations of unfair competition law. Rules of conduct which restrict a provider's action on the market are therefore dubious under European antitrust law where they restrict an action which subsequently proves to be irrelevant and neutral in the light of unfair competition law.

But the additional question arises whether it is possible to impose sanctions for the violation of codes of conduct. In the United States, the discussion focuses on Alternative Dispute Resolution (ADR) which might lead to the introduction of an internet jurisdiction and arbitration proceedings in the internet. However, serious attempts to establish such internet courts have never been made. And indeed, the introduction of internet courts would probably not solve the problem of execution, as the decisions of such courts would not be enforceable.

D. Data Protection and Depersonalization

The internet also leads to a depersonalization of law. All legal rules which relate to a specific 'person' have to be reconsidered. People can create new persons, change their identity, build up virtual realities and virtual entities. For instance, new ways of building up a corporation are establishing in the area of electronic commerce. Virtual corporations are working on a spontaneous, trans-border basis. One of the mayor problems caused by the depersonalization is the concept of personal data in the context of data protection. Especially, the possibilities of

---

[26] This thesis has extensively been justified by *Hoeren*, in: *Becker* (Hrsg.), Rechts-probleme internationaler Datennetze, 1996, pp. 35.

dynamic addresses lead to the question how a concrete person is identifiable via
an IP address. Until now, no solution has been found for that problem in data
protection law; further research is necessary.

E. Technology instead of Law

The question therefore arises whether the answer to the machine might be found
in the machine itself.[27] A number of difficult legal questions may become
obsolete in the internet by the introduction of certain technical procedures. For
instance in the area of copyright, one has to think of digital watermarking
techniques and digital fingerprints.[28] These procedures guarantee that the owner
of a right can positively be identified and that cases of piracy can as easily be
prosecuted. Reference may also be made for cryptographic procedures.[29]

However, the role of technical means within the legal system has to be
considered. Technology as such is not more than a fact which per se cannot
claim legitimacy. For instance, it would be dangerous to qualify the circumvention of any anti-copying device as illegal. As the anti-copying device could
very well be set up by someone who himself is not in the position of a right-
holder; the circumvention of security measures which have been established by
a software-pirate can not be prohibited. Technical devices do not create
themselves legitimacy which causes specific problems in relation to the digital
signature.[30] The German *Signaturgesetz* has for instance been praised as it
combines very extensive technical standards of certification with a free market
economy orientated model of institutions.[31] But this combination is problematic
in two aspects. To begin with, the technical security standards have been
established so high that hardly any company will be able to meet them. This
might just be tolerated in Germany. In an international context however this
attempt will be rejected as a discriminating obstruction of access, especially as
Germany on its own in the world with these high standards. However, it is not a
alternative solution to reduce the value of security standards to zero as it has
been done in the draft for a EU Signature Directive. I fully agree with Germany
and France who disapproved the draft so that the text is no longer in discussion.

---

[27] See *Hoeren*, Law, Computers and Artificial Intelligence 4 (1995), pp. 175.
[28] *De Selby*, ACM Management Review 1997, pp. 467.
[29] See Imprimatur, The Law and Practice of Digital Encryption, Amsterdam 1998.
[30] Cf. *Roßnagel*, Neue Juristische Wochenschrift-Computerreport 1994, pp.96; *Bieser*,
   Computer und Recht 1996, pp.566.
[31] Cf. *Timm*, Datenschutz und Datensicherheit 1997, 525 (528); *Rieß*, Datenschutz und
   Datensicherheit 1997, 284 (285); *Hohenegg/Tauschek*, Betriebs-Berater 1997,
   pp. 1541.

F.   Electronic Commerce and the Problem of Trust

The deciding factor in relation to Electronic Commerce will be the question of trust.[32]

I.   Trust in the 'Analogous' Environment

Contracts are only concluded by someone who can trust in the performance of the contract by the other party. Such a trust exists if parties are in a long standing business relation and therefore have no doubts concerning the compliance with the contract. However, new connections may contain some difficulties. Apart from problems such as the ability and the willingness to pay, every party has to make sure who the other party is and how the contractual statements of the other party have to be understood. In the 'analogous' life, the guarantee of authenticity and identity is given by personal contact or by observance of the written form. If contract negotiations take place in the presence of both parties, either party knows whom one is dealing with and is aware of the content of the declarations of intent. The written form guarantees at least a certain authenticity of the communication; in relation to the declaring person certainty can be reached by introduction of a notary.

II.   Trust and Digital Signature

These trust-building measures will in the long run not be applicable to the internet. Here, the parties do not know each other, they only meet in the anonymity of the digital world. Personal contacts are missing as much as the possibility to find a safeguard in the written form. Hence, when an electronic order is placed no one knows whether it actually is placed by the person who pretends to be the orderer. The content of an order may also be changed on the long through the internet to the recipient. In this crisis, asymmetric encoding techniques promise relief. By digital signature they secure the identity and the correctness of the declaring person and protect against undue inspection by encoding with the help of a public key.

But who guarantees that an encoded message really does origin from the person who created the text under a specific name? Here, the German *Signaturgesetz* and the EU draft for a Signature Directive refer to the fact that the identity of the sender is guaranteed by the certification organisation (§5 I Signaturgesetz). In so far this organization acts a kind of notary. Yet, the

---

[32]   See in connection with this *Khare/Rifkin*, Weaving a Web of Trust, in: World Wide Web Journal, Summer 1997, pp. 77.

certification organizations are governed by private law. Anyone can establish such an institution; according to the draft of the European Commission even without a specific license. It therefore has to be asked which requirements have to be met in order for the certification institutions to be trusted. It is difficult to create trust via private certification organizations. In this private sector trust can only be created by a security infrastructure which has to be provided by the certification institutions. An advanced level of technology is supposed to create trust.

But this concept has its weaknesses: to begin with, the high security standards promoted in the German *Signaturgesetz* are seen by some European states as exaggerated and are rejected by the European Commission for being anti-competitive. In so far, the level of security will be lowered throughout Europe, which will give rise again to the question of trust. Secondly, trust in technology cannot not be created through technology itself. As soon as technology improves, the trust in conventional encoding devices vanishes. Cryptographic methods which are now considered to be safe may soon become obsolete; and then one has to wonder what to do with those keys which have already been distributed. Therefore I think a legislator should not specify the evidential value of a digital signature. As the digital signature has no established a fixed evidential value; this varies intertemporally.[33] The concept of the European Commission implemented in the Draft Signature Directive is not convincing. According to the Commission, everybody should be able to establish a certification agency without a license and should only repressively be held responsible via a liability for defects. It is questionable in how far this can establish trust, especially as a certification agency can at any time limit the risk of liability simply by choosing a suitable legal form.

G. Summary

The previous reflections may be summarized as follows:
1. The internet does not create net-specific legal problems. Rather, the internet law itself is only part of the general search for an international information order and the specifications of an information justice.
2. In the information society, a number of new property rights come into existence which cannot be classified within traditional property concepts.
3. The internet is leading to a dematerialization, deterritorialization, detempo-ralization and depersonalization of law; the legal system thereby loses its traditional (Roman law) roots (person, space, time).

---

[33] See in connection with this §§ 17 II, 18 *Signaturverordnung (SigV)*, which came into force on the 1.11.1997.

4. Self-regulation in the internet may assist law, but can never substitute it. Especially questions of antitrust law caused by business self-regulation need of further clarification.
5. Technology can never legitimate technology. Problems of trust in the integrity and authenticity of electronic texts are becoming more and more important.

LAW APPLICABLE TO TORTS AND COPYRIGHT INFRINGEMENT THROUGH THE INTERNET

by Masato Dogauchi, Tokyo

Contents

A. Introduction

People can access the cyberspace, which is imagined to exist in the computer, through the Internet. All that such people are interested in is information itself. The distance on the earth does not matter at all. People can communicate with each other by just clicking their mouse and nobody thinks about how far away the counter-party is. It is said that 'there's no "there," there.'[1]

---

[1] Resnick, Cybertort: The New Era, Nat'l L.J., 18 July 1994, at A21.

In the present nation state system, however, the legal framework is built on the basis of sovereignty, territory and nationals. Private international law is based upon such territoriality of law. According to the choice-of-law rules, any legal problem is thought to have its '*Sitz*'(place) in one of the jurisdictions in the real world. Consequently, the Internet provides many interesting problems in the field of private international law.

Nevertheless, it is important to note at the beginning that the Internet does not require special treatment in choice-of-law rules.[2] It is not a totally new means of communication. It is, in one of its features, just an advanced mode of traditional means of communication, such as facsimile, telephone, and mail. In another feature of the Internet, it is an advanced mode of traditional mass media, such as television, radio, newspaper, and magazine. Applicable law to contract between two parties across the borderline of the jurisdictions has been considered for over one hundred years. Libel by a newspaper article issued in country A and distributed in country A, B and C has also caused choice-of-law problems for more than one hundred years. The only new phenomenon introduced by the Internet is that ordinary people can easily be a party to international transactions and a wrongdoer in libel, violation of privacy, or copyright infringement without knowing of their international character. It is hard for them to image that clicking a mouse would cause legal consequences across the border and that a foreign law might be applied to their obligation.

From this viewpoint, there is no problem 'in cyberspace' but there are problems 'through the Internet.'[3] The main topic in this paper is copyright infringement through the Internet, which will be dealt with in Part C. Before exploring the problems in the field of copyright law, however, choice-of-law problems concerning torts through the Internet in general will be dealt with in Part B. Part D. is the conclusion of this paper.

---

[2]   See, Kronke, Applicable Law in Torts and Contracts in Cyberspace, in K. Boele-Woelki and C. Kessedjian eds., Internet: Which Court Decides? Which Law Applicable?, at 65 (1998). I attended the international colloquium held at Utrecht University on 28 June 1997 where Professor Kronke made a presentation to the same effect and I supported his view there.

[3]   There are some authors who purport to invent new legal framework for cyberspace. According to them, new *lex mercatoria* shall be formed for contracts in cyberspace and discussions with regard to torts on the high sea or in Antarctica shall be referred to for determining the law applicable to tort in cyberspace. See, Hardy, The Proper Legal Regime for 'Cyberspace', 55 U.Pittsburgh L.Rev. 933(1994); Note (Burnstein), Conflict on the Net: Choice of Law in Transnational Cyberspace, 29 Vanderbilt J. of Transnat'l L. 75 (1996).

B. Torts through the Internet

I. *Lex loci delicti*

In private international law founded by Savigny[4] in the middle of nineteenth century, the law applicable to a certain group of legal problems, such as the formal validity of marriage, is to be determined by one or a combination of two or more connecting factors, such as the place of celebration or nationality of one of the parties. The principle governing which factor is to be picked as a connecting factor is that the law with the most significant relationship to the group of legal problems shall be designated as the applicable law.[5] Considering the function of the connecting factors, they must be territorial notions, such as nationality, habitual residence, the place of acting, or the place where the property is situated.[6] Otherwise, no law can be designated as a governing law.

---

[4] Friedrich Karl von Savigny (1779–1861). One of his works, *'System des heutigen römischen Rechts'*, volume 8 (1849) had a fundamental impact on the choice-of-law method. According to him, on the assumption that the sovereign state and the civil communities can be divided and the communities have different but interchangeable laws based upon the same basic values, every civil law problem has a homeland or *'Sitz'* whose law is the most appropriate one to govern them. See, Tanaka, *Savigny ni okeru Kokusai-shugi to Shizen-hô-shisô* (Internationality and Natural Law in Savigny), Saburô Yamada-Fschr., p. 3 (1930); Sakurada, *Savigny no Kokusai-shihô Riron: Toku ni sono Kokusai-hô Kyôdô-tai no Kannen ni tsuite* (Zur IPR-Theorie von Savigny: Insbesondere über seinen Gedanken der völkerrechtlichen Gemeinschaft), Hokudai Hôgaku, Vol. 33, No. 3, p. 589; No. 4, p. 1039; No. 6, p. 1463; Vol. 35, Nos. 3 & 4, p. 319 (1982–84).

[5] There was and is another idea for determining the governing law. In the eleventh century through the middle of nineteenth century, the theory of statutes was developed. The most eminent scholar who purported this theory was Bartolus de Saxoferato (1313–57). According to this theory, on the one hand, the law of person (*statuta personalia*) was applied personally, and, on the other, the law of goods (*statuta realia*) was applied territorially. A similar idea was asserted in the American Conflicts Revolution in the middle of the twentieth century as the governmental interest analysis. According to this theory, the territorial scope of application of the individual law is determined in accordance with its public interests. One has to scrutinize the aim of the parliament that enacted the law before deciding whether it shall apply to the problem at hand. Both the theory of statutes and the governmental interest analysis do not use the connection factor. Therefore, it might be easier for these theories to cope with the problems in cyberspace. See, Acker, Choice-of-Law Questions in Cyberspace, 1996 U. Chicago Legal Forum 437, at 453.

[6] With regard to the governing law of contract, trust, and certain other juristic acts, party autonomy is admitted. This has its roots in French theory in the sixteenth century. Among others, Charles Dumoulin (1500–1566) is famous for his emphasis on the parties' intentions to decide the governing laws in matrimonial matter. In terms of Savigny's theory, the parties' intention is not an objective one like the others

cont. ...

In accordance with Article 11(1) of the *Hôrei* (Application of Law (General) Act)[7], 'the creation and effect of claims arising from the management of affairs without mandate, unjust enrichment, and unlawful acts are governed by the law of the place where the facts giving rise to the claim occur.'[8] With regard to torts, 'lex loci delicti', that is, the law of the country where an alleged tort is committed, is applied. The reasonableness of this provision is explained by the idea that dealing with torts has significant impacts on the public interests of the place where the event concerned occurs.

In the case of a traffic accident or fight, because the alleged wrongdoer and the victim are situated at the same place when the event happened, it is easy to determine the *lex loci delicti*. On the other hand, in the cases of libel, defamation or violation of privacy by the writings on the message board on a homepage, or invasion into another person's computer and violation of data therein, which is the *lex loci delicti*, the law of the place from where the wrongdoer struck his key-board, the law of the place where the receiving computer is situated, or the law of another place?

II.   Cross-Border Torts

The discussion on the *lex loci delicti* in cross-border torts in which the alleged wrongdoer and the victim are situated in different jurisdictions has gone on for many years. Product liability or libel by newspaper are typical examples in which the alleged wrongdoer (the manufacturer of the product or the mass media) and the victim (the consumer or the person whose honor is injured) are in distant places across a border.[9]

---

but can be deemed as a subjective connecting factor by which the designation of a certain territory is to be determined in each case.

[7]   Law No. 10, 1898 as amended by Law No. 27, 1989, etc. As to the full text of the *Hôrei*, see, Japanese Annual of International Law, No. 39, p. 186 (1996).

[8]   Article 11 (2): As to unlawful acts, the preceding paragraph does not apply where facts occurring in a foreign country are not unlawful under Japanese law.

(3): Even if facts occurring in a foreign country are unlawful under Japanese law, the injured person shall not recover damages or have any other remedy not available under Japanese law.

[9]   For example, in Tokyo District Court judgement, 28 August 1989 (Hanrei Jihô, No. 1338, p. 121), an article on a Japanese monthly journal issued in Japan allegedly violated the honor of a Japanese person who lived in California. No judgment was delivered on the issue of choice-of-law, because, in this case, the Japanese court denied its jurisdiction over the claim filed by the publisher for declaratory judgment that it was not liable for any claim by the California-living person on whom the article was written. And, in Tokyo District Court judgment, 30 September 1992 (Hanrei Times, No. 825, p. 193), a Japanese professional horse rider who was racing
                                                                         cont. ...

The law applicable to product liability is one of the most debated issues in this field. In 1973 the Hague Conference on Private International Law concluded the Convention on the Law Applicable to Products Liability.[10] According to Articles 4 through 6, the deliberate stage-by-stage connection method (*alternative Anknüpfung*) as follows is adopted. Suppose the habitual residence of the person directly suffering damage is in country A, the principal place of business of the person allegedly liable is in country B, the place where the product was acquired by the person directly suffering damage is in country C and the place of injury is in country D. At the first stage, if A=B or A=C, then the law of A applies. Otherwise, at the second stage, if D=A, D=B or D=C, then the law of D applies. Otherwise, at the third stage, unless the claimant chooses the law of D, the law of B applies.

However, as far as the interpretation of the present rules are concerned,[11] it would be difficult to interpret Article 11(1) of the *Hôrei* as mentioned above as

---

in Malaysia filed a lawsuit for damages against a Japanese newspaper publisher whose article allegedly libeled the plaintiff. The court did not distinguish the damage caused in Malaysia and that caused in Japan nor mention the choice-of-law problem at all. It ordered the defendant to pay money in accordance with Japanese law. See, Deguchi, *Kokusai-shihô jô ni okeru Meiyo Kison* (Libel in Private International Law), Jôchi Hôgaku, Vol. 38, No. 3, p. 131 (1995).

[10] Signed in 1973, Taking effect in 1977. Eight European countries are parties to the convention. Japan has not signed it. See, Sano, *Seisanbutsu Sekinin no Hôsentaku ni kansuru Ichi Kôsatsu* (Products Liability and Choice of Law) (1), Hôsei Ronshû, No. 91, p. 1 (1982); Dyer (translated by Dogauchi and Oda), *Shihan-seiki wo mukaeta Seizô-butsu Sekinin no Junkyo-hô ni kansuru Hague Jôyaku* (Twenty-five Years of The Hague Convention on the Law Applicable to Products Liability), Minji Hô Jôhô, No. 93, p. 8, and No. 94, p. 8 (1994).

[11] As *de lege ferenda,* the stage-by-stage connection method seems to be appropriate because of its deliberate consideration to find out the law of the place that has the closest connection with the matter at issue. The author, however, cannot support the rule that allows a party to choose the law applicable to tort, even within the very limited alternatives at the last stage for the following reasons: First, such method destroys the static legal order, for the law applicable to the product liability cannot be determined before the party in fact decides to choose the law of D or not. Liability of the person should be conceptually fixed at the time when the victim suffers the damage. Second, the victim does not necessarily know which law is more favorable for him. Without knowing the contents of the laws concerned, giving the ability to choose the governing law would not protect the victim at all. In addition, even if he knows the content of the laws concerned, it would still be difficult to determine which is more favorable. As the results of comparative law studies show, one part of the law of country D's law might be more favorable than the same part of the law of country B, but another part of country D might be more favorable than the same part of the law of country B. Third, considering the second point above, a victim who chose one law may want to change his choice when he has realized his own mistake in face of unexpected, disadvantageous results of its application to his claim. If such

cont. ...

excluding product liability.[12] Consequently, the problem is which law shall be applied, the law of the place of acting where the manufacture did the work resulting in the damage, or the law of the place where the victim suffered the damage. In the case where these two places are different, the latter should be the connecting factor in torts because the torts are perfected when the damage happens and the central issue in torts is to enable the victim to recover his loss. Thus, when a car manufactured in Germany caused an accident and injured a person in Japan, Japanese law rather than German law shall be applied to the claim of the victim based upon the tort.

The same rule shall be applied to the claims of the victims of torts committed through the Internet. For the purposes of private international law at least, libel through the Internet is not different from the libel by a newspaper article. The place of access to the information in cyberspace is the place of damage whose law shall be applied.[13] The place from where the wrong doer uploads the Internet does not a matter at all. In the case of Internet torts, everywhere on earth can be the place where people can access such information. Will this cause any problem or confusion?

III. How to Count the Numbers of Torts

As opposed to the above view that the law of the place where the contents in cyberspace can be read shall govern whether it is libel or not, and what kind of remedies shall be ordered, including the amount of the damages, one can find a different idea in the Draft Articles on the Law Applicable to Contractual and Non-Contractual Obligations made by the Study Group of the New Legislation of Private International Law[14] in Japan as follows:

---

change of choice were easily allowed, then the stability of legal order and efficiency of the judicial process would be severely impaired.

[12] This opinion might be a minority one. There are many Japanese scholars according to whose view the law applicable to product liability shall be determined in accordance with natural justice (*jôri* in Japanese) on the presumption that Article 11 does not apply to contemporary type of torts such as product liability because the liability there tends to be absolute and protection of the victim must weigh heavily. However, concrete rules thereon are not the same. One view suggests that the law of the place of market where the products are placed in the stream of commerce should be applied. See, Sano, *supra* note 10 (Hôsei Ronshû, No. 99), at 246 (1984).

[13] Dogauchi, *Cyberspace to Kokusai-shihô* (Cyberspace and Private International Law), Juristo, No. 1117, p. 63 (1997).

[14] The Study Group consists of eleven scholars including the author. See, Japanese Annual of International Law, No. 39, p. 185 (1996) (Articles 1 through 7) and No. 40, p. 57 (1997) (Articles 8 through 17). Japanese language version is found in Minshôhô Zasshi, Vol. 112, No. 2, p. 106 and No. 3, p. 133 (1995).

Article 10 [Invasion of Privacy or Right of Personality by Way of the Media]:
Proposal A: Liabilities that arise from the invasion of privacy or right of personality by way of any publication, broadcast or similar media action providing unspecified individuals with information shall be determined by *the law of the habitual residence of the injured party.* (emphasis added)

According to this proposal, in such tort cases, the place of the victim's habitual residence should be considered as the most closely connected with the cases, because invasion of privacy or right of personality occurs in his habitual residence irrespective of the place of publication.[15] This view is based on the idea that there is only one tort as far as there is only one victim. The damage which occurred in the world is calculated under a single law under this view.
However, Proposal B is as follows:

Proposal B: Liabilities that arise from the invasion of privacy or right of personality by way of any publication, broadcast or similar media action providing unspecified individuals with information shall be determined by *the law of the place where the damage occurs* (emphasis added).

Although the above proposals are just de *lege ferenda*, this conclusion can be drawn as the result of interpretation of the words 'the law of the place where the facts giving rise to the claim occur' in Article 11 (1) of *Hôrei*. The author's view is the same as Proposal B. According to this view, the number of alleged torts is the number of places where the damage occurs even when there is only one victim. He can claim damages under the law of the country A as compensation for damages suffered there, and can also claim damages under the law of the country B as compensation of damage suffered there, and so on. However, it is a matter of course that the result of the application of the law applicable to torts might be the denial of the claim by the victim because the alleged matter in not a tort at all. Also, whether the victim can really get damages under so many laws is a different matter. He has to prove the damage that he suffered in individual country. It would be rare for ordinary people to prove that they really suffered damage in so many countries. A world famous actress might acquire damages under the laws of many countries where she is popular. On the other hand, a libel case of a famous politician would make it clear that Proposal A above does not result in a sound conclusion. Considering that there are some differences in the extent of allowance of criticism for the purpose of public interest, even if he lives in country A where such freedom of press is restricted, injunction of the publication in country B where such criticism is free should not be allowed in accordance with the law of country A.

---

[15] See also, Deguchi, *supra* note 9, at 125; Deguchi, *America Teishoku-hô ni okeru Meiyo Kison* (Libel in American Conflict of Laws), Jochi Hôgaku, Vol. 42, No. 1, p. 415 (1998).

With regard to the number of torts, the 1995 Shevill case[16] in the EC Court of Justice is indirectly concerned. In this case, the plaintiffs included, among others, one individual, a U.K. national living in England, and two companies, one of which was incorporated and doing business in France and the other of which was incorporated in Belgian and controlling the former French company. The defendant was a French company publishing a French newspaper.[17] According to the plaintiffs, an article in the defendant's newspaper was defamatory in that it suggested that they were part of a drug-trafficking network for which they had laundered money. They filed a lawsuit in the English court for damages. The defendant disputed the jurisdiction of the English court under Article 5(3) of the Brussels Convention.[18] According to Article 5(3), a person domiciled in a Contracting State may, in another Contracting State, be sued: 'in matters relating to tort, delict or quasi-delict, in the courts for *the place where the harmful event occurred.*' (emphasis added).

The House of Lords referred the question to the EC Court of Justice. The EC Court of Justice held that 'the victim of a libel by a newspaper article distributed in several Contracting States may bring an action for damages against the publisher either before the courts of the Contracting State of the place where the publisher of the defamatory publication is established, which have jurisdiction to award damages *for all the harm* caused by the defamation, or before the courts of each Contracting State in which the publication was distributed and where the victim claims to have suffered injury to his reputation, which have jurisdiction to rule *solely in respect to the harm caused in the State of the court seised.*' (emphasis added).[19] These holdings do not mention the law applicable

---

[16] Judgment on 7 March 1995. Case-C-68/93. See, Nakanishi, *Shuppan-butsu ni yoru Meiyo Kison Jiken no Kokusai Saiban Kankatsu ni kansuru Ôshû Shihô Saibansho 1995 nen 3 gatsu 7 nichi Hanketsu ni tsuite* (European Court of Justice Judgment on 7 March 1995 on the Jurisdiction over the Case of Libel by Publication), Hôgaku Ronsô, Vol. 142, No. 5 & 6, p. 181 (1998).

[17] It was estimated that more than 237,000 copies of the issue in question were sold in France and approximately 15,500 copies distributed in the other European countries, of which 230 were sold in England and Wales.

[18] Convention of 27 September 1968 on Jurisdiction and the Enforcement of Judgments in Civil and Commercial Matters, as amended by the Convention of 9 October 1978 on the Accession of the Kingdom of Denmark, Ireland and the United Kingdom of Great Britain and Northern Ireland and by the Convention of 25 October 1982 on the Accession of the Hellenic Republic.

[19] According to the rules on international jurisdiction, which are to be determined in principle in reference to the provisions on jurisdiction among domestic courts prescribed in the Code of Civil Procedure, jurisdiction based on the jurisdiction over a related action is admitted in reference to Article 7 of the Code of Civil Procedure, which provides for jurisdiction over consolidated objectively related actions, provided that Japanese courts have jurisdiction over one of such related actions. Therefore, in Japan, if a case like Shevill were to happen, Japanese courts would
cont. ...

to the libel. In fact, the Court held, as *obiter dicta*, that '(t)he criteria for assessing whether the event in question is harmful and the evidence required of the existence and extent of the harm alleged by the victim of the defamation are not governed by the Convention but by the substantive law determined by the national conflict of laws rules of the court seized, provided that the effectiveness of the Convention is not thereby impaired.' However, the Court seems to count the number of torts as Proposal B of the draft Article 10 of the Study Group of the New Legislation of Private International Law does as above.

Accordingly, under the rule of Proposal B, it shall be the law of the place from where the information can be accessed that determines the legal problems concerning torts committed through the Internet and causing damage through it.

C.   Copyright Infringement through the Internet

I.   Choice-of-Law Rules Embedded in the Berne Convention

Where one can find a rule in the Berne Convention regarding the law applicable to copyright infringement, it forms a special rule and, to that extent, excludes the application of Article 11 of the *Hôrei*. The provision that attracts attention in this respect is Article 5(2).

> Article 5(1): Authors shall enjoy, in respect of works for which they protected under this Convention, in countries of the Union other than the country of origin, the rights which their respective laws do now or may hereafter grant to their nationals, as well as the rights specially granted by this Convention.
> (2): The enjoyment and the exercise of these rights shall not be subject to any formality; such enjoyment and such exercise shall be independent of the existence of protection in the country of origin of the work. Consequently, apart from the provisions of this Convention, the extent of protection, as well as the means of redress afforded to the author to protect his rights, *shall be governed exclusively by the laws of the country where protection is claimed.* (emphasis added)
> (3): (omitted)

---

have jurisdiction with respect to all of the harm caused in the world based upon the jurisdiction over the claim for damages with respect to the harm caused in Japan. In contrast, under the Brussels Convention, there is no such jurisdiction over consolidated objectively related actions, so the Shevill case had significant impact on the practices of the Contracting States. With regard to the rules on international jurisdiction of Japan, see Supreme Court Judgment on 16 October 1981, Japanese Annual of International Law, No. 26, p. 122 (1983); Supreme Court Judgment on 24 June 1996, Japanese Annual of International Law, No. 40, p. 132; Supreme Court Judgment on 11 November 1997, Hanrei Jihô, No. 1626, p. 74. See also, Dogauchi, Concurrent Litigations in Japan and the United States, Japanese Annual of International Law, No. 37, p. 72 (1994).

Although other possibilities cannot be excluded,[20] it seems natural to understand that Article 5(2) provides for the application of the substantive law of the place where the copyright infringement happens.[21] It should be noted that 'the country where protection is claimed' is not necessarily the country of the forum, because the plaintiff may file a lawsuit in country A where the person who committed infringement in the country B lives. According to this interpretation, the words of 'the country where protection is claimed' means that 'the country where' the infringement of copyright against which 'protection' is to be 'claimed' happens. In other words, the law of the country where the matter against which protection is claimed occurs, occurred or is about to occur is the governing law in this regard. For example, when injunctive relief is claimed, the law applicable to such claim is the law of the country where such relief needs to be implemented to protect the copyright. And, when damages are claimed, the applicable law thereto is the law of the country where damage resulted from the infringement.

Incidentally, there are other provisions in the Berne Convention that provides for the law of the country where protection is claimed to govern as follows (emphasis added):

> Article 7(8): In any case, the term *shall be governed by the legislation of the country where protection is claimed*; however, unless the legislation of that country otherwise provides, the term shall not exceed the term fixed in the country of origin of the work.
>
> Article 10bis(1): It shall be a matter for legislation in the countries of the Union to permit the reproduction by the press, the broadcasting or the communication to the public by wire of articles published in newspapers or periodicals on current economic, political or religious topics, and of broadcast works of the same character, in cases in which the reproduction, broadcasting or such communication thereof is not expressly reserved. Nevertheless, the source must always be clearly indicated; the legal consequences of a breach of this obligation *shall be determined by the legislation of the country where protection is claimed*.
>
> Article 14bis(2)(a): Ownership of copyright in a cinematographic work *shall be a matter for legislation in the country where protection is claimed*.

---

[20] According to Motonaga, *Chosakuken no Kokusaiteki no Hogo to Kokusaishihô* (International Protection of Copyright and Private International Law), Juristo, No. 938, p. 58 (1989), Article 5(2) should be read to provide for the application of the forum's choice-of-law rules. Under this view, Article 11 of the *Hôrei* is to be applied. See also, E. Ulmer, Intellectual Property Rights and the Conflict of Laws, p. 12 (1978). There is another view that, on the same assumption that the Berne Convention does not have its own choice-of-law rule, the law of the country where the availment of the work is done shall be applied. See, Komada, *Chosakusha no Kenri no Seishitsu Kettei to Hô no Teishoku ni kansuru Rironteki Kôsatsu* (Étude theorique sur la qualification du droit d'auteur et les conflits de lois), (doctor thesis, not yet published) (1998).

[21] See, Y. Tamura, *Chosakuken-hô Gaisetsu* (Copyright Law), p. 467 (1998).

In light of the embedded choice-of-law rules in the Berne Convention as above, the problems with respect to copyright infringement through the Internet will be considered in the next section. Before that, it should be noted that there is one substantive legal difference between ordinary tort and copyright infringement. In the case of an ordinary tort, the wrongdoing and harmful results are indispensable components of one complete tort, and the events as a whole are evaluated under a single governing law. Even when the torts are divided into several ones according to where the damage happened as written above, the chosen law applies to the set of wrong doing and harmful results thereof. In contrast, in copyright law, the rights of the authors are fragmented into many sub-rights and the infringement of such individual sub-right is to be evaluated under the law. Such right does not necessary require real damage. The right itself is protected under copyright law. This difference will cause some unsound conclusion in the case of copyright infringement through the Internet.

II. Copyright Infringement through the Internet

In the field of copyright law, Japan is one of the most advanced countries in amending its domestic laws to cope with the Internet. The Japanese Copyright Law was the first law in the world to be amended to make provisions with respect to the interactive transmission by wire in 1986. In 1992, the Multimedia Subcommittee was established in the Copyright Council of the Agency for Cultural Affairs to discuss the issues which had stemmed from the development of digitization and network, and the so-called 'Japanese Green Paper' was reported in 1995, which listed the relevant issues to be discussed and exemplified possible legislation. After receiving public comments from the many interested institutions when the Multimedia Subcommittee was about to start amendment of the Copyright law, the forum of discussion moved to Geneva as the schedule for the new treaties of WIPO was accelerated.

In December of 1996, the WIPO Copyright Treaty and the WIPO Performances and Phonograms Treaty were adopted at the Diplomatic Conference.[22] With respect to the protection necessary in the age of the Internet, the following provisions are important:

> Article 8 of WIPO Copyright Treaty [Right of Communication to the Public]:
> Without prejudice to the provisions of Article 11(1)(ii), 11bis(1)(i) and (ii), 11ter(1)(ii), 14(1)(ii) and 14bis(1) of the Berne Convention, authors of literary and artistic works shall enjoy the exclusive right of authorizing any communication to the public of their works, by wire or wireless means, including the making available to

---

[22] These treaties are called 'Internet Treaties.' See, Ficsor, Copyright for the Digital Era: The WIPO 'Internet' Treaties, 21 Columbia-VLA J. Int'l L. & Arts, 197 (1997).

the public of their works in such a way that members of the public may access these works from a place and at a time individually chosen by them.

Article 10 of WIPO Performances and Phonograms Treaty [Right of Making Available to Fixed Performances]:

Performers shall enjoy the exclusive right of authorizing the making available to the public of their performances fixed in phonograms, by wire or wireless means, in such a way that members of the public may access them from a place and at a time individually chosen by them.

Article 14 of WIPO Performances and Phonograms Treaty [Right of Making Available of Phonograms]:

Producers of phonograms shall enjoy the exclusive right of authorizing the making available to the public of their phonograms, by wire or wireless means, in such a way that members of the public may access them from a place and at a time individually chosen by them.

The right of authorizing the making available to the public of one's work is a very unique one. It is indispensable in the age of the Internet because it would be extremely difficult to identify who copied the work and transmitted it through the Internet due to the system of the computer network. Without any access and without any transmission, this right enables one to demand that the homepage maker shall delete the work in question from the server.

Taking into account the provisions of the above two treaties, Japan amended her Copyright Law in 1997 (entered into force on 1 January 1998), the major purpose of which was to establish the new right of 'authorizing the making available' of authors, performers and phonogram producers. This amendment was one of the steps towards the ratification of these treaties. The relevant provisions are as follows:

Article 23(1) [Right of Public Transmission]:

The author shall have the exclusive right of authorizing public transmission[23] (including the making transmittable[24] in the case of interactive transmission[25] of his work.

---

[23] According to the definition (Article 2(1)(vii-ii)), ''public transmission' means the transmission of wired or wireless telecommunication intended for direct reception by the public (excluding the transmission of wired telecommunication within the same premises other than the case of the transmission of computer programs).'

[24] According to the definition (Article 2(1)(ix-v)), ''making transmittable' means putting in such a state, by either of the following acts, that 'interactive transmission' can be done:

a) for an 'interactive transmission server' already connected to a telecommunication network for the use of the public:
 – to store information in its public transmission memory;
 – to add new memory with information into public transmission memory; or
 – to input information to it continuously without storage;

b) for an 'interactive transmission server' already with information stored in its public transmission memory or inputted to it continuously without storage:
 – to connect it to a telecommunication network for the use of the public.'

Article 92–2(1) [Right of Making Transmittable of Unfixed/Fixed Performances]:

Performer shall have the exclusive right of authorizing the making transmittable of their performances.

Article 96–2 [Right of Making Transmittable of Phonograms]:

Producers of phonograms shall have the exclusive right of authorizing the making transmittable of their phonograms.

Accordingly, in Japan it is copyright infringement to upload a work into one's computer that is connected to the Internet without permission of its author. Then, is it copyright infringement for a person in a foreign country to upload the same work into his computer in the foreign country without permission of its author? Members of the public in Japan can access such work from Japan at any time they want. Suppose the author plans to make available his work through the Internet to those who pay money by way of a certain method, and suppose his prospective market is Japan. What law shall be applied?

III. Application of the Law Applicable to the Copyright Infringement through the Internet

In accordance with the embedded choice-of-law rule in the Berne Convention, as stated above, the law of the country where protection is claimed, that is the law of the country where the matter against which protection is claimed occurs, shall be applied. The matter against which protection is claimed in this case is the act of 'making available' of the work to the public. What the wrongdoer does is to upload the work without permission of the author into a computer connected to the Internet in a foreign country and transmit it from abroad upon the requests of members of the Japanese public. So, the law of that foreign country shall be applied to the matter. As long as this is done in a foreign country whose law has not yet provided for such right of authorizing the making available to the public, however, such matter is not actionable under that law.

With regard to an event that happened in Japan, Japanese law governs. But, it is not possible for the claimant to prevent the Japanese public from accessing the Internet to enjoy the work on the unauthorized homepage, because it is not copyright infringement even under Japanese law. Of course, when the members of Japanese public make a copy of the work or transmit it to another party, it is copyright infringement. However, considering that it would be impossible to identify when, where, and by whom the copyright is infringed, it is not practical to claim remedies against those people. This is the reason why the right of

---

[25] According to the definition (Article 2(1)(ix-iv)), 'interactive transmission' means the 'public transmission' automatically done upon request by member of the public (excluding those included in broadcasting or wire diffusion).'

'[authorizing the] making available' to the public is created under the WIPO new treaties and Japanese law. Without such new right under the governing law, the copyright cannot be protected from infringement through the Internet. The author loses the Internet market for the Japanese public, and there is no remedy for it.

Very similar discussion has gone on with regard to copyright infringement by satellite broadcasting. In the case where from country A one transmits a work to an artificial satellite and the transmission from the satellite reaches the country B, C and D, which law is to be applied to such broadcasting? According to the draft articles of the Group of Experts on the Copyright Aspects of Direct Broadcasting by Satellite in 1985, the laws of the receiving countries (B, C and D) shall be applied. This is called 'Bogsch doctrine.'[26] Against this doctrine, however, the majority asserted that it would be difficult to clear the legal problems in so many countries and that it would be technically impossible to identify the size of the 'footprint', that is the territorial scope in which the satellite broadcasting can be received. According to them, the larger the parabola antenna one has, the more broadcasting signal one can receive. The law of the country from which the broadcasting signal is transmitted is asserted to be applicable to the right of broadcasting. This solution is favorable for the broadcasting companies, because once they have acquired the right of broadcasting in accordance with the law of transmitting, then they do not care about the size of the 'footprint' of the satellite signal. Finally, the EC Directive 93/83 of 27 September 1993 on the Coordination of Certain Rules Concerning Copyright and Rights Related to Copyright Applicable to Satellite Broadcasting and Cable Retransmissions[27] was issued. This directive localizes the act of transmission 'solely in the Member State where, under the control and responsibility of the broadcasting organization, the programme-carrying signals are introduced into the uninterrupted chain of communication.'[28] Because the territorial scope of this rule is Europe, evasion of the law may not be so realistic in this field. But, with regard to the Internet, applying the law of the country of initiation would yield no effective protection, because it would be easy for the originator of the transmission to relocate its transmitting point to a country with underprotective copyright law. Even the European Commission itself indicated that it might be difficult to identify a single point of transmission in the case of the Internet and that the point of origin could be in a country in this field.[29]

---

[26] Copyright (in Japan), May 1985, p. 181. Incidentally, Mr. Bogsch was the Secretary General of the WIPO at the time.

[27] 1993 O.J.(L.248) 15. See, Tagaya, *Kokkyô wo koeru Eisei Hôsô Cable Densô to Chosakuken Hôsei* (Trans-border Satellite and Cable Transmission and Copyright Law, Copyright, September 1996, p. 13.

[28] Behind this rule, there may be a view that broadcasting means not receiving a signal but transmission of signal by definition.

[29] COM(96)568 final, 20 November 1996, pp. 23–24, and n. 35.

As stated above, choice-of-law method, in any event, would not be enough to protect the copyright in the cyberspace age.

IV. Technological Means

Considering the inadequate protection of copyright against the infringement through the Internet, the main road to save the situation is raising the protection level by the unification of substantive rules. This has been done in the forum of WIPO for over one hundred years. In the case of satellite broadcasting, unification among the certain inter-related countries would be enough, as shown in the case of the territorial scope of the EC Directive as above. In the case of Internet transmissions, in contrast, unification of the laws of all countries would be necessary because one can make the work available in cyberspace from everywhere on the earth. Yet, it would be almost impossible to induce all countries, including a number of developing countries, to make the rules on the right of authorizing the making available to the public, at least, not within a reasonable period.

Then another way should be found. One alternative means is the technological means which appears in Articles 11 and 12 of the 1996 WIPO Copyright Treaty as follows:

> Article 11 [Obligation concerning Technological Measures]:
> Contracting Parties shall provide adequate legal protection and effective legal remedies against the circumvention of effective technological measures that are used by authors in connection with the exercise of their rights under Treaty or the Berne Convention and that restrict acts, in respect of their works, which are not authorized by the authors concerned or permitted by law.
> Article 12 [Obligations concerning Rights Management Information]:
> (1) Contracting Parties shall provide adequate and effective legal remedies against any person knowingly performing any of the following acts knowing, or with respect to civil remedies having reasonable grounds to know, that it will induce, enable, facilitate or conceal an infringement of any right covered by this Treaty or the Berne Convention:
>> (i) to remove or alter any electronic right management information without authority;
>> (ii) to distribute, import for distribution, broadcast or communicate to the public, without authority, works or copies of works knowing that electronic rights management information has been removed or altered without authority.
> (2) As used in this Article, 'rights management information' means information which identifies the work, the author of the work, the owner of any right in the work, or information about the terms and conditions of use of the work, and any numbers or codes that represent such information, when any of these items of information is attached to a copy of a work or appears in connection with the communication of a work to the public.

The goal at which these provisions are aimed is the security of information by technological means of protection. Such provisions, though strange in the field of copyright law, are inevitable in the era of cyberspace given the insufficiency of the remedy for copyright infringement through the Internet as stated in Section 3 of Part III.[30]

V. Extraterritorial Application of the Criminal Law

Apart from civil law protection and technological protection, criminal sanctions are another method to protect copyright. According to Article 119 of the Japanese Copyright Law, those who violate copyright shall be punished with less than three years of imprisonment or with less than a one million yen fine. In addition, Article 27(i) of the Implementation Law of the Criminal Code provides that Article 119 of the Copyright Law is to be applied extraterritorially as long as the person who committed this crime is a Japanese national.

This personal principle of extraterritorial jurisdiction is also provided for with regard to certain kinds of crimes listed in Article 3 of the Criminal Code. Such crimes as listed in Article 3 of the Criminal Code are very serious ones like murder, robbery, and others. Even with regard to these serious crimes, the reasonableness of the personal principle is not easily explained. Comparing these crimes in the Criminal Code with copyright infringement, it would hardly be possible to explain its reasonableness.[31] Copyright law has become too complex for ordinary people to know what is legal and what is illegal. Consequently, they would be surprised at its extraterritorial punishment under Japanese Copyright Law with respect to an act that is legal under the law of the place where it had been done.

Therefore, criminal punishment seems to be inadequate to cope with the situation of the copyright infringement through the Internet.

D. Conclusion

Copyright infringement through the Internet will increase dramatically because of its ease and low cost. Ordinary people will knowingly or unknowingly commit some form of unlawful acts. Accordingly, it would be very difficult to enforce the legal measures, if any, to protect copyright. And, because territorial distance has no meaning at all for people enjoying the convenience of the cyberspace, an adequate legal solution should be built with worldwide perspectives. However, as stated above, effective protection through designation of the law applicable to the problems in accordance with choice-of-law rules

---

[30] The amendment to add the provisions to this effect was implemented in Japan on 1 October 1999.

[31] See, Y. Tamura, *supra* note 21, at 468, n. 4.

would be difficult. The connecting point adopted in the Berne Convention, that is 'the country where protection is claimed,' may be easily relocated by the wrongdoers. Private international law cannot guarantee a sound conclusion given such differences between the heaven and the hell of the copyright laws among countries.

The straightest and most effective way to cope with the situation is to unify the copyright laws of all countries at a high level. In addition, in order to secure the actual enforcement of such harmonized substantive laws, the rules of jurisdiction and the enforcement of foreign judgments should be unified and guaranteed among them. In order to accelerate the unification process, it would be more effective to negotiate in a forum other than WIPO. For example, in the WTO negotiations, even the low copyright protection countries can deal with the high protection countries in other fields, such as bananas or shoes, and then can reach a high level protection agreement in the field of copyright law, which would have been impossible to attain by negotiating a single item. The contents of the TRIPs Agreement[32] are not a satisfactory result of such negotiations, but it seems to be a first step in this direction.

After such a fundamental unification of substantive laws among countries, private international law would play its role to deal with a few differences among the laws that still remained.

---

[32] Agreement on Trade-Related Aspects of Intellectual Property Rights, Annex 1C of the Marrakesh Agreement Establishing the World Trade Organization of 1994.

Part 2: The Law and International Finance

GLOBALIZATION OF CAPITAL MARKETS: A PERSPECTIVE FROM JAPAN

by Hideki Kanda, Tokyo

Contents

A. Introduction

The astonishing speed of globalization of financial markets inevitably affects, and is affected by, Japanese financial markets and Japanese financial institutions. Globalization of financial markets does not mean that there is one market emerging on our planet. It means that many markets coexist in a multi-layered fashion, from a local domestic market to an international wholesale market. These multiple markets interact with one another. Also, financial transactions take place, and financial institutions act, across national borders in these multi-layered markets. In this environment, a risk which arises in one market can be easily transmitted to another market, but from a regulatory standpoint, it is difficult to regulate these multi-layered financial markets.

The interaction between Japanese and global financial markets is not entirely clear. In December of 1989, a historic drop in stock prices on the Tokyo Stock

69

Exchange began. Accelerated by the discovery of the 'loss compensation' scandal in 1991,[1] the stock price decline led to a sixty percent drop in the market in 1995.[2] This market decline spread to real estate and other financial markets, and led to the worst banking crisis in Japan's history, driving the real economy into recession. Although this bursting of the stock market and real estate 'bubbles' resulted in unprecedented damage to Japanese institutions and the national economy, it did not spread to other countries' markets.

From a Japanese perspective, however, the competitiveness of Japanese financial institutions and Japanese financial markets inevitably declined.

Elsewhere I had examined the Japanese response from the crash until 1996, and made the following tentative conclusions: (1) a country which suffers from scandals, market crashes or unfavorable economic conditions within the country has a stronger stimulation to move toward 'global standards'; (2) the speed of a particular country's move toward these standards depends on its domestic situation; and (3) not everything is moving toward these global standards.[3]

In this paper, I describe the developments in Japan since 1996. More specifically, this paper examines the impact of 'Japan's Financial Big Bang' on the Japanese legal system. Japan's Big Bang, which was announced in November 1996, suggests a drastic move in the Japanese regulatory and institutional settings in the financial sector toward the Western model, particularly the American model, with the increased weight of capital markets in resource allocation. This move also suggests a change in the Japanese legal system. Exactly in what direction and to what extent the Japanese legal system will change, however, is a separate and difficult question.

In this paper I focus on the following issues. I basically argue that Japan's Big Bang program, in some respects, serves as a force to change the entire legal system in Japan. Section B. provides a brief sketch of the Big Bang's program. Section C. examines its impact on the Japanese legal system. Section D. is my preliminary conclusion.

---

[1] For the details of the loss compensation scandal, see Curtis J. Milhaupt, Managing the Market: The Ministry of Finance and Securities Regulation in Japan, 30 Stanford Journal of International Law 423 (1994).

[2] In the 10 years preceding 1989, stock prices rose sixfold.

[3] Hideki Kanda, Globalization of Financial Markets and Financial Regulation in Japan, Zeitschrift für Japanisches Recht, No. 4 (1997), at 9.

B. Overview of Japan's Big Bang Program

I. Background

Japan's Big Bang is a program to undertake an extensive overhaul of the regulatory and institutional structure regarding the financial sector in Japan. The program was launched on the initiative of Prime Minister Ryutaro Hashimoto in November 1996. He pointed out three fundamental principles for the program: free, fair and global. The reform is expected to be accomplished by the year 2001.

The Japanese economy suffered from the bursting of the 'bubbles' in the stock and real estate markets in 1991. Stock prices dropped more than 60% between 1991 and 1995, and land prices recorded a similar drop, driving the Japanese economy into recession. As a result, financial institutions and financial markets in Japan lost competitiveness. In Japan, the process of deregulation and the proper response to the rapidly changing environment in the world financial markets were delayed because the Diet and the government had to spend (and are still today spending) an enormous amount of time resolving the banking crisis. The Big Bang program is aimed at remedying this delay, and thus has two notable characteristics: (1) the reform is drastic and the scope of the reform is extensive, and (2) the time-table of the reform is specifically shown.

II. Selected Items of the Big Bang Reform

While this is hardly the place to describe in detail the content of the Big Bang program, several items of the reform are worth mentioning briefly.[4]

Lifting the ban on pure holding companies (effective, December 1997, for non-financial firms; March 1998, for financial institutions). The Anti-Monopoly Act, which prohibited 'pure holding companies' per se, was amended in 1997, and relevant statutes in the financial sector were amended to respond to this change. Thus, a financial group may emerge with a holding company structure where banking, insurance and securities businesses are offered through subsidiaries under centralized management of a holding company. In fact, Daiwa securities group established a holding company structure on 26 April 1999.

Abolishment of exchange control (effective, 1 April 1998). The Foreign Exchange Act was drastically amended. For instance, anyone may open and maintain a bank account outside Japan without regulatory permission or

---

[4]   The details of the Big Bang program are available in English at the web site of the Ministry of Finance <http://www.mof.go.jp>. See also Valentine V. Craig, Financial Deregulation in Japan, FDIC Banking Review, Volume 11, No. 3, at 1 (1998).

clearance. Part of the amount of individuals' financial assets in Japan, which total to U.S. $10 trillion, may be moved outside of Japan.

Abolishment of regulation on currency exchange industry (effective, 1 April 1998). Also as the result of the Foreign Exchange Act amendments, anyone may engage in the currency exchange industry. Convenience stores and other firms have already announced their entry into this business. For instance, travelers can now buy U.S. dollars at the airport counter of the air carrier.

Establishment of new regulatory bodies (effective, 22 June 1998). A new agency called the Financial Supervisory Agency ('FSA') was established and given power to regulate banks, securities firms, and insurance companies. This power was transferred from the Ministry of Finance to the FSA. Also, in December 1998, a new agency called the Financial Reconstruction Commission ('FRC') was established on top of the FSA, and is responsible for licensing and other regulatory activities in the financial sector. The FSA engages in the implementation of financial regulation. The creation of this new regulatory structure suggests that the style of financial regulation in Japan will also change from consensus-based regulation to rule-based regulation.

Abolishment of fixed commission system of securities brokers (partly effective, April 1998; fully effective, 1 October 1999). This will inevitably make the securities brokerage industry more competitive.

Entry into securities business: from licensing to registration system (effective, 1 December 1998). The entry level became lower for the securities industry. This change also accompanies the abolishment of prohibition on securities firms from engaging in non-securities activity. For instance, a manufacturer will be permitted to enter the securities industry while maintaining a manufacturing business. The number of securities firms may increase drastically.

Sale of mutual funds by banks (partly effective, December 1997; fully effective, 1 December 1998). Only 4% of the U.S. $10 trillion in individuals' financial assets in Japan are invested in Japanese mutual funds. Sixty-five percent are invested in bank deposits and postal service deposits. When mutual funds become marketed by banks, the picture may drastically change. Also, important reforms for the mutual fund system were made. For instance, a company-type fund (which is popular in the U.S. but was not permitted in Japan) became available (effective, 1 December 1998). Also, private funds (funds marketed to a limited number of institutions) became permitted (effective, 1 December 1998).

Asset management by securities firm (effective, 1 December 1998). Securities firms are now permitted to offer asset management service, typically by offering a product known in the U.S. as a 'wrap account.'

Improvement in accounting (effective, fiscal year 1999). Consolidated accounting with market-value accounting of financial assets will be required. The new accounting rule must be consistent with the International Accounting Standards.

Defragmentation among banking, securities and insurance industries. This is an ongoing liberalization program of fragmented industry regulation in Japan. Liberalization measures include permitting mutual entry among banking, insurance and securities industries through the subsidiary or holding company structures, and reducing firewall regulations among banking, securities and insurance industries. Implementation dates vary, but the greater part will be completed on 1 October 1999.

Securitization of loans, receivables and real property. A special statute was passed in the Diet in June (effective, 1 September 1998). This special legislation permits a low-cost method of securitizing financial assets, so that financing in the capital markets will become more attractive. Also of importance in this connection is the fact that the secondary market of securities among institutions was liberalized; certain qualified institutions may trade (non-equity) securities freely among themselves as under Rule 144A of the Securities Act of 1933 in the U.S. (effective, June 1998).

III. Impact on the Japanese Economy

While the impact of the Big Bang on the Japanese legal system is addressed in Section C., brief notes on the possible impact of the reform on the Japanese economy may be worthwhile.

From Bank Centered System to Capital Market Centered System. In the past, bank lending dominated the financial sector in Japan. This infrastructure successfully helped Japan catch up and undertake high economic growth during the thirty years following World War II. Once the Japanese economy reached a matured stage, however, the bank centered system began to produce costs to the national economy due to the relatively high cost of banking services. Other major countries, notably the U.S., today have well-developed capital markets, and the globalization of financial markets inevitably requires the increased role of capital markets in Japan. The Big Bang program thus encourages drastic improvement of the Japanese capital markets.

From Stability to Adaptability. Related to the above, in the past, the Japanese system emphasized stability, especially employment stability. This policy again made great contributions to Japan's economic growth. Stability, however, is not compatible with adaptability, and thus Japan was poor at adapting rapidly to changing environments in the world financial (especially capital) markets. The U.S. system, in contrast, represents a system emphasizing adaptability. The Big Bang program includes various measures toward increasing adaptability of the financial system in Japan. The price may be some loss in stability.

Increased Choice for Consumers. As the Big Bang includes drastic deregulation in the financial sector, it obviously will give Japanese consumers and investors more choice.

Increased Business Opportunities for Foreign Institutions. Obviously, the Big Bang will open more doors to foreign institutions. Some name the Big Bang reform as a 'Wimbledon' style reform. While Wimbledon is located in the UK, most players are foreigners. Whether this will happen depends on language, business custom and other cultural contingencies.

C. Impact on the Legal System in Japan

I. Characteristics of the Japanese Legal System

While many characteristics were pointed out about the Japanese legal system in the past decades, I think that three distinctive features existed during the period when Japan experienced high economic growth after World War II: (1) solid basic laws, (2) strong bureaucracy, and (3) small judicial system.[5]

Solid Basic Laws. Japan imported basic statutes in the early Meiji era from Europe, and thus prepared solid basic statutes as early as the late 19th century. Japan enacted basic statutes such as the Civil Code, Commercial Code, Code of Civil Procedure, and so on. Japan also prepared a Western-style solid judicial system, including the court system. While how these imported components of the legal infrastructure contributed to the high economic growth in Japan may be a separate question, it is noteworthy that the process of these imports was relatively smooth and Japan was quite successful in the transplant of basic components from the Western legal system to its legal system.

Strong Bureaucracy. Aside from the existence of solid basic laws, however, it must be noted that strong bureaucracy played a significant role during the post-war high growth period. The Japanese economy, including the financial sector, was controlled, protected and carefully taken care of by the government, which was armed with a very strong bureaucracy. Universities successfully sent their qualified graduates to the central bureaucracy in the government, and rules made by, and developed under the initiative of, this strong bureaucracy governed the business and financial sectors in Japan, which in turn led the Japanese economy to unprecedented success.

Small Judicial System. Under the above-mentioned circumstances, while the judicial system was kept solid since its inception in the Meiji era, the actual role or activity of the judicial sector remained 'small.' The business sector, including the financial sector, developed rulemaking and dispute resolution mechanisms within themselves and without resorting to courts or the judicial sector. Most bureaucratic rules were promulgated by business participants and bureaucrats,

---

[5] These findings were based on a research project by the Asian Development Bank. See Katharina Pistor and Philip A. Wellons, The Role of Law and Legal Institutions in Asian Economic Development 1960–1995 (1998).

and were almost never challenged before the courts. Also, disputes tended to be resolved within the business sector under the influence of the strong bureaucracy, rather than by means of court litigation. As a result, the national budget allocated to the judicial sector was very small, and the number of judges and private attorneys remained minimal in Japan, compared with other major industrialized countries.

II.   Impact of the Financial Big Bang on the Legal System in Japan

As noted in Section B., the Big Bang reform indicates that the style of financial regulation will change from consensus-based regulation to rule-based regulation. On the one hand, drastic deregulation will permit financial institutions and other private parties great freedom in creating and offering new and innovative financial products in the market place. Ex ante prohibition for certain risk-bearing financial products will be lifted. Instead, rules will be enforced ex post; that is, the key to the new system is that the party who violates a rule will be sanctioned ex post. This change suggests a change in the three features of the legal system identified above. I describe the expected change in the reverse order: the judicial system, bureaucracy, and the basic law.

First, the judicial system must become larger. This must take place simply to respond to the rule-based system of finance. The effort in increasing the number of those who pass the national bar examination in recent years is just one indication of the change. The number of lawyers will, and must, increase drastically. Also, the number of court litigation in the finance and business areas is already increasing, and today, judges are required to have an increased amount of knowledge and experience about complex financial transactions. For instance, in a recent case, judges faced the need to calculate damages in complicated swap transactions. More generally, both the court system and alternative dispute resolution systems should expand in response to increasing 'legal' disputes in the finance and business areas. The government will have to allocate more of the budget and resources to the judicial sector.

Second, while I am not sure whether the power of the Japanese bureaucracy will become weak in the future, the style of bureaucratic governance will inevitably change. In the past, bureaucratic rules were promulgated by means of lengthy rulemaking processes.[6] The Big Bang basically announced the abandonment of these rules; in the future, there will be an increased number of straightforward 'conduct' rules for market participants, which must be enforced ex post. This does not mean that regulators will become unimportant. They will

---

[6]   See, for example, Hideki Kanda, Politics, Formalism, and the Elusive Goal of Investor Protection: Regulation of Structured Investment Funds in Japan, 12 University of Pennsylvania Journal of International Business Law 569 (1991).

remain important, but the style of regulation will change from ex ante regulation to ex post regulation. The role of regulators will be to police compliance with rules, and to detect and sanction when rules are violated. In this vein, the role of the courts will inevitably become important. To take one example, the Securities and Exchange Act in Japan has a provision that the regulator may seek an injunctive order from the court to stop any illegal activity (section 192). This provision has never been triggered in the past. In the future, the provision of this type should be triggered in Japan.

Third, what about solid basic statutes? I predict that Japan will need to add more specific legal rules to the existing solid basic laws. To take one example in the finance area, Japan enacted a special statute in June 1998, (as a part of the Big Bang program) that confirms the validity of so-called close-out netting agreements popularly used in swap transactions worldwide. This legislation is already popular in the U.S. and Europe, and shows a new trend in the Japanese legislative history: enhancing legal predictabilities (or reducing legal uncertainties) in the finance area. The package of new statutes that was enacted in October 1998, to deal with the banking crisis includes various special provisions to the general rules on mortgage and related matters under Civil Code and related basic statutes. Thus, I expect that Japan will build up more intricate specific rules over the existing solid basic statutory base in the future.

D. Conclusion: Where Will the Japanese System Go?

As described above, Japan's Financial Big Bang suggests an extensive change in the Japanese legal system in certain important respects. Does this suggest that the Japanese legal system will converge to the Western system? This is not an easy question to answer. Elsewhere I had examined substantive legal rules on corporate governance converge.[7] There, a hypothesis was submitted that the cost of enforcement is the key and that in any given jurisdiction, unless various enforcement mechanisms change, substantive legal rules on corporate governance will not change, except for the rules for which the cost of enforcement is either very low or too high. Japan's Big Bang will probably require the increased role and function of legal rules. Whether the Japanese legal system as a whole will change, and more generally whether legal systems in countries experiencing a similar reform in the financial regulation will converge, are both interesting questions worth future research.

---

[7] See Gérard Hertig and Hideki Kanda, Rules, Enforcement, and Corporate Governance (draft, 1998). See also Hideki Kanda, Notes on Corporate Governance in Japan, in Klaus J. Hopt, et al. (eds.), Comparative Corporate Governance 891 (1998)

GLOBALIZING CAPITAL MARK
AND POSSIBLE REGULATORY
RESPONSES

by Harald Baum, Hamburg[*]

Contents

---

[*] Thanks are due to *Susanne Kalss* and *Katharina Pistor* for valuable comments on an earlier draft of this paper.

Harald Baum

A. Globalization of Capital Markets in Perspective

In the 1990s, 'globalization' has probably become one of the most frequently used terms at international conferences dealing with political, economic, or legal issues. The talk is already no longer about the process of 'Globalisierung', but rather about the result of that process: 'Globalität' ('globality').[1] This sounds as if we are confronted with new, inevitable, and irreversible phenomena which already encompass our economies in full and render our national politicians and regulators helpless. These three basic assumptions seem to be causal for some of the widespread xenophobic anxieties about the internationalization of markets and the resulting increased competition. Especially after the Asian financial crisis of 1997/1998, it has become an easy but mostly unjustified excuse to blame the internationalization of finance for unwelcome results of *domestic* policy failures.[2] However, a closer look at these assumptions shows that they are misleading. To briefly highlight this point, we must broaden our perspective for a moment to encompass the political and economic aspects of the globalization of the capital markets before focusing on the legal issues surrounding this development. Our discussion then proceeds as follows:

In Part B we will define the regulatory challenge that globalization poses for the national policymaker. Different regulatory options and possible strategies to cope with that challenge are discussed in Parts C through E. The classification starts with non-integrative strategies and proceeds towards increasingly integrated policies. Non-cooperative (unilateral) strategies are not viewed as promising solutions (Part C). Partly cooperative policies are also regarded as of limited use only (Part D). That leaves us with truly cooperative strategies as the best and increasingly practiced solutions for globalizing capital markets. This is especially true for international cooperation in enforcement and mutual recognition of securities regulation. However, the most intense form of cooperation, legal harmonization, is viewed with skepticism because it impedes regulatory competition (Part E). In Part F an attempt is made to draw some general conclusions.

Given the complexity and scope of our topic, the following analysis is limited in various aspects. First, it intends to give (only) an *overview* of basic regulatory options, recent developments, and the current discussion in the regulatory context of globalizing capital markets. The analysis therefore takes a rather *general* view without putting too much weight on details of specific regulatory issues in the different sections of the markets. Furthermore, examples for illustration will be taken from different regulatory areas: they may concern

---

[1]   Cf. speech of the former German president, *Roman Herzog*, at the World Economic Forum in Davos, January 1999, cf. Frankfurter Allgemeine Zeitung, No. 24, January 29, 1999, p.8.

[2]   See, e.g., NUNNENKAMP 1999 and BEDDOES 1999.

the regulation of transactions or of institutions as well as of the market itself. Second, the perspective is basically limited to *capital* markets and international *securities* regulation[3] and the arguments concentrate mostly on *legal* strategies; the topic of self-regulation as an alternative to state legislation is only briefly touched upon. Also, the focus is on *mandatory law* and not on private law; thus the development of law merchant (lex mercatoria) in the area of capital markets will not be discussed. Third, as far as the comparison of law is regarded, a certain emphasis will be laid on the *U.S.* securities regulation and its practice. For a long time, the U.S. market has been the most important of all securities markets, and the Securities and Exchange Commission (SEC) has been the world's most active guardian of these markets. In an international comparison, the U.S. securities legislation created in the 1930s and 1940s may probably be the most developed and sophisticated of its kind.[4] Securities regulations in other countries have often been influenced by American regulatory concepts;[5] in some instances they were even directly modeled on them, as in the case of Japan.[6] Additionally, we will put the regulation of the securities markets within the European Union by Community Law in the comparative perspective.

I. Globalization as an Advantage

Broadly speaking, the integration of global capital markets has two distinctive advantages, one economic and one political.[7] First, at the global level it allows world savings to look for their most productive uses regardless of their location. Furthermore, integrated markets create possibilities for an international pooling of risks and diversification of investment. By buying foreign securities, investors can diversify away some of the systemic risk connected with their home market and achieve increased risk-adjusted returns. Countries in a temporary recession or with little capital can borrow abroad to finance invest-

---

[3] The term 'international securities regulation' shall hereafter refer to rules and regulations that deal with cross-border securities activities in the primary, secondary, and takeover market.

[4] However, some critical voices point out that the U.S. already had the best capital market long before the present securities regulation and the SEC; cf. MACEY 1994; WALLMAN 1998.

[5] Cf., e.g., the adoption of prohibitions against insider trading in various European countries; cf. HOPT/WYMEERSCH 1992.

[6] Cf. BAUM 1997.

[7] For a comprehensive appraisal of the pros and cons of a global capital market, see OBSTFELD 1998; the effects of globalization on the German financial markets are discussed with BÜTTNER AND HAMPE 1997. A balanced discussion of the general economic advantages of globalization can be found, e.g., with v. WEIZÄCKER 1999 and KRUGMAN 1999.

ment for promoting economic growth. From the issuers' perspective, offering securities globally provides them with a range of benefits not to be obtained in their home markets, such as additional capital, increase in share value, additional liquidity, increased publicity, and others.[8] Venture capital missing at the domestic level may be found in foreign markets.[9] In short, the welfare gains of free capital flows are by most measures significant.

Second, international capital markets have a disciplinary function on national policymakers who might otherwise be tempted to exploit captive domestic capital markets. As could be seen in times when capital mobility was severely restricted by tight domestic financial regulation, quite a few governments regularly helped themselves to their citizens' savings through inflation and negative real interest rates. If capital is allowed to flow, policy failures will be punished. This pressure is also being felt by the national regulator: a capital market that is too tightly regulated and thereby imposing non-competitive costs on transactions will be avoided, as well as a market that is underregulated and thereby too risky to attract foreign investors' money.

II. Globalization in Historical Perspective

Given its obvious advantages, one would expect a global capital market to have been functioning for a long time. However, this has not been the case. For decades the market has been fragmented and limited in scope. Only *now* are we beginning to experience levels of capital internationalization that are comparable to the cross-border capital flows a century ago during the period of the gold standard through 1914.[10] International investment flows during the four decades between 1870 and 1913 on average exceeded 3 percent of GDP in major industrial countries. In the 1930s they had fallen to less than half that level due to World War I and the Great Depression when tighter restrictions were imposed. The final breakdown came with the arrival of World War II. Only in the 1970s did international investment flows begin to rise again significantly. But even today, with an average of 2.3 percent of GDP between 1990

---

[8] See GEIGER 1997, 258–260, with further examples; however, not all hopes of multiple listings are fulfilled and there seems to be a significant difference whether an issuer has his *initial* listing in a small or large market, cf. LICHT 1998.

[9] This is especially true for small or unsophisticated markets. A well-known example is the phenomenon that as of 1998, more than 100 companies incorporated in Israel— 70 of those being high-tech companies—were listed on the three big American exchanges; cf. COFFEE 1998.

[10] See VERDIER 1998.

and 1996, cross-border capital flows have not yet reached their pre-World War I level.[11]

The *long-term* historical perspective clearly shows that capital internation-alization is *not* a new phenomenon and that it can at least theoretically be reversed by regulatory change. Fortunately, however, it seems highly unlikely in today's networked world that any democratic government could be able to drastically curtail personal liberty again and reimpose strict capital controls. So most probably the free flow of capital as a prerequisite for further integration of national capital markets is here to stay. This brings us to the *short-term* historical perspective. From this point of view, one aspect sticks out: globalization is a fairly *recent* phenomenon. The process started some 25 years ago and has accelerated rapidly over the last decade.[12] To name but a few examples:

At the New York Stock Exchange (NYSE), the number of foreign listed companies increased from 38 in 1980—half of which were from Canada—to 290 companies from 42 countries in 1996.[13] The number of foreign companies traded on the three sections of the German stock exchanges more than tripled from 432 to 1,385 between 1987 and 1996. This compares with 802 listed or registered domestic companies.[14] The Swiss Exchange's list of foreign companies more or less equaled the domestic one in December 1998 (193:232).[15] In 1993 the London Stock Exchange (LSE) handled about 53 percent of the trade in French blue chips.[16] In 1995 over 50 percent of the total daily turnover was foreign equity turnover.[17] Alternative (proprietary) trading systems are operating globally, too. For example, in the mid-1990s Instinet already had terminals in 13 different countries and about 15 percent of its trade was created by cross-border transactions.[18] Another sign of internationalization are cross-border mergers and alliances between stock exchanges, such as the joint trading platform of the German-Swiss futures exchange Eurex or the

---

[11] OBSTFELD 1998, 11 et seq., with further references. The global integration of *trade* had already reached its pre-WW I level relative to GDP by the 1980s, and since then has experienced substantial further growth; cf. FEENSTRA 1998.

[12] For an overview of the developments in the 1990s, see, e.g., GRASSO 1997; developments in the 1980s are covered, e.g., by BAUM AND BREIDENBACH 1990; VAN ZANDT 1991. See further SECURITIES AND EXCHANGE COMMISSION 1984; SECURITIES AND EXCHANGE COMMISSION 1988.

[13] Cf. GRASSO 1997, 1108.

[14] Cf. DEUTSCHES AKTIENINSTITUT 1997, p. 02–1.

[15] Cf. FEDERATION OF EUROPEAN STOCK EXCHANGES, European Stock Exchange Statistics, December 1998.

[16] Cf. STEIL 1996, 10.

[17] Cf. GEIGER 1997, 249.

[18] Cf. RUDOLPH AND RÖHRL 1997, 152.

surprising alliance between the LSE and its former archrival Deutsche Börse in 1998.

Portfolio investment strategies are becoming increasingly international, too. In the first half of the 1990s, the non-U.S. stocks component of U.S. portfolios nearly doubled; the number of global and international mutual funds grew fivefold between 1990 and 1996 and their assets grew tenfold.[19] Net purchases of foreign stocks by U.S. investors grew from an average of less than $3 billion in the 1980s to more than $50 billion in 1995.[20] In Germany the share of foreign investors in the bond market rose from less than one percent in 1985 to some 22 percent ten years later.[21] On average, more than 10 percent of the stock in major industrial countries is at present held by foreigners.[22] Cross-border mergers and acquisitions, including international takeovers by tender offer bids, are by now commonplace in the headlines of major newspapers.

The list of examples could be easily continued, but the dynamics of that trend should be clear. The chairman and chief executive officer of the New York Stock Exchange, *Richard A. Grasso*, regards the confluence of a major shift towards equity finance in most industrialized countries with the fundamental shift of U.S. retail investors and U.S. institutions in their approach to ownership of non-U.S. equities as one of the 'biggest business opportunities placed before NYSE in the past one hundred years'. He compares it to the secular change in the U.S. financial markets a century ago when the infra-structure and industrial enterprises we know now were created and financed.[23]

III. Forces of Change

Which are the driving forces behind the recent changes at the international capital markets? We can see a couple of different factors which are mutually reinforcing and partly dependent on one another. In other words, inter-nationalization has a 'dynamic, historical character: it feeds on itself'.[24] An appropriate analysis would therefore require the development of a dynamic model, but as this cannot be done here, we will stick with the traditional approach and only focus briefly on the individual aspects as such.[25] The globalization of investment and finance must be seen in connection with

---

[19]   Cf. GRASSO 1997, 1111–1112.
[20]   Cf. GEIGER 1997, 249.
[21]   Cf. BRANDT 1997, 163.
[22]   Cf. HOPT AND BAUM 1997, 293.
[23]   GRASSO 1997, 1109.
[24]   VERDIER 1998, 3.
[25]   For a more detailed analysis of these changes, see, e.g., SECURITIES AND EXCHANGE COMMISSION 1994; RUDOLPH AND RÖHRL 1997, 146–161.

- innovation in information and communication technologies,
- government policies easing cross-border capital flows and market access by deregulation,
- institutionalization (and professionalization) of market participants, and
- increasing importance of equity financing accompanied by disintermediation, securitization, and development of new financial products.

If one views the securities markets basically as a device for the transmission of information, it becomes clear that their globalization corresponds with and is enhanced by the technical improvements of the telecommunications markets. But for all technical advances, globalization would not have been possible without a massive deregulation leading to a decline of prohibitive regulatory barriers to market access, capital movements, currency convertibility, etc. Furthermore, it was professional market participants who had the means to use both the technical possibilities as well as the regulatory freedom. In turn, they are creating demand for more sophisticated trading possibilities and they are pushing for a further deregulation. The more national economies become structured along the lines of a continuing cross-border flow of international finance, the less likely is a return of the currency control and tax measures that impeded the market after World War II. The 'genie' of international finance is probably too much 'out of the bottle', and taxes and regulation are an anathema for the financial services industry.[26]

All these rapid and fundamental changes notwithstanding, one caveat seems necessary. We may have permanently left the era of totally fragmented capital markets for the foreseeable future. However, we have not yet arrived in a world of truly integrated and internationalized securities markets (and may never do so). There are various counterfactors resisting such a market, not least the considerable regulatory barriers still impeding access to different markets. A look at the pattern of investor holdings shows that they do not contain shares of issuers of different countries in proportion to the country's respective total market capitalization, as one would expect in a truly international market. Rather, investors continue to display a very strong home bias.[27] This corresponds with another observation. Despite the increase of companies labeled 'multinationals', by far the greater part of economic activity is undertaken by enterprises whose economic center of gravity is clearly located in one country. The headquarters are located in the home country, the firm was taken public there, and the biggest part of its operation is carried out there.[28] Securities transactions remain mainly local in character. Multijurisdictional offerings—while growing in number—are still rare, and secondary trading is still mostly focused in the home market. Even where securities are cross-listed on different national

---

[26]   Fox 1997, 2530.
[27]   Fox 1997, 2507.
[28]   Fox 1997, 2506.

exchanges, the price is established in the home market and only mirrored in the satellite markets where the secondary listings are obtained.[29]

In other words, given the diversity of actors and interests involved, there is a long way to go before—if ever—we see a truly globalized market. For the foreseeable future, a strong home bias will prevail. This observation has to be kept in perspective when discussing regulatory issues. However, even if progress may not be as rapid as is commonly assumed, the relative importance of transnational securities transactions will continue to grow, and the integration and internationalization of the securities markets over the last two decades is far from being meaningless from a regulatory perspective. To the contrary.

B. Regulatory Challenge

The regulatory challenge posed by globalization has two basic aspects: one technical (I) and one competitive (II).

I. *Policy Trilemma*

To the extent that capital markets become globalized, policymakers are challenged to 'regulate' such international markets with national laws. From a technical point of view, delocalized screen-based securities trading poses the greatest challenge to securities regulators who are trying to allocate jurisdiction based on a territorial approach.[30] This can be difficult, as the Japanese Ministry of Finance discovered. When the volume of trading in Nikkei 225 futures on the Osaka Stock Exchange grew too heavy in the view of the Ministry, it caused a rise in transaction costs. This reduced the number of traded contracts from 5.4 million in 1991 to 1.6 million in 1993. At the same time, the trading of those contracts at the Singapore Monetary Exchange rose correspondingly, so the overall number of trades was not reduced. This means the regulatory aim was not reached and the overall effect of the administrative action was negative, as the trading fees were no longer generated in Japan but abroad.[31]

This example illustrates a general problem. Globalized markets confront the national policymakers with a specific trilemma which can be labeled the 'impossible trinity'.[32] A policymaker may likely want to achieve three goals when designing a financial system: (1) continuing national sovereignty; (2) financial markets that are regulated, supervised, and somehow protected; and

---

[29]   VAN ZANDT 1991, 59.
[30]   TRACHTMAN 1994, 72.
[31]   The example is taken from RUDOLPH AND RÖHRL 1997, 157.
[32]   BEDDOES 1999, 4.

(3) the advantages of a globalized capital market. Unfortunately, however, these three objectives are incompatible. Any coherent reform cannot avoid favoring two parts of the trinity at the expense of the third. If the regulation of the market as well as the maintaining of national sovereignty are the primary objectives, capital market integration will have to be sacrificed. If, on the other hand, capital market integration and global regulation are the dominant aims of reform, this can only be achieved at the expense of national sovereignty. If, thirdly, the policymaker wishes to keep sovereignty and at the same time allow the integration of capital markets, he has to accept an entirely free market structure at the global level.

The consequence of the impossible trinity for the global financial architecture is that any radical blueprints for reform are unrealistic. No policymaker will be prepared to sacrifice one of the three objectives in favor of the other two. Any realistic option can offer no more than an improvement of the trade-offs between them.[33]

II. Regulatory Competition

The dynamics described above have already led to significantly intensified competition, not only among market participants, but also among exchanges and other trading systems and, finally, among national markets and their regulatory systems as such. Globalization makes weaknesses in individual capital markets more transparent than before.[34] At the same time do open markets and advanced technology provide institutional investors with the chance of a regulatory arbitrage. If insufficient regulation—be it too much, too little, or just faulty—makes raising capital and trading in a given market too expensive, there is now a ready exit to other markets.[35]

A competitive market for regulatory regimes challenges not only the cross-border or international aspects of securities regulation, but to an even greater extent the domestic regulatory substance. Here lies the core of the 'regulatory challenge' in the securities markets for the national legislators and administrators. To the extent that a national regulation only requires what the market would provide in any case, no difficulties will arise, but the rule seems rather pointless. If, however, something is required that the market would otherwise not provide because market participants are disinterested and not willing to pay for it, regulatory competition will undermine the specific market design.

---

[33] BEDDOES 1999, 5.
[34] MAILANDER 1997/98, 391.
[35] For a general discussion of the political implications raised by the exit option that the Internet technology is increasingly providing, see ENGEL 1999a, 23–27, with further references.

Regulators can only enforce such a market structure if they have the means to suppress regulatory competition successfully. The 'classic way' to do so is an agreement with your competitors not to compete.[36] In a globalized market the only acceptable way to suppress regulatory competition is by legal harmonization. From this perspective, an international harmonization arrangement can be viewed as something similar to a 'cartel arrangement' that limits competition among national regulatory regimes for the sake of keeping market forces at bay.[37] Thus, the basic regulatory question posed by the gobalized capital market is whether we favor competition or harmonization among national securities regulations. Depending on the perspective, one can regard globalization and the resulting possibility of regulatory arbitrage as a threat or as a chance. The answer to this question will depend on how one evaluates the likely outcome of competition with respect to the regulation of products, players, transactions, and markets, as will be discussed later.[38]

III. Effects of Regulatory Arbitrage

The possibility of regulatory arbitrage can render misguided regulation expensive. Accordingly, the regulator must strike the fine balance between a justified blocking of needless evasions of useful rules that correct market failure and a hindering of beneficial transactions by imposing unnecessary costs. The gains from getting the balance right are potentially significant,[39] as are the costs of not getting it right. A look to the U.S. capital market may illustrate this.

An often-cited example of a *misguided* regulatory policy is the Equalization Tax imposed by the U.S. between 1963 and 1974. Various observers regard the tax as one of the major causes for the development of the Eurobond market and the rebirth of London as a leading financial center at the expense of New York. The Act imposed a 15 percent tax on such purchases in an attempt to discourage investment in foreign securities by U.S. residents.[40] Even if, as described above, the number of foreign listings on the New York Stock Exchange is rising, the world's biggest and most liquid exchange so far has attracted only a very small percentage of the large number of non-U.S. firms which principally qualify for a listing there. In comparison, in 1994 the London Stock Exchange—although much smaller in any measure than NYSE—had more than twice as many foreign companies listed.[41] The LSE is still the largest international market for

---

[36]   KITCH 1996, 242.
[37]   Cf. KITCH 1996; for a critical view of that comparison, cf. BASEDOW 1998, 55.
[38]   See infra Part E. at I.
[39]   FOX 1997, 2503.
[40]   See FOX 1997, 2518, 2530 with further references.
[41]   Cf. HOPT AND BAUM 1997, 295–297 with further references.

secondary trading: in 1995 the daily foreign equity turnover was $2.8 billion compared with $1.7 billion on NYSE and NASDAQ[42] combined.[43]

More generally, in recent years U.S. investors have increasingly seen themselves expressly excluded from initial public offerings placed in the international capital markets. Foreign issuers who are in compliance with their home states' accounting and disclosure requirements try to avoid the additional costs of complying with what is often perceived as cumbersome U.S. securities regulation and fear the risk of becoming involved in frivolous securities litigation.[44] As a consequence, U.S. investors who cannot reach the foreign target of their investment choice will leave the U.S. market and will thereby forgo *all* of the protection the domestic securities regulation intended to provide them with.[45]

The same counterproductive results can be seen in the context of international tender offer bids. When the number of U.S. security holders are small in a given foreign company, it has become common practice for bidders for the securities of that company to exclude U.S. holders from the offer. Foreign bidders often undertake considerable efforts to avoid any contact with U.S. shareholders.[46] A sample of 31 tender offers compiled in 1997 by the U.K. Takeover Panel showed that in 30 of the offers U.S. holders were expressively excluded by the bidder.[47] Thus U.S. shareholders are deprived of the chance to participate in the tender offer premium, as the bid price normally is significantly higher than the market price—a perverse result of regulatory paternalism.

So it is no surprise that the SEC's policy of broad extraterritorial application of the U.S. securities regulation with respect to cross-border activities[48] has increasingly become the target of massive criticism by some U.S. academics and practitioners.[49] Generally speaking, these critics call for a deregulation leading to a more restrictive and more flexible use of the U.S. securities laws in those

---

[42] National Association of Securities Dealers Automated Quotation System, a U.S. automated inter-dealer quotation system.

[43] GEIGER 1997, 249.

[44] FERRI 1997.

[45] LONGSTRETH 1995, 320. A German example might be the Auslandsinvestmentgesetz (Foreign Investment Law) of 1969 that constituted an excessive overregulation in the aftermath of the IOS scandal. The result was that most foreign funds avoided the German market altogether to the disadvantage of German investors; see BÖHLHOFF 1991, 55–56.

[46] Not always successfully, though. Cf. the famous case *Consolidated Gold Fields Plc. v. Minorco, S.A.*, 871 F.2d 252 (2d Cir. 1989).

[47] U.S. ownership of the target was less then 15 percent in these cases, cf. SECURITIES AND EXCHANGE COMMISSION 1998.

[48] See infra Part C. II.

[49] See, e.g., ROMANO 1998; CHOI AND GUZMANN 1996, 1997 and 1998.; FOX 1997 and 1998; LONGSTRETH 1995; COX 1992; for a general critical appraisal of the SEC's policy, see MACEY 1994.

cases.[50] The critics persist despite the fact that in recent years the Commission itself has at least cautiously started to curb the scope of their international application by exemption.[51] Others, however, strongly defend the SEC's international policy and strictly oppose a lowering of U.S. standards in favor of regulatory arbitrage and interjurisdictional competition.[52]

The two views are more or less diametrically opposed and seem to depend critically on a factual evaluation of the U.S. capital market and its degree of internationalization. Those in favor of a strict regulatory regime and its extensive application in the international securities market do not regard the examples mentioned above as overly important. Rather, they stress the fact that the U.S. has long been and will be the largest capital market in the world. Furthermore, they point out that an increasing number of profitable foreign firms deliberately accept additional regulatory costs when listing on the U.S. market in spite of strong international competition from, among others, the LSE. In this view, the greater the likelihood of the continuing predominance of the U.S. market, the less U.S. regulators will have to fear foreign arbitrage.[53]

IV. Regulatory Options

A policymaker has quite a variety of options to address the core question of an internationalized market: Which jurisdiction or jurisdictions are supposed to regulate a given conduct in connection with a cross-border securities trans-action? The picture of possible strategies to handle potential jurisdictional conflicts is complex, and may even be chaotic. Although fundamental reforms of capital market regulation are underway or have just been completed in various countries,[54] the questions of international securities regulation have only fairly recently become one of the central issues, and as yet there are only few internationally accepted solutions.[55]

---

[50] The different proposals are discussed infra at Part E.

[51] Cf. infra Part D.

[52] See, e.g., COFFEE 1998; GEIGER 1997; BREEDEN 1994.

[53] See COFFEE 1998, 43; the former SEC Commissioner *Steven Wallman*, however, takes a rather different view and warns against 'too much solace' from the fact that others have not yet caught up, see WALLMAN 1998, 350.

[54] A comparative overview can be found in the country reports in HOPT, RUDOLPH AND BAUM 1997.

[55] For a broader perspective of globalization and international economic regulation with respect to the possible development of an international or world economic law, see, e.g., BEHRENS 1986; STOBER 1999 and STEPHAN 1999. The general consequences for private international law are discussed, e.g., by BASEDOW (in this volume) and BASEDOW 1994; for an analysis from the perspective of the New Institutional Economics, see SCHMIDTCHEN 1995.

Solutions will differ with respect to the specific problem addressed. Jurisdiction regarding disclosure of cross-border offerings may be different from that appropriate to broker-dealer regulation or that of international insider cases. Put differently, the outcome will vary whether we try to regulate transactions, institutions that are components of markets, or the market as an institution.[56] Furthermore, it might make a difference whether the activities take place within a regional market that is partly harmonized—such as the internal capital market of the European Union—or whether the transaction is between countries with fundamentally different regulatory policies.

For a classification, different viewpoints are possible.[57] A useful criterion for evaluating law and policymaking in the international arena may be whether the chosen strategy is non-cooperative, partly cooperative, or truly cooperative.[58] Among the group of cooperative strategies, one can further differentiate between flexible, regulatory competition-enhancing or -inhibiting solutions.[59] Our classification starts with the non-integrative policies.

C. Non-cooperative Strategies

Non-cooperative strategies come in two diametrically opposed forms. They can be friendly or hostile.[60]

I. Disinterested (Laissez-faire) Approach

A state may decide to apply its securities regulation in a strictly territorial manner. Law and enforcement are confined to transactions taking place in the state's territory; contact with other countries is avoided. No legal protection is offered for securities transactions undertaken by its nationals cross-border, and domestic effects of transactions in foreign markets are disregarded. In this case, the policymaker is betting on the self-regulatory forces of markets and may hope for international standards to emerge. The positive aspect of the territorial approach is that it enhances regulatory competition and the resulting regulatory

---

[56] Cf. TRACHTMAN 1994, 74.
[57] See with varying perspectives SYKES 1999; CHOI AND GUZMANN 1998 and 1997; ROMANO 1998; GEIGER 1997; SCHUSTER 1996, 590–693, and 1994; SCHNYDER 1996; LONGSTRETH 1995; BAUMS 1994; TRACHTMAN 1994 and 1993; BAUM AND BREIDENBACH 1990; GRUNDMANN 1990.
[58] See especially SCHUSTER 1994 and TRACHTMAN 1994.
[59] See CHOI AND GUZMANN 1998.
[60] SCHUSTER 1994, 174.

separating equilibrium. Thus, in the view of some, a regime of territoriality may in the long run be best suited to advance global welfare.[61]

Viewed from the perspective of the regulatory trilemma described above, this approach to international securities activities maintains the state's sovereignty and makes use of the advantages of the globalized capital market. However, a possible price is paid with respect to the third side of the triangle: if all countries adopted this strategy, the international market would often not be regulated at all. This approach has a tendency to create a legal vacuum for cross-border transactions. Domestic regulatory policies could then be systematically circumvented by simply executing forbidden transactions abroad in other markets. Even though, in principle, that market may not accept such a transaction either, it does not care to intervene in the given case because the damages occur abroad.

II. Aggressive Unilateralism

The other extreme would be a unilateral strategy that more or less completely disregards the interests of other states. In this case, the state will assert jurisdiction over transactions outside its territory whenever its self-defined national interests are affected. This is normally the case if activities undertaken abroad are having an effect in the domestic market. As far as unilateral non-cooperative strategies are concerned, in international economic law the effects principle is the extraterritorial alternative to the territoriality principle.[62]

The legislative method differs from the classical choice of law approach under private international law. It is a statutory approach asking under which circumstances a specific statute needs to be applied. Typically, mandatory economic law ('Eingriffsnormen', 'loi d'application immédiate') is applied that way.[63] Basically, the SEC and the U.S. courts are using this method when determining the international application of the American securities laws and deciding about subject matter jurisdiction in a given case.[64]

---

[61] See CHOI AND GUZMANN 1997, 1889.

[62] The passive personality principle (= protection of nationals residing abroad) no longer plays a significant role in the extraterritorial enforcement of international securities laws; see SCHUSTER 1994, 187–188.

[63] For a recent general analysis of the international application of mandatory economic law, see, e.g., BASEDOW 1998 (exemplified in the field of competition law); see further BASEDOW 1994 and SCHNYDER 1990. The latter contains the most fundamental treatment of this question so far.

[64] An overview and a comparison between the U.S. and the German international securities regulation can be found with KIEL 1994; with respect to the German practice see also SCHNEIDER 1997.

Fundamental parts of the U.S. securities legislation were created in the 1930s and 1940s, at times when cross-border capital flows were at a historical low. The Securities Act dates from 1933[65] and the Securities Exchange Act dates from 1934[66]. Even later reforms were largely conceptualized in a market environment that was focused on domestic as opposed to cross-border trade.

In principle, the U.S. securities law regime extends U.S. jurisdiction over all securities offerings in the world, wherever they are located, if they only have some connection, however remote, with the U.S.[67] A telephone call into the U.S. in connection with a sales transaction already triggers—in principle—the application of the registration duty under the Act.[68] The same may be true in case of a later resale into the U.S. of securities initially traded on third markets only[69]. However, in recent years the excessive protection of U.S. investors wherever they may be located has given way to the more narrow protection of the U.S. capital market as such.[70]

With respect to the international application of the anti-fraud rules of the Exchange Act, we see a similar picture. Rule 10b-5 under Section 10(b), covers all transactions 'in connection with the purchase or sale of any security'.[71] As with registration requirements under the Securities Act, it is only restricted by the requirement that some use is made of interstate commerce.[72] Once more, the extraterritorial application of the anti-fraud rules is very broad in principle and somewhat ambiguous, as the SEC has not clarified the reach of Rule 10b-5 outside the U.S. Rather, the reach of Section 10(b) of the Exchange Act has been left to the courts.

The question of to what extent U.S. securities laws govern activities that have taken place across the border is connected with the question of whether a

---

[65]　15 U.S.C. § 77.

[66]　15 U.S.C. § 78.

[67]　Section 5 of the Securities Act addresses all offers (and sales) of securities that make use of 'any means or instruments of transportation or communication in interstate commerce'(15 U.S.C. § 77e). 'Interstate commerce' is defined in Section 2(7) of the Securities Act and includes communication 'between any foreign country and any State, Territory, or the District of Columbia' (15 U.S.C. § 77b(7)). For a short overview over the extraterritorial application of the U.S. securities laws, see RATNER 1996, § 42.

[68]　CHOI AND GUZMANN 1996, 210.

[69]　BAUM AND BREIDENBACH 1990, 9.

[70]　CHOI AND GUTZMANN 1996, 221.

[71]　17 U.S.C. § 240.10b-5.

[72]　Section 10(b) of the Act declares it unlawful to make use of 'any manipulative or deceptive device or contrive . . . by the use of any means or instrumentality of interstate commerce or of the mails' in connection with the 'purchase or sale of any security' (15 U.S.C. § 78j(b). The term 'interstate commerce' is defined similarly to the definition in the Securities Act; cf. Section 3(a)(17) of the Exchange Act, 15 U.S.C. § 78c(a).

court has subject matter jurisdiction in the given case.[73] The courts apply two tests to answer that question. Under the 'conduct test', jurisdiction is asserted if the acts causing a loss from transactions in securities to American investors have occurred within the U.S. Thus it can be qualified as a territorial approach. The 'effects test', on the other hand, embraces an extraterritorial approach. Jurisdiction is conferred—although the incriminated conduct took place abroad—if negative effects are generated in the U.S. market, at least insofar as the transactions involve stock registered and listed on a U.S. exchange and the interests of American investors are harmed.[74] If the effects principle is applied without restrictions, it results in an aggressive unilateral strategy and can be qualified as a non-cooperative behavior.[75]

The usefulness of such a strategy is more than doubtful. First, it may be questioned to what extent extraterritorialism is really necessary to achieve the aims of a national securities regime. Second, often it will not be effective in any case and, third, it will frequently render unintended results that are rather counterproductive.

If the primary regulatory aim is the protection of a domestic *market* and not of every national *investor,* regardless of where he or she is involved in a securities transaction, it does not seem plausible to apply the domestic laws on frivolous actions concluded on foreign markets.[76] Such transactions may defraud domestic investors but—as a rule—do not impose a negative externality on the domestic market.[77] Probably the price on those markets will be lower, thereby discounting a perceived greater possibility of fraud. The picture may be different if a country allows itself *systematically* to become a safe harbor for fraudulent trading. But then an even better answer for dissolving that externality might be bilateral agreement to achieve mutual cooperation.[78]

The drawbacks of an unfettered unilateral approach are obvious. Jurisdictional conflicts with other states are inevitable.[79] As these states are induced to pass counteractive laws to protect their own interests and their citizens, the unilateral strategy is not effective. These come in the form of bank secrecy laws

---

[73]   Literature and cases covering this question are numerous; a good overview with further references can be found with SCHUSTER 1996, 506–549; shorter CHOI AND GUZMANN 1997, 1884–1889.

[74]   The leading case is *Schoenbaum v. Firstbrook,* 405 F.2d 200 (2d Cir.1968).

[75]   For possible restrictions, cf. infra Part D. II.

[76]   Our analysis is restricted to international securities regulation. A different picture may emerge with respect to anti-trust law. There an extraterritorial application may often be the only way to keep markets open; cf., e.g., BASEDOW 1998; MESTMÄCKER 1988.

[77]   CHOI AND GUZMANN 1996, 222.

[78]   Cf. infra Part E.IV.

[79]   Those conflicts have written legal history in the 1970s and 1980s.; cf., e.g., SCHLOSSER 1985.

and so-called blocking statutes which prohibit the disclosure of information and presentation of documents under certain circumstances. In the mid-1980s, some 23 countries had either explicit bank secrecy laws or corresponding customs or precedents, and some 26 countries used blocking statutes.[80] In the worst-case scenario, the clash of extraterritorial application of one state's laws with the blocking statutes of another result in contradictory rules of conduct for the parties concerned. If both laws simultaneously sanction a non-compliance with their respective obligations, the parties will be punished whatever they do. This rather bizarre but not unreal situation amounts to nothing less than a complete and unacceptable failure of the legislations involved.[81]

Besides causing conflicts of sovereignty with other states and not being effective, the strict unilateral approach has another serious drawback. As already mentioned, the former scarcely restricted unilateral application of U.S. securities laws has led to adverse consequences: foreign issuers were kept out of the U.S. market and U.S. investors were locked into the domestic securities regime. As a perverse result of that paternalism, lucrative business and investment possibilities were lost.[82] A strictly unilateral approach once more demonstrates our policy trilemma. While national sovereignty is maintained and the capital market is regulated, no or only very limited use is made of the advantages offered by the globalized market.

D. Partly Cooperative Strategies

Under this heading, two different approaches can be subsumed. Again, the U.S. securities regulation will be used as an example. The first approach refers to the formulation of explicit and general exemptions restricting the extraterritorial application of the securities laws by the SEC, while the second encompasses a balancing of interests on a case-by-case basis by the courts. Both approaches have in common that they are not truly cooperative in the sense that the other states—whose interests are possibly affected by the exercise of extraterritorial jurisdiction—are not actively involved in the process of accommodation of the conflicting jurisdictions. Rather, consideration of their interests is made only unilaterally by the acting state.[83]

---

[80] Cf. COMMITTEE ON GOVERNMENT OPERATIONS 1988, 4.
[81] See BAUM 1989; BAUM AND BREIDENBACH 1990.
[82] Cf. supra Part B. III.
[83] SCHUSTER 1994.

I.   Unilateralism Restricted by Exemption

In the mid-eighties, the SEC had become increasingly frustrated with obstacles to its extraterritorial application of the U.S. securities laws.[84] In 1984 the Commission floated the idea of the so-called 'waiver by conduct' principle as a possible solution.[85] The proposal suggested that a foreign businessman entering the American capital market automatically waived all protection possibly granted by secrecy laws or blocking statutes of his home country.[86] After receiving a more than cool reception by academics as well as market partici-pants, the project was quickly dropped for good.

In a shift of policy, the SEC has instead intensified its attempt to limit the extraterritorial reach of the securities laws by adopting a number of explicit and sometimes rather complex exemptions in the form of general rules. In this way, the Commission has tried to accommodate the laws and regulations under its administration to operate within a globalizing context. Three recent examples may illustrate this trend.[87]

In 1990, the so-called 'Regulation S' was adopted as an exemption to the registration duties under the Securities Act.[88] The new regulation sets forth the proposition that offerings made outside of the U.S. are not subject to the registration duty of the Securities Act, as long as they are not merely concluded offshore as a prerequisite for a later distribution in the U.S.[89] by creating two safe harbors, one for issuers and one for resales.[90] The two main requirements for an application are that the offer is made in an 'offshore transaction' and no 'direct selling efforts' take place within the United States in connection with the distribution or resale of the securities.[91]

Regulation S takes a primarily *territorial* approach to jurisdiction, whereas formerly the regulatory goal of Section 5 of the Securities Act was interpreted as

---

[84]   See KAUFFMAN, 1985.

[85]   See SECURITIES AND EXCHANGE COMMISSION 1984.

[86]   See FEDDERS, WADE, MANN AND BEIZER 1984.

[87]   For a more comprehensive picture, see, e.g., LONGSTRETH 1995; BAUM AND BREIDENBACH 1990.

[88]   Regulation S—Rules Governing Offers and Sales Made Outside the United States without Registration under the Securities Act of 1933, Securities Act Release No. 6863, Exchange Act Release No. 27942, Investment Company Act Release No. 17150, April, 1990.

[89]   Rule 901 (17 U.S.C. § 230.901).

[90]   Rule 903 and 904 respectively (17 U.S.C. § 230.903, § 230.904). For a detailed description, see STEINBERG AND LANDSDALE 1995; cf. further CHOI AND GUZMANN 1996, 210–215; ROQUETTE 1994, 579–584; BAUM AND BREIDENBACH 1990, 24–27.

[91]   Rule 902 (17 U.S.C. § 230.902).

the protection of U.S. *investors* regardless of where they were located.[92] With respect to the registration, the SEC has decided to rely upon the laws in the jurisdictions in which the transactions are concluded rather than the U.S. securities regime.[93] Thus the Commission has recognized the primacy of the laws in which a market is located and concludes: 'As investors choose their markets, they choose the laws and regulations applicable in such markets.'[94] This shows a certain change in emphasis from the protection of U.S. investors to a protection of the integrity of the U.S. *market,* from which all participants of that market profit regardless of their nationality.[95]

Regulation S is generally appraised as progress in the right direction by decreasing undue regulatory restraint.[96] However, the fact that the anti-fraud and anti-manipulation provisions of the Exchange Act continue to apply unchanged with respect to transactions that are otherwise covered by Regulation S is viewed as inconsistent with the territorial principle and unnecessarily protective, if the primary regulatory aim is the protection of the U.S. market.[97]

Basically, the same territorial approach is taken by the SEC in an interpretive release it issued in the spring of 1998 with respect to securities offerings and sales on the Internet.[98] As publishing an offer on the Internet is qualitatively different from mailing an offer into the U.S.—in effect, the audience 'finds' the offerer, rather than the reverse[99]—Regulation S applied directly would not be of much help in restricting the extraterritorial reach of the Securities Act with respect to such 'cyber' offerings. As long as it could be viewed from the U.S., any offer placed somewhere in the world on the Internet would be potentially subject to the Act. The Commission has realized that this approach is untenable and has clarified that Internet postings as such do not result in a registration obligation under the U.S. securities laws, provided the issuer has implemented measures reasonably designed to prevent sales into the

---

[92] Cf. Regulation S's predecessor, Securities Act Release No. 4708, 29 Fed. Reg. 9828 (July, 1964).

[93] STEINBERG AND LANDSDALE 1995, 47.

[94] Regulation S, Securities Act Release No. 6863 (supra).

[95] STEINBERG AND LANDSDALE 1995, 47; CHOI AND GUZMANN 1996, 221.

[96] Cf., e.g., STEINBERG AND LANDSDALE 1995, 63. This has, however, been criticized for being unnecessarily complex in view of its rather simple and clear purpose; see LONGSTRETH 1995, 326.

[97] See CHOI AND GUZMANN 1996, 221–224.

[98] Statement of the Commission Regarding Use of Internet Web Sites to Offer Securities, Solicit Securities Transactions or Advertise Investment Services Offshore, Release Nos. 33–7516, 34–39779 (March, 1998), text available at *http://www.sec.gov/ rules/concept/33–6516.htm*; for an analysis see RUTLEDGE 1998. The release precedes a report of IOSCO published in September 1998 that addresses the same questions; cf. infra Part E. IV. 2; for the British perspective, see LONG 1998.

[99] See COFFEE 1997, 1231.

U.S.[100] The relevant test is whether offers are *targeted* to the U.S. market. However, the anti-fraud and anti-manipulation provisions of the Acts will continue to reach all activities on the Internet that satisfy the relevant jurisdictional tests described above.

Another example of limiting the extraterritorial reach of the U.S. securities laws by stipulating an exemption uses a somewhat different method. Under the present takeover regulation added in 1968 by the Williams Act to the Securities and Exchange Act, a foreign bidder who wants to acquire a foreign issuer that also has U.S. residents as shareholders must not only comply with the takeover regulations of the target's home jurisdiction, but also with U.S. securities laws.[101] So far, the only way for the bidder to stay away from additional disclosure and filing obligations under the Securities Acts which are in conflict in various aspects with European takeover regulations, namely the British City Code on Takeovers and Mergers,[102] is to expressly exclude all securities holders in the U.S. and to undertake considerable efforts to avoid any contact with the U.S.[103] Because this practice has increasingly deprived American investors of participating in lucrative tender offer premiums,[104] the SEC proposed a new Rule on Cross-Border Tender Offerings in late 1998.[105] The 1998 release proposes *general* exemptions, focusing relief in the areas where U.S. ownership is small or where there is a direct conflict between U.S. and foreign regulation.[106] This investor-oriented approach contrasts with the (more modern) market-oriented approach taken with Regulation S.

If adopted, the Rule would make available a general exemption in regard to a foreign target (private issuer) in which U.S. investors hold a record 10 percent or less of the securities, as long as the offer treats U.S. securities holders no less favorably than those in other jurisdictions. A second, more restrictive exemption would be available when the record holdings of U.S. securities holders do not exceed 40 percent of the subject class. It would provide more limited relief to

---

[100] See Release at p. 2–4. A reasonable measure could be a disclaimer posted at the Web site making it clear that the offer is directed only to countries other than the U.S.

[101] An overview of the federal takeover regulation can be found with RATNER 1996, § 15.

[102] Cf. BROWN, HANTZ AND BUDLONG 1998.

[103] Cf. the leading cases *Plessey Company Plc. v. General Electric Company Plc.*, 628 F. Supp. 477 (D. Del. 1986); *Consolidated Gold Fields Plc. v. Minorco, S.A.*, 871 F.2d 252 (2d Cir. 1989); a good overview of the U.S. approach toward international takeovers can be found with SCHUSTER 1996, 573–589.

[104] See supra Part B. III.

[105] Proposed Rule: Cross-Border Tender Offerings, Business Combinations and Rights Offerings, Release Nos. 33–7611, 34–40678 (November, 1998); text available at *http://www.sec.gov./rules/proposed/33–7611.htm*. The proposed changes are commented on by BROWN, HANTZ AND BUDLONG 1998.

[106] See Release 33–7611, at 5.

eliminate frequent areas of conflict between U.S. and foreign regulatory require-ments.[107] However, the general anti-fraud provisions of the Exchange Act would continue to apply without restriction by exemption.[108]

Again, the proposed rule seems to be a step in the right direction, but a rather limited one. From a European conflict of laws perspective, it would be more convincing if the applicable law and the competent authorities controlling the tender offer bid are those—and only those—of the jurisdiction in which the target company is registered (or has its principle place of business) *and* where its shares are admitted to trading. If a given firm is registered in country X, does its principle business there, and has its shares listed on an exchange located in X—as is the case with even most of the 'multinational' firms[109]—it seems hard to think of any reasonable argument why a bid for that firm by a bidder domiciled in X should be subject in a cumulative way to every foreign jurisdiction where shareholders happen to be located. This evaluation does not change if 11 percent of securities holders happen to be resident in one foreign jurisdiction.[110]

II. Unilateralism Restricted by Comity

The second possible type of restriction on the extraterritorial reach of the U.S. securities laws is on a case-by-case basis and is applied by the courts. It becomes especially relevant with respect to the application of the anti-fraud provisions of the Exchange Act in cases involving cross-border securities fraud. The international scope of Section 10(b) of the Exchange Act, the major anti-fraud provision, has not been clarified by the SEC. Rather, their limitation has been left to the courts, which follow an extraterritorial approach by using the so-called 'effects test' and asking if negative effects are generated in the U.S. market.[111] If unrestricted, the effects principle results in an aggressive unilateral, non-cooperative strategy.[112]

---

[107] A variety of potential conflicts is addressed, cf. Release 33–7611, at 9–18.

[108] For a critical view, see BROWN, HANTZ AND BUDLONG 1998, 14.

[109] See supra Part A. III.

[110] Things may become more complicated if the target company is cross-listed on other exchanges or if registration and listing are in different jurisdictions. But even in these cases, it is obvious that it is not feasible to subject the bid to various conflicting procedural regulations. Furthermore, the application of varying laws for different groups of securities holders based on their nationality would seem to be incompatible with the principle of an equal treatment of investors, which is the common goal of takeover regulation worldwide. These questions cannot be discussed in greater detail in this context; for a comprehensive recent discussion, see ZIMMER 1996, 85–100.

[111] Cf. supra Part C. II.

[112] For a general evaluation of the effects principle, see BASEDOW 1994, 430 et seq.

However, the effects principle can be used at least partly cooperatively if extraterritorial jurisdiction based on that principle is reduced to substantial, direct, and foreseeable effects, and if an additional 'test of reasonableness' is made asking whether the exercise of jurisdiction is not unreasonable under the specific circumstances. This comity-oriented approach is laid down in the Restatement (Third) of the Law of Foreign Relations of the United States, which was drafted by the American Law Institute in 1987.[113] § 416 of the Restatement translates the general principle of reasonableness into the field of securities legislation, modifying the conduct and effects tests somewhat. Courts have started to use at least some of the (non-binding) rules of the Restatement as a basis for their judgments, thus transferring them into law.[114]

Beyond the test of reasonableness, the Restatement proposes a further restraint on jurisdiction. Even if the exercise of jurisdiction is not unreasonable, in case the prescriptions of the two states involved are in conflict, the court should balance their interests—the so-called 'balancing test'.[115] Seen from the property rights perspective, this approach simulates negotiations on property rights of states.[116] Although the costs of the procedure of discovering and evaluating the other state's interests are higher compared with the use of the unrestricted effects principle, costs are ultimately saved as the other state will probably not retaliate if it sees that its interests are taken into account.

However, from a practical point of view, the test of reasonableness and especially the interests balancing test have been criticized as impractical and not sufficiently precise.[117] Furthermore, the multilateral approach to extraterritoriality is criticized in general, first for exacerbating the tendency toward underregulation because the state assigned with legislative jurisdiction may not have an incentive to correct market failures in another state. Second, critics regard the courts as ill-equipped to achieve multilateral solutions in international regulatory conflicts. In this view, judicial unilateralism helps to promote international negotiations by creating a moderate amount of conflict. These are the truly multilateral solutions to such conflicts.[118]

Indeed, cooperative strategies—to the extent they can be realized—seem to be preferable to both an aggressive *and* a restricted extraterritorial application of securities regulation which, in the long run, can be considered as second-best

---

[113] Cf. §§ 402, 403 Restatement (Third); for a general comment, see SCHNYDER 1990, 138–141; MENG 1989; with respect to securities regulation, see SCHUSTER 1996, 522–525; KIEL 1994, 147–151; for a recent evaluation with respect to the international enforcement of anti-trust rules, see BASEDOW 1998, 23–26.

[114] See SCHUSTER 1996, 522 with further references.

[115] § 403(3) Restatement (Third); the balancing of interests is analyzed by VEELKEN 1988.

[116] See SCHUSTER 1994, 190–191.

[117] See KIEL 1994, 150–151.

[118] See DODGE 1998.

solutions only.[119] With respect to our policy trilemma, truly cooperative strategies promise the most: sovereignty is kept or at least given up in a controlled and restricted manner, the positive effects of the global market are allowed to enhance welfare, and the international markets are not completely unregulated. As will be shown in the following section, international securities fraud might be best tackled by information and enforcement cooperation, while disclosure and other regulatory concerns may be taken care of by recognition.

E.   Truly Cooperative Strategies

I.   Overview

Cooperative strategies are driven by a variety of reasons that range from a necessity to cooperate in cross-border enforcement to political prudence to business facilitation.[120] In contrast to the partly cooperative approaches, truly cooperative strategies actively involve all sides concerned. They can be roughly divided into three different groups: first, *harmonization of securities regulation* (see infra at II.; second, *mutual recognition* (see infra at III.); and third, *cooperation in enforcement* (see infra at IV.). Compared with mutual recognition or harmonization, the least intrusive and troublesome form of cooperative strategy is cooperation. The strongest form of integrative regulatory policy is, of course, legal harmonization.

II.   Harmonization

1.   Types of Harmonization

Legal harmonization comes in different forms and aims at different targets. First, in a fairly modest but flexible way, players in the market may try to promote an informal development of *shared international standards* in specific areas of cross-border securities business. These activities are located below the level of formal legal harmonization, and can be described as harmonization from below. Second, legislative harmonizing efforts may come in the form of *minimum harmonization*. This is limited to basic principles and concentrates on some key regulatory elements only. This form of minimum harmonization is the current practice of capital markets regulation in the EU. It is usually combined with a concept of mutual recognition that it serves to facilitate.[121] Third,

---

[119] For a similar view, see BAUMS 1994, 11–12.
[120] See TRACHTMAN 1994, 75–81.
[121] See infra at C.2.

comprehensive harmonization resulting in uniform law may be attempted on the government level if a completely integrated market is to be achieved. It may also indirectly serve the purpose of imposing a leading jurisdiction's regulatory concept in a specific market segment on smaller jurisdictions. International (multilateral) treaties will probably be the base for legislative harmonization. Often legal harmonization will be accompanied by the establishing of an international or interregional organization, be that a court or an administrative agency.

However, it seems rather doubtful whether a comprehensive legislative harmonization can be considered a realistic option for international securities regulation on a *global*—as opposed to regional—scale in the foreseeable future[122]. Another question might be whether we will see some kind of '*de facto harmonization*' along the lines of the U.S. securities laws, as at least some observers deem possible given the gravity of the U.S. capital market.[123] A possible scenario might be a further increased role of the U.S. market with its jurisdiction and regulatory regime becoming dominant in the global market place. As already mentioned, the U.S. capital market is by far the biggest, and it probably has the most sophisticated securities regulation. Network externalities and the phenomenon of low-risk herding may attract a continuous migration of the largest firms.[124] This kind of 'first mover' advantage may not be easily competed away and may restrict a direct regulatory competition with other juris-dictions. However, with respect to development of an increasingly integrated European capital market with significant depth, this scenario does not seem to be inevitable, although in certain market segments—such as accounting standards, for example—the U.S. concepts clearly dominate at present.

With respect to its *substance*, harmonization can be procedural or substan-tive. The latter has the greater potential of being detrimental to regulatory competition. This feature makes a critical difference: whereas mutual recogni-tion and cooperation in enforcement have the potential to *enhance* regulatory competition, comprehensive harmonization, on the contrary, will often *inhibit* such competition. This brings us to a basic policy question: How shall competi-tion and harmonization in international securities regulations be evaluated? Put differently, having discarded non-cooperative and partly cooperative strategies, the question remains as to which of the truly cooperative strategies serves the globalizing capital markets best?

---

[122] Cf. CHEEK III 1996, 255.
[123] See, e.g., COFFEE 1998.
[124] COFFEE 1998, 41–43.

2. Legal Harmonization or Regulatory Competition?

To our policy question there will be, of course, no general answer. The outcome of competition or harmonization in international securities regulation depends on the specific regulatory context and the different types of objectives at stake. In any case, it would be beyond the scope of this article to even try to find definite answers. The discussion of whether harmonization is a more desirable aim in international securities regulation than competition, and if so, where and to what extent sectorial harmonization should be tried,[125] is part of the broader controversial discussion about the usefulness of harmonization of business law.[126] And this discussion itself is best viewed as a part of the ongoing general debate about the advantages and disadvantages of legislative and extra-legislative unification and harmonization of law.[127] Also, regulatory competition is increasingly understood from an institutional perspective as one aspect of competition among institutions.[128] In spite of the complexity of the issue, some general considerations may be proposed with respect to future discussions, for it will be difficult to develop a coherent strategy to make the best use of the chances provided while coping with the dangers caused by globalizing capital markets without a clear, *principled* evaluation of the issue.

It has already been mentioned that legal harmonization is the only feasible way to suppress regulatory competition and arbitrage in a globalized market if we do not accept extraterritorialism.[129] Accordingly, there exists a great temp-

---

[125] An excellent overview can be found with WHITE 1996; see further with varying results, e.g., ROMANO 1998; LICHT 1998; CHOI AND GUZMANN 1997; GEIGER 1997; KITCH 1996; FORD AND KAY 1996. A discussion of the pros and cons of regulatory competition within the *domestic* U.S. securities market can be found, e.g., with WALLMAN 1998, COFFEE 1995, or MACEY 1994.

[126] The most comprehensive analysis so far—mostly focused on corporation law—will be BUXBAUM AND HOPT 1988, together with BUXBAUM, HERTIG, HIRSCH AND HOPT 1991; both studies are reviewed by v. WILMOWSKY 1992; see also MERKT 1995; KÜBLER 1994. For a critical analysis of regulatory harmonization in the international goods and services markets, see SYKES 1999; also TRACHTMAN 1993.

[127] Cf., e.g., the various contributions to the two conferences held at the Max Planck Institute for Foreign Private and Private International Law in 1985 and 1991 respectively; reprinted in 50 *Rabels Zeitschrift für ausländisches und internationales Privatrecht*, 1986, 1–250, and 56 *Rabels Zeitschrift für ausländisches und internationales Privatrecht*, 1992, 215–316. For a recent sceptical analysis with respect to international commercial law see STEPHAN 1999; for a discussion in the European context with respect to a possible unification of private law see REMIEN 1999.

[128] Cf., e.g., the various contributions in GERKEN 1995 (especially ENGEL and KERBER AND VANBERG); also STREIT 1996; STREIT AND MUSSLER 1995. For a general understanding of institutions, see ENGEL 1999b.

[129] Cf. supra Part B.II.

tation for the regulator to harmonize in order to reduce the strain put on national regulation by a globalized market. However, harmonization comes at a price. Three questions of special interest shall be briefly discussed: (1) Is there actually a need for comprehensive legal harmonization in international securities regulation as claimed by many regulators? (2) What are the costs of harmonization? and (3) Are there cheaper alternatives?

a) The call for legal harmonization is commonly based on two main reasons. The first aims at enhancing competition in the markets for financial products and services. To the extent that it is used to lower entry barriers to national markets, substantive harmonization may intensify competition in those markets. It may thus help to create a level playing field and reduce protectionist national regulations that have created market power for domestic firms which have been sheltered against international competition.[130] But actually, this is less a question of harmonization than of deregulation and liberalizing markets. Another aspect is the lowering of transaction costs by harmonizing the rule of the game in the national markets. If financial services can be provided in various markets, obeying one set of identical rules only will without doubt cause transactions to become cheaper.[131] However, in most cases the same result can probably be achieved by mutual recognition. Again, only one set of rules has to be taken care of by a financial service provider. To make this option workable some minimum harmonization might be necessary, but not a comprehensive one.[132]

The second argument is more complex and more controversial. Is regulatory competition fostering a competitive and potentially destructive 'race to the bottom' among national regulators that would ultimately be harmful to market participants? This common assumption of regulatory competition has become increasingly challenged.[133] Theory might suggest that the possibility of migration to various capital markets should give rise to a regulatory arbitrage under which companies try to play the national legal regimes against each other by threatening to switch to other less intensely regulated markets.[134] If anything, however, the 'most visible contemporary form of migration', as one U.S. observer states, obviously is motivated by the opposite goal: an increasing number of foreign firms opt into the higher regulatory or disclosure standards of

---

[130] See WHITE 1996, 29.
[131] For a general appraisal of the pros and cons of uniformity versus diversity, see KITCH 1991, 39–42.
[132] Cf. infra at 3. and III.
[133] See, e.g., ROMANO 1998, taking the positive experience of American interjurisdictional competition for corporate charters as a basis to propose a similar 'market approach' to international securities regulation; see also STREIT AND MUSSLER 1995; KÜBLER 1994.
[134] Cf., e.g., the detailed theoretical analysis with GEIGER 1997; see also KAMAR 1999; FOX 1997.

the U.S. market.[135] At least profitable foreign firms deliberately accept additional regulatory disclosure when cross-listing on the U.S. market, as the attached costs are more than offset by higher stock prices.[136] These are accredited to the assumed better protection of dispersed shareholders under U.S. securities regulation. By opting into more rigorous standards, firms implement a kind of bonding under which they commit to stricter governance standards than their home countries provide and thus voluntarily reduce the danger of exploitation of minority shareholders.[137] Other examples are European firms listing on the LSE that voluntarily choose to meet higher local disclosure requirements than in their home market.[138] In general, there is no reason to assume that firms will list on an exchange with the lowest disclosure require-ments; instead, they will choose one where their *costs* are lowest. As investors value information and accordingly discount share prices, this will probably *not* be the exchange which requires the least amount of disclosure.[139]

Of course, not all foreign issuers try to list on one of the U.S. exchanges. On the contrary, as already mentioned, many try to *avoid* the U.S. market exactly because of the costly regulation.[140] However, this fact does not render the observation void that a significant 'race to the top' does take place. It rather indicates that the dichotomy of either a 'race to the bottom' or 'race to the top' may be too simplistic in the international context. Given the differences among issuers, investors, and countries, the ultimate outcome of regulatory competition may in general be none of those, but rather the evolution of a greater variety of regulatory options associated with different markets.[141] Assuming that no individual state has too great a given advantage with respect to its own issuers and investors, to that extent something like a 'separating equilibrium' may develop under which different states will design their regulatory regime according to particular types of issuers and investors.[142] The former will choose which state's regime best suits their specific needs, and the latter will then discount the price they are willing to pay for securities based on the perceived risk associated with a specific legal regime. If the U.S. securities regulation may

---

[135] COFFEE 1998, at 22–24, referring to the fact that the foreign listings on NYSE tripled between 1992 and 1998. CARBONE AND MUNARI 1998 draw a similar conclusion for the EU financial market, where market opening has given rise to a competitive regulation among the Member States enhancing their regulatory standards (359).

[136] FÜRST 1998; but see LICHT 1998, cautioning about the complex and not necessarily successful outcome of multiple listing.

[137] COFFEE 1998; this may explain the remarkable influx of Israeli high-tech companies effecting IPOs on NASDAQ to raise venture capital.

[138] See ROMANO 1998, 159.

[139] ROMANO 1998, 213.

[140] See supra Part B.III.

[141] Cf. the extensive analysis by CHOI AND GUZMANN 1997, 1869–1883.

[142] CHOI AND GUZMANN 1997, 1876, 1882.

be especially attractive for large firms with dispersed ownership, other jurisdictions might attract firms with concentrated ownership averse to extensive
disclosure and thus might specialize in marketing different legal products.[143]

One further aspect that may be of importance has been mostly ignored so
far: national securities regulations not only compete as substitutes for one
another, but they also interact with one another at the same time. The effects of
regulatory arbitrage may thus be wider and deeper than commonly perceived.[144]

Whatever the final outcome, the danger of a general 'race to the bottom' in a
globalized market without harmonized regulation and a global supervisory
agency seems highly improbable. Rather than harmonization of national
securities regimes, the goal of international securities regulation should be to
allow for regulatory competition in principle.[145] The most efficient way to attain
the trade-off between regulatory quality and cost which optimally meets the
needs of market participants is to offer them a choice of markets, and let them
choose.[146]

Yet another question, not specifically addressed here, is who should be the
competitors. The benefits of regulatory competition might be best realized by
giving some regulatory authority back to those institutions that were the first
regulators anyway: the exchanges. This, of course, is the question of self- vs.
state regulation.[147]

b) Comprehensive legislative harmonization incurs various costs. Three major
disadvantages shall be shortly addressed.

By definition, harmonization stops regulatory competition and puts an end to
regulatory arbitrage. This has negative consequences. Regulatory competition
can be understood as part of an institutional competition among jurisdictions.
This competition among institutions or systems—as all competition[148]—has a
quality as a knowledge-creating (discovery) process.[149] Given the constitutional
lack of knowledge of all societal agents (including that of regulators),
institutions can best be understood as fallible hypotheses about a way of
organizing human coexistence that must pass permanent tests.[150] A variety of
systems—or regulations in our case— is a prerequisite for finding the solution
which serves the desired purposes at the lowest costs. As no agent is in

---

[143] COFFEE 1998, 43.
[144] See LICHT 1998, 635–637.
[145] ROMANO 1998, 208.
[146] KITCH 1996, 241; see also BÖHLHOFF 1991.
[147] See MAHONEY 1997; also HOPT AND BAUM 1997; KÖTZ 1992; MERTENS 1992.
[148] Cf. VON HAYEK 1969, who first emphasized the interpretation of competition as a
       discovery process.
[149] FÜLBIER 1998, 293–296; STREIT 1996, 524–525; STREIT AND MUSSLER 1995, 78–79;
       KERBER AND VANBERG 1995, 42–48.
[150] GERUM AND WAGNER 1998, 356; STREIT 1996, 525; STREIT AND MUSSLER 1995, 78.

possession of the perfect model in most areas of social science, nobody can say what is the best regulatory system.[151] The potential and probability for the development of new and better institutional arrangements are much smaller in a non-competitive setting such as that found under a harmonized legal regime. Institutional competition also has a controlling function.[152] Private competitors can compare the quality of institutions, and the possibility of regulatory arbitrage acts as a strong incentive for the political competitors to be responsive to investors' needs and to offer attractive regulatory solutions.[153] These incentives are lost in a world of harmonized regulation. If a monopoly of regulation is obtained, national regulators have considerable incentive to overregulate and institute regulations of ever-increasing complexity.[154] And, as with all regulation, there is always a bias for regulators to opt for specific and detailed rules that 'constrain behavior and channel activities to what is known and safe'.[155] Thus potential liabilities of the regulators might be reduced, but only at the expense of imposing costs on innovation and flexibility.[156]

A second major disadvantage is the loss of regulatory diversity. Only legal heterogeneity pays respect to national preferences in regulatory policy that reflect local differences in risk tolerance, income, and other factors.[157] Harmonized regulation, on the other hand, results in a great loss of diversity and of valuable adaptations to national conditions.[158] Accordingly, regulatory competition will not lead to a complete harmonization 'from below' by the market.[159] Rather, different solutions will develop that respond to the varying needs of different actors, although, of course, good regulations will often be copied, thus leading to some kind of (limited) harmonization.[160]

A further serious drawback of legal harmonization is the quality of the resulting harmonized or uniform law. Given the time it takes to reach an international agreement, the harmonized result may be outdated before it is even applied in practice, especially in the fast-changing field of financial services. Even worse, once an agreement is reached, it is extremely difficult to be changed again, resulting in a dangerous petrification of the harmonized provisions.[161] Again, this is especially true in fields with rapid changes such as capital markets. Additionally, due to its character as a political compromise

---

[151] Cf. SCHMIDT 1991b, 91.
[152] STREIT 1996, 525–526.; STREIT AND MUSSLER 1995, 79–80.
[153] MAHONEY 1997, 1454.
[154] See CHOI AND GUZMANN 1998, 950; MACEY 1994.
[155] WALLMAN 1998, 346.
[156] FORD AND KAY 1996, 154.
[157] SYKES 1999, 51–52.
[158] WHITE 1996, 30; see also KÖTZ 1986, 12; SCHMIDTCHEN 1995, 109.
[159] STREIT 1996, 525.
[160] Cf. SCHMIDT 1991a, 57
[161] Cf. SCHMIDT 1991a, 58.

resulting from a rather non-transparent political process, harmonization may only be possible on some kind of shared minimum standard, or it may follow a dominant regulatory solution not suitable for other local situations. In any case, to the extent that harmonization is deepened and broadened, almost inevitably the overall level of regulation will be raised.[162] More likely than not, this will have a negative effect on the market in the long run, even if harmonization was primarily used to lower transaction costs. Furthermore, harmonization may not only be used to lower entry barriers; to the contrary, it can also be misused to create new barriers.[163]

Where does this leave us? Basically, the same rule should be applied in the international context as with the regulation of the national market: if no market failure is obvious, then there is no need or justification for regulating the market. By harmonizing national securities regulation, the international capital market becomes regulated. National legal concepts are lifted via harmonization on an international level, and thus the overall level of regulation will be raised. Therefore, legal harmonization in the field of international securities regulation should be used only as an *exceptional* policy instrument and *not* as a rule. As is argued by *White*, 'in the absence of a strong showing that there is a substantial market failure and that the problems of government failure can be overcome so as to create a reasonable likelihood that government intervention will improve outcomes, the competitive outcome should prevail'; competition ought to be the 'default option'.[164]

With respect to our initial question, one important general conclusion can be drawn: those who favor harmonization of specific areas of national securities regulations bear a *double burden of proof*. First, they have to show convincingly that a substantive market failure exists that calls for regulatory harmonization. Second, advocates of harmonization are required to produce a quantified cost benefits analysis that takes into account the disadvantages of harmonization. They have to prove that the assumed positive results of intervention outweigh the dangers of internationally harmonized government failure. As is mostly overlooked when market failure is analyzed, it cannot be taken for granted that regulatory action—which is itself prone to (government) failure—really does improve and not exacerbate market imperfections.[165]

In short, if in doubt, do not harmonize through international agreements, however big the temptation may be to reduce the strain put on national regulation by a globalized market. This is especially true as less intrusive and costly regulatory options exist.

---

[162] See KÖNDGEN 1998, 129.
[163] Cf. MESTMÄCKER 1989, 288.
[164] WHITE 1996, 30; see also WOLF 1993.
[165] The way the Japanese financial crisis of the 1990s was mishandled by bureaucrats is a vivid example of government failure; see, e.g., MILHAUPT AND MILLER 1997.

c) Regulatory diversity comes along with the benefits of congruence with differing cultures and the competition for survival of the most effective regulatory regime. Unfortunately, however, it also provides opportunities for bad conduct by market participants and allows for externalization of costs by states. The positive, disciplinary benefits of regulatory arbitrage can thus only be achieved when it is possible to avoid an externalization of regulatory costs raised by the activities of firms and the social costs allocable to the individual national regulation or the lack thereof.[166]

This can be achieved by developing rules of regulatory jurisdiction on an international level. These have to be agreed upon among states to be effective; horizontal cooperation is therefore necessary. Such rules have similar functions as the agreed rules of tort and property on the domestic level, namely, to facilitate the operation of the market and to assign the distributive consequences of specific actions.[167] An effective allocation of regulatory jurisdiction can be an alternative to harmonization of substantive regulation without suppressing regulatory competition.

The same is true for fraud enforcement. As fraud can be and always has been carried out on an international scale, effective enforcement requires international cooperation, but again does not call for harmonization.[168] Thus, as a rule, regulatory competition accompanied by enforcement cooperation might serve the purpose of the globalizing capital market best.

3.   Minimum Harmonization

As already briefly mentioned above, the opening of markets and lowering of transaction costs does not require a comprehensive legislative harmonization. Instead, some kind of minimum harmonization combined with mutual recognition can, as a rule, achieve the same results while avoiding the pitfalls of the former. Minimum harmonization offers a middle way between the two extremes of unfettered regulatory competition and full-scale harmonization.

The most prominent example of a regionally-based effort to establish a regime of minimum harmonization in the field of international securities regulation is the capital markets law of the European Union.[169] This has to be

---

[166] TRACHTMAN 1993, 102.
[167] ID.
[168] KITCH 1996, 241; see infra D.
[169] For an overview of the capital market regulation within the EU, see, e.g., SULGER 1998; GRUNDMANN 1996; ASSMANN AND BUCK 1990; WARREN 1990; for a comparison between the U.S. and the EU securities regulation, see ROQUETTE 1994. A short list of some major works giving a comprehensive analysis might contain FERRARINI 1998; STEIL 1996; WEBER 1996; ANDENAS AND KENYON-SLADE 1993.

seen as a complementary device to the principle of mutual recognition applied within the EU.[170]

In 1966 the European Communities adopted the goal of establishing an integrated securities market and the creation of a European capital market law.[171] This undertaking was based on the principal objectives laid down in the EEC Treaty: the free movement of goods, persons, services, and capital between the member states.[172] Through a series of directives, that goal has by and large been achieved some three decades later, although *not* by establishing *one* capital market but rather by fostering the integration of the *national* securities markets.[173] In spite of considerable progress, in many areas fragmentation and impediments to cross-border financial services still remain. This prompted the Commission—upon invitation of the European Council—to speed up integration by introducing the so-called 'Financial Services Action Plan' in May 1999.[174]

At the beginning, a concept of strict harmonization was employed. However, as that proved difficult to implement, this approach was later rejected. Detailed harmonization was too complicated and too slow to achieve; often it even proved impossible to unite the different legal concepts of the Member States around a common denominator. Therefore, in the Commission's White Paper of 1985, 'Completing the Internal Market',[175] the concept of mutual recognition combined with a harmonization of minimum standards as a precondition for recognition was adopted as an alternative.[176] This competition of systems as a coordinating mechanism is also reflected in the subsidiarity principle established in the Maastricht Treaty.[177] Thus a compromise was chosen: neither the

---

[170] Cf. infra C.2.

[171] See KOMMISSION DER EUROPÄISCHEN WIRTSCHAFTSGEMEINSCHAFT 1966, based on an expert report, the so-called Segré Report.

[172] A basic analysis of the economic constitution of the EU can be found with MESTMÄCKER 1994; BEHRENS 1994; BASEDOW 1992.

[173] Cf. GRUNDMANN 1996, 103. Actually, the relative success in creating a European securities regulation contrasts with the much greater difficulties in developing a European company law; cf. HOPT 1998.

[174] COMMISSION OF THE EUROPEAN COMMUNITIES 1999.

[175] COMMISSION OF THE EUROPEAN COMMUNITIES 1985.

[176] Paragraphs 102, 103 of the White Paper state: 'The Commission considers that it should be possible to facilitate the exchange of such "financial products" at a Community level, using a minimal coordination of rules . . . as the basis for mutual recognition by Member States of what each does to safeguard the interests of the public. Such harmonization . . . should be guided by the principle of "home country control".'; cf. STREIT AND MUSSLER 1995, 88–90; LOMNICKA 1993, 84–86; FITCHEW 1991, 7–11.

[177] Cf. GERUM AND WAGNER 1998, 355; MOLITOR 1996; BAUMS 1995. The most recent decision of the European Court reflecting the idea of a competition of systems is the *Centros* decision from March 9, 1999 (NZG 1999, 298; ZIP 1999, 438).

establishment of one capital market with a completely harmonized (uniform) market regulation, nor development left to legislation on the Community level only, nor to market forces in an unconstrained laissez-faire approach.[178]

However, the discussion rages on as to whether too much or too little harmonization has taken place.[179] A major point of criticism is the lack of a basic concept of harmonization within the EU.[180] Although harmonization is—at least theoretically—constrained to minimum standards, de facto it can be rather far-reaching. This makes the drafting process time-consuming and the directives complex and difficult to change later, as has been criticized by the Commission itself.[181] In any case, it should be recognized that minimum harmonization is *not* a 'transitory stage on the way toward European legal unity'—rather, it was designed 'to safeguard national autonomy and to keep open competition between national legal orders'.[182]

An illustrative example for this approach is the Proposed Thirteenth Council Directive on Company Law, Concerning Takeover and Other General Bids, of January 19, 1989[183] as amended in 1990[184], in 1996[185], and again in 1997[186]. The complicated history of the proposed Directive—yet another amended version is expected for the summer of 1999[187]—exemplifies the difficulties in harmonizing different national concepts and customs.[188] The original version of the proposal had stipulated a so-called 'mandatory bid' obliging everyone who had acquired more than one-third of the shares of a company listed in a regulated market

---

[178] However, there are also contrary developments: in certain areas, such as, e.g., consumer protection, the Single European Act of 1987 (1987 O.J. No. L 169/29) has paved a way toward a greater harmonization at the cost of reducing the potential for a competition of systems; for details, see STREIT AND MUSSLER 1995, 90–93.

[179] For a detailed analysis, see GRUNDMANN 1996, 124 et seq., and especially BUXBAUM AND HOPT 1988, together with various contributions in BUXBAUM, HERTIG, HIRSCH AND HOPT 1991; see also COMMISSION OF THE EUROPEAN COMMUNITIES 1999.

[180] Cf., e.g., ASSMANN AND BUCK 1990, 110–112; against such criticism FITCHEW 1991, 1–3.

[181] See KOMMISSION DER EUROPÄISCHEN GEMEINSCHAFTEN 1998. 3–6. As an example of a misguided regulatory process, the Capital Adequacy Directive is cited. According to the Commission, the original proposal had 26 pages, the final version of the Directive had 79 pages, and it had to be changed already four years later—the changes alone consumed another 28 pages .

[182] KÖNDGEN 1998, 129; see also CRUICKSHANK 1998, 133–134.

[183] 1989 O.J. No. C 64/8.

[184] 1990 O.J. No. C 240/7; for an analysis of the earlier version, see, e.g., HOPT 1992; BAUMS 1995; SEALY 1993.

[185] 1996 O.J. No. C 162/5; for an analysis of the later version, see, e.g., HOPT 1997; ANDENAS 1997.

[186] COM (97) 565 fin.; reprinted together with an introduction with NEYE 1997.

[187] Cf. Börsen-Zeitung, No. 115, June 19, 1999 and No. 117, June 22, 1999.

[188] See HOPT 1997, 379–384.

within the EU to submit a public offer for all of the other outstanding shares.[189] This provision was modeled after the concept of the British City Code. The basic idea was to offer minority shareholders protection *at the time* of a change of ownership. However, put simply, this concept collided with (among others) the German model of granting protection for the time *after* such a change by providing special legal protection for minority shareholders *in* a combine (*Konzernrecht*). Furthermore, the concept of *legal* regulation was contrary to the British idea of *self-regulation* in this area. Negotiations were suspended in 1991 because of strong opposition from these two and other Member States. The proposal became part of the discussion about the subsidiarity principle.

After the Member States had signaled a principle agreement to a restricted directive that only established general principles, work was resumed by the Commission in 1993.[190] The revised version of the proposed Directive was reduced to a so-called 'framework' directive, and although even the 1989 proposal had been a typically minimum-standards directive, the basic concepts were significantly watered down, leaving it now up to Member States to introduce *either* a mandatory bid in accordance with the directive *or other* measures that would provide equal protection.[191] This proposal has been characterized as an uneasy political compromise trying to accommodate all sides.[192] However, at least there is room for regulatory competition, which interestingly has ultimately *not* been successfully implemented by Germany.[193]

4.   Shared International Standards

The most important example of developing internationally acceptable (non-binding) standards of securities regulation has been undertaken by the *International Organization of Securities Commissions (IOSCO),* as will be described below.[194] A good example is IOSCO's Resolution Concerning Mutual Assistance of 1988, which formulates the basic principles of mutual assistance among securities regulators and has been approved by a majority of its members. This kind of harmonization with its focus on cooperational and

---

[189]   Cf. Art. 4 of the 1989/1990 versions.

[190]   ANDENAS 1997, 103.

[191]   Cf. Art. 3 .1 of the revised versions of 1996/1997.

[192]   HOPT 1997, 384.

[193]   A flexible self-regulatory Takeover Codex introduced in 1995 has not been accepted by major parts of the German industry, resulting in what will probably be a more strict legal solution expected for the year 2000.

[194]   Cf. infra at IV.1.

jurisdictional questions allows for competition in substantive regulation and avoids most of the pitfalls of legislative harmonization.[195]

In the future, one might even think of the establishment of an international organization capable of internalizing jurisdictional conflicts in the field of securities regulation.[196] As IOSCO is only a consultative body, no such dispute settlement organization currently exists.

III. Mutual Recognition

Mutual recognition may come on the administrative or the legislative level. It is opposed to extraterritorialism and has the potential to enhance regulatory competition. However, the greater the degree of legal harmonization required as a precondition for recognition, the less beneficial is the effect on regulatory competition. Recognition refers to financial products as well as to market participants licensed or supervised in other jurisdictions. It lowers entry barriers to the domestic market and thus fosters competition in the market for financial services.

If one wants to keep confrontational extraterritorial application of laws in cross-border transactions at bay, and if one further does not wish to apply all involved and most probably contradicting laws in a cumulative way (thus making such transactions unnecessarily burdensome), one must choose from the world of non-harmonized securities law regimes. The traditional dichotomy in recognition is home country law versus market place law. However, at least with respect to product-oriented regulation such as disclosure duties attached to securities, this rather limited picture could be enlarged in transnational markets by a third possibility: the choice of legal systems (applicable law and juris-diction) by the issuer or the 'architects' of new financial instruments. This third possibility of accepting a—probably somehow preconditioned—use of the global 'market for laws' may become especially important in the complex world of innovative financial instruments increasingly used in cross-border securiti-zation. Answers given so far to the question of home vs. market rule vs. choice of legal systems can possibly best be sorted out by taking a horizontal perspec-tive and distinguishing among different types of recognition on a bilateral, regional, and multilateral level.

---

[195] Another source of developing international standards may be the law merchant or lex mercatoria not treated here; cf., e.g., KÖTZ 1992.
[196] See SCHUSTER 1994, 192–194.

1. Bilateral Recognition

An example of accommodation to foreign ways by bilateral recognition is the U.S.-Canadian multi-jurisdictional disclosure system worked out in 1991 after lengthy negotiations.[197] Basically, the system allows Canadian issuers to offer securities in the U.S. using their domestic, rather than U.S., offering documents. However, although the Canadian regulatory system is very similar and adequate to the SEC's way of investor protection, the drafting process is highly complicated and in the end, to some extent, U.S. accounting standards still have to be taken into account by Canadian issuers. As a result, very limited efficiency gains were achieved. Thus it is highly unlikely that the SEC will take up such a recognition approach again in the foreseeable future with other countries.[198] Accordingly, it was not even discussed in the SEC's Market 2000 Study of 1994[199] and can, for all practical purposes, be regarded as dead in spite of the great expectations attached to the idea when introduced.[200]

2. Regional Recognition

Once more, the integrated capital market created by the European Union over the last three decades may serve as an example. The EU has established the world's only truly and functional multi-jurisdictional securities regime.[201] At least since the policy change in 1985, the concept of mutual recognition based on minimum harmonization has served as the cornerstone of the system of liberated cross-border financial services among the Member States described above.[202] Mutual recognition refers to market participants and their activities —by way of the so-called 'European Passport' under the Investment Services Directive[203]—as well as to the financial products offered by them.

Significant examples for the latter are the Listing Particulars Directive[204] and the Public Offer Prospectus Directive[205] referring to mutual recognition for listing purposes and prospectus requirements. These directives contribute to the development of an integrated capital market by establishing the concept of mutual recognition with respect to the vast array of disclosure requirements in

---

[197] See ROQUETTE 1994, 574–576; BAUM AND BREIDENBACH 1990, 27–29.
[198] LONGSTRETH 1995, 329.
[199] SECURITIES AND EXCHANGE COMMISSION 1994.
[200] LONGSTRETH 1995, 330.
[201] See WARREN III 1990, 193.
[202] See supra II.3.
[203] See infra IV.2.
[204] Council Directive 80/390, 1980 O.J. No. L 100/1 as amended.
[205] Council Directive 89/298, 1989 O.J. No. L 124/8.

the Member States.[206] The Listings Particulars Directive establishes a minimum disclosure standard for the disclosure document necessary as a prerequisite to list on any European stock exchange. The mutual recognition regime has significantly reduced national barriers to multiple (simultaneous and consecutive) cross-border listings. However, there are certain limits to the effectiveness because Member States are allowed to maintain higher disclosure standards that have to be met by the issuer, and as a rule the information load is rather heavy.[207] In any case, mutual recognition refers to the listing particulars *form* only; the exchanges are not obliged to actually list a specific security.

The Prospectus Directive has a wider scope of application and requires the publication of a prospectus if securities are offered to the public, regardless of whether or not those are listed. But in case of a listing, these requirements are fulfilled if the requirements of the Listing Particulars Directive are met. If a prospectus is prepared in accordance with the complete Directive in a Member State that has not made use of possible exemptions in the Directive, and if the prospectus has been approved by the competent authority, another Member State cannot refuse a recognition even if that state itself has adopted a higher disclosure standard.[208] But the pertinent securities have to be offered simultaneously or within a short period of time.

3.   Multilateral Recognition

Outside the Common Market there is no regulatory harmonization to speak of. Here, recognition becomes truly multilateral. This describes the situation the U.S. sees itself confronted with in a globalizing capital market. The extremely cautious approach taken by the SEC in the past with respect to recognition of foreign regulatory regimes has just been mentioned.[209] This practice has caused growing criticism by U.S. academics and practitioners.[210] The shared base of that criticism is an uneasiness about the barely constrained extraterritorial application of the U.S. securities laws.[211] However, the consequences drawn and the rationale underlying the proposed remedies differ significantly.

---

[206]   Cf. SULGER 1998, 224 et seq. GRUNDMANN 1996, 109 et seq.; ROQUETTE 1994, 589 et seq. WARNER 1992, 21 et seq.; WARREN III 1990, 209 et seq.

[207]   For the recent criticism of the Commission concerning a perceived overregulation with respect to information duties in listing documents, see KOMMISSION DER EUROPÄISCHEN GEMEINSCHAFTEN 1998, 8; cf. also GRUNDMANN 1996, 132 et seq.

[208]   For the rather complicated details with respect to recognition, see GRUNDMANN 1996, 117–119.

[209]   Cf. supra 1.

[210]   See, e.g., ROMANO 1998; CHOI AND GUZMANN 1996, 1997 and 1998; FOX 1997 and 1998; and cf. supra Part B.III.

[211]   Cf. supra Part C.II.

A recent proposal focused on the *nationality of the issuer* criticizes both the SEC's traditional approach of trying to protect all U.S. investors as well as the Commission's more recent approach of trying to protect the U.S. capital market.[212] The proposal is based on the observation that a cross-border securities transaction has (at least) three dimensions of nationality: the residence of the buyer, the place of transaction, and the nationality of the issuer.[213] The author regards efficiency as the only rationale for mandatory disclosure. In his view, efficiency in transnational securities transactions strongly suggests a clear principle of statutory reach. As the author is equally skeptical of the notion of a potential single regime for all issuers around the world and the notion of unconstrained regulatory competition which he regards as leading to an unavoidable 'race to the bottom', issuer nationality is proposed as a solution. Each country should regulate the disclosure behavior of issuers of its nationality and no others. Where the issuer's shares are traded should be of no concern, and neither should the nationality of the buyer.[214]

The issuer-nationality approach is criticized for eliminating regulatory competition and undermining international capital mobility.[215] The alternative concept criticizes especially the underlying assumption of a necessary regulatory 'race to the bottom'; rather, evidence is interpreted as indicating a likely 'race to the top'.[216] This more flexible concept under the label 'market approach' emphasizes the desirability of regulatory competition and advocates a regulatory control of the *issuer's domicile* regardless of where the shares are traded.[217] The market approach provides issuers with a choice of their securities domicile for trading purposes abroad. As a result, the disclosure and registration obligations as well as the anti-fraud provisions of the jurisdiction where the securities are traded are of no importance for the foreign issuer.[218] This concept is much broader than the Canadian-U.S. multi-jurisdictional disclosure system mentioned above.[219]

Very similar to the market approach is a concept labeled 'portable reciprocity'.[220] Normal reciprocity only allows an issuer seeking capital in a foreign market to carry his domestic regime abroad. Portable reciprocity extends that concept to include multiple countries, diverse regulations, and greater issuer choice.[221] This approach rejects territorial considerations with respect to

---

[212] See Fox 1997 and 1998.
[213] Fox 1997, 2504.
[214] See ID. 2628–2629.
[215] See CHOI AND GUZMANN 1998, 949.
[216] See ROMANO 1998, 212–214; see also the discussion supra II.2.
[217] ID. 207–209.
[218] ID. 208.
[219] Cf. supra 1.
[220] See CHOI AND GUZMANN 1998.
[221] See id. 921 et seq.

jurisdiction and allows the market participants to *choose* the most appropriate regulatory regime for themselves. Any combination of issuer nationality, investor nationality, regime choice, and transaction location is deemed permissible under that concept. As a consequence, the regulatory regime 'travels' with the securities it issues.[222] Portable reciprocity is seen as a way to increase the intensity of regulatory competition between different countries. This in turn is supposed to give regulators an incentive not to overregulate but rather to maximize the welfare of *all* securities market participants. Furthermore, regulatory competition is expected to lead to a separation between countries in their type of securities regulation. Rational investors will then discount the price they are willing to pay depending on the specific risk of fraud and other opportunistic behavior in a given market.[223] The concept of portable reciprocity differs from the market approach by offering more choice for the issuer because choice is not constrained to the state of incorporation.[224]

The more flexible concepts may also be better suited for the innovative financial instruments increasingly used in cross-border securitization that is by definition not governed by one or even two legal regimes.[225] Because securitization is an intermediation system that combines different components, linked together through markets, financial intermediaries can choose legal regimes in the global 'market for laws' either fully or partly by contracting to supplement inadequate national laws.[226]

IV. Cooperation in Enforcement

Cooperation or assistance in enforcement is the least intrusive and troublesome form of cooperative strategy when compared with mutual recognition or harmonization. In a way, it can be viewed as a kind of limited scope mutual recognition.[227] As a rule, cooperation in enforcement takes place on an administrative level. It respects regulatory differences and other states' jurisdictions. It is most widely used in the area of market regulation and will be backed by bilateral agreements and, possibly, multilateral treaties. It may function as an alternative to both extraterritorialism and harmonization and is a prerequisite for allowing regulatory competition. Enforcement cooperation may be backed by procedural harmonization on the legislative level.

---

[222] ID. 922.
[223] ID. 950–951.
[224] ID. 948.
[225] See FRANKEL 1998.
[226] FRANKEL 257. These highly specific private laws are then repeated, and as they become slowly accepted as customs a modern law merchant develops.
[227] TRACHTMAN 1994, 85.

1. Dynamics

Beginning in the mid-1980s, efforts in international cooperation have significantly intensified over the last decade.[228] In the international arena, the *International Organization of Securities Commissions (IOSCO)* has become a
leading force in initiating and coordinating securities law enforcement on an
international level.[229] IOSCO is a private nonprofit organization that developed
out of the former regional *Inter American Association of Securities Commissions (AASCO)* in 1983. Some 15 years later it had grown to 73 regular and 35
affiliate members. A secretariat is based in Montreal. IOSCO's members are
committed to the following purposes: (1) cooperation in order to maintain just
and efficient markets; (2) exchange of information designed to further the
development of domestic markets; (3) establishing of standards and effective
surveillance of international securities transactions; and (4) providing of mutual
assistance to ensure market integrity and effective enforcement.[230]

In 1986 IOSCO passed the Resolution Concerning Mutual Assistance, the
so-called Rio Declaration, and in 1989 a Resolution on Cooperation. Others
followed.[231] The 1986 and 1989 Resolutions constituted the initial base for an
increasingly deeper and broader cooperation on the bilateral level designed
according to international principles. At least in the beginning, the SEC was
probably the primary mover behind the IOSCO's enforcement activities and
especially the Rio Declaration.[232]

In the U.S., the efforts of the SEC to maintain the high level of regulation in
a globalizing market by extraterritorial implementation had become increasingly
frustrated.[233] This intensified the agency's interest in an international enforcement cooperation as a workable alternative. The legal basis for such a
cooperation was finally established in 1990 when several earlier legislative
proposals of the SEC were enacted as the International Securities Enforcement
and Cooperation Act.[234]

Within the European Union, the implementation of the Investment Services
Directive (ISD)[235] has created a specific dynamic toward increased supervisory
cooperation. The ISD introduces a European Passport for investment firms that
allows them to offer their services throughout the Union, and further permits

---

[228] See also SCHNYDER 1996, 158–164; BEARD 1996; GREENE 1994.
[229] See JORDAAN 1998.
[230] The organization, its purposes, and activities are described in greater detail by
SOMMER 1996; ZARING 1998, 292–297.
[231] The reports are available at the organization's Internet address at *http://www.
iosco.org*.
[232] See ZARING 1998, 297.
[233] Cf. supra Part D.I.
[234] See the overview with BAUM AND BREIDENBACH 1990, 12–17.
[235] Council Directive 93/22/EEC, 1993 O.J. No. L 141/1; see WYMEERSCH 1998.

cross-border expansion of exchange trading systems via remote membership.[236] An increased exchange of information is a precondition for the admission of these cross-border investment activities.[237] Thus the main goal of enforcement assistance is obtaining information that can be used for supervisory purposes and investigations and may later serve as evidence in a possible prosecution and trial.

2.   Instruments of Cooperation

Means and instruments to enhance international cooperation in deterring securities fraud can be viewed from different perspectives. First, from a *horizontal* perspective, we can distinguish among multilateral, regional, and bilateral means of cooperation. Second, from a *vertical* perspective, we can differentiate according to the degree of formality between legally *binding* measures, like multi- or bilateral treaties, and *non-binding* ones, like the IOSCO principles or administrative agreements between two supervisory agencies. Finally, we can characterize instruments with respect to their *regulatory focus*. Multilateral treaties may intend to facilitate international legal procedures in *civil* cases. Bilateral treaties on mutual legal assistance typically focus on *criminal* procedures, whereas agreements between securities commissions serve primarily *administrative*—namely supervisory—goals. The latter are of increasing importance.[238] In the following we will once more take the horizontal differentiation as a guide.

a) Multilateral Efforts: An important example of an international treaty designed to assist internationally in procuring information is the Hague Convention on the Taking of Evidence Abroad in Civil and Commercial Matters.[239] The Convention enables signatories to request each other's assistance in obtaining evidence. The request will be executed to the extent compatible with that state's domestic law. The Convention is a useful general instrument in fostering international cooperation; however, as its application is limited to civil judicial proceedings, it is of little help in fighting cross-border securities fraud that is typically the target of investigations or administrative proceedings by a securities regulator.

Better suited to facilitate the cooperation in market supervision and combating securities fraud are the resolutions and principles drafted by IOSCO,

---

[236] See HOPT AND BAUM 1997, 316–321, STEIL 1996,115–145.

[237] BERGSTRÄSSER 1998, 373.

[238] Cf. infra at (3).

[239] Opened for signature March 18, 1970. Signatories to the Convention are among others the U.S. and Germany (cf. BGBl. 1977 II, 1472).

although these—in contrast to international treaties—are legally non-binding. The resolutions and principles are specifically tailored for regulatory purposes and have become increasingly accepted. In 1998 IOSCO's Rio Declaration had been approved by 54 of its 73 regular members, and the 1989 Resolution on Cooperation by 26 members.[240] In 1991 the 'Principles for Memoranda of Understanding'[241] were drafted to serve as a guideline for the negotiation of bilateral assistance agreements.[242] These Principles specifically deal with problems arising in the context of sharing of information between securities regulators.[243]

So far, the most recent effort in dealing with problems in international cooperation is the report 'Securities Activities on the Internet'.[244] Among other issues, the Committee promotes enhanced cooperation and sharing of information by the regulators to effectively monitor and police securities activity on the Internet. It recommends the use of the Net for supervision and tackles the difficult question of who should exercise regulatory authority over cross-border securities activities on the Internet. The analysis starts with a 'conducts test' and an 'effects test'.[245] If the offer or sales activities occur within the regulator's jurisdiction or if these have a 'significant' effect upon residents or markets in that jurisdiction, a regulator may impose its regulatory requirements.[246] However, these factors are not regarded as determinative or exhaustive. In some kind of refined 'balancing test',[247] the report lists additional factors that 'may support the assertion of regulatory authority' and those that may not.[248]

---

[240] Cf. BERGSTRÄSSER, 1998, 374.

[241] Report of the Technical Committee, September 1991; available at the organization's Internet address at *http://www.iosco.org*.

[242] Cf. infra (3).

[243] See JORDAAN 1998, 274–285.

[244] Report of the Technical Committee, September 1998; text available at the organization's Internet address at *http://www.iosco.org*.

[245] This approach is more or less in accordance with the general practice of the SEC and the U.S. courts described above, as well as with the SEC's interpretive release regarding offerings on the Internet from 1998; see supra Part C.II. and Part D.I. respectively.

[246] Cf. REPORT 1998, Part IV.B. (Key Recommendations).

[247] See supra Part D.II.

[248] Assertion of jurisdiction is supported if the relevant information is targeted or pushed (via e-mail) to residents. The same is true if the issuer or financial service provider accepts purchases from residents of the regulator's jurisdiction. On the other hand, if issuer or service provider clearly states to whom the Internet offer is directed or takes precautions that are reasonably designed to prevent sales to residents in the regulator's jurisdiction, it may be appropriate for that regulator not to assign jurisdiction; cf. REPORT 1998, Part IV. B.

The Principles appear to be a promising effort to solve jurisdictional conflicts by coordination on a procedural level rather than turning to a substantive harmonization of laws.[249] But they do not tackle questions of enforcement that may pose bigger problems than jurisdiction: How can a judgment supported by proper jurisdiction be turned into meaningful economic relief?[250]

b) Interregional Cooperation: The most prominent example of an interregional cooperative framework is, again, the integrated securities market within the EU.

Allowing cross-border investment activities based on the home country laws—as has become standard within the Common Market—requires an effective supervision by the authorities of the home state.[251] In this sense, cooperation among supervisory agencies is a prerequisite for a functioning internal financial market. Effective supervision in turn needs an extensive exchange of information in matters concerning surveillance and enforcement between the competent agencies. Such an exchange including otherwise confidential information is only possible if the supervisory agencies are authorized by law to communicate these data. Under the Investment Services Directive (ISD)[252] and other directives, the national authorities are empowered as well as obliged to cooperate and share information. Experiences so far seem to show that in practice the exchange of information has been functioning well.[253] On the other hand, in a report from October 1998 about the future tasks concerning the financial services within the EU, the Commission has stated that the national supervisory systems have not yet been sufficiently adapted to the rapid market integration.[254]

With the implementation of the ISD, the exchange of information has to be further increased and consultation procedures are required in addition to cooperation and information. The former 'static' cooperation based on a passive flow of data has given way to a dynamic process between the supervisory agencies of two Member States with a shared competence toward the same intermediary.[255] Art. 19 ISD regulates when host country authorities may excise jurisdiction over the activities of an intermediary from another Member State using the European Passport. Direct intervention is permitted in matters administered by the host country. This will be the case mostly with respect to

---

[249] For a comprehensive discussion of the general issues raised by securities offering and trading on the Internet, see, e. g., ENGEL 1999a; COFFEE 1997; CELLA AND STARK 1997.

[250] See TRUDEL 1998, 1123 et seq.

[251] The home rule is regarded as the most important concept of coordination at present, see SCHNYDER 1996, 158.

[252] Council Directive 93/22/EEC, 1993 O.J. No. L 141/1.

[253] See BERGSTRÄSSER 1998, 375.

[254] See KOMMISSION DER EUROPÄISCHEN GEMEINSCHAFTEN 1998, 3–4.

[255] See BIANCHERI 1998, 364.

conduct of business rules. The authorities have a right to request information directly from the intermediary while at the same time contacting the home country supervisory agency.[256]

The possibility for the host country authorities to intervene with respect to conduct of business has recently been criticized by the Commission: the national authorities have been unwavering in applying their conduct of business rules, thus creating unnecessary obstacles to cross-border business.[257]

Cooperation with third-country authorities is, as a rule, not specifically taken care of in the various Directives. However, in general, at least the same amount of confidentiality is required as a guarantee if information is passed within the framework of a Memorandum of Understanding.[258]

In December of 1997 in Paris, the 15 supervisory agencies of the Member States plus those of Iceland and Norway, following the model of IOSCO, established the *Forum of European Securities Commissions (FESCO)*. This pursues similar goals as IOSCO within the EU, namely close cooperation and the development of joint supervisory standards.[259] The first and most important challenge the European supervisory agencies have to cope with is the *practical* implementation of the Investment Services Directive; the most ambitious project in this context is a planned harmonization of the conduct of business rules.[260] As mentioned above, so far even when using the European Passport a financial services firm has to comply with the specific conduct of business rules of each Member State—in a worst-case scenario this means 15 different sets of rules.

c) Bilateral Treaties and Agreements: Bilateral cooperation is often institutionalized in the form of Mutual Legal Assistance Treaties (MLATs) or Memoranda of Understanding (MOUs). MLATs are negotiated through formal diplomatic channels, have the force of law, and oblige the signatories to provide assistance in proceedings concerning criminal matters.[261] MLATs provide for various kinds of assistance ranging from production of information to asset freezes. However, there are several restrictions on their effectiveness, primarily the dual criminality requirement under which the offense being investigated must constitute a criminal violation in both states.

Unlike MLATs, MOUs are non-binding statements of intent that are tailored according to the needs of securities regulators and are directly negotiated and

---

[256] A detailed description of rights and duties under the ISD can be found with BIANCHERI 1998.
[257] Cf. COMMISSION OF THE EUROPEAN COMMUNITIES 1999, 5.
[258] Cf., e.g., Art. 25 III ISD. The relationship between the EU and non-member states with respect to securities regulation is discussed with BUCK 1994.
[259] Cf. WITTICH 1999.
[260] WITTICH 1999.
[261] For an overview from the U.S. perspective, see GREENE 1994, 640–649; BEARD 1996, 272–274.

implemented by the parties concerned. Therefore, MOUs are regarded as more efficient and reliable than MLATs in obtaining information,[262] although adherence to them cannot be enforced by law. However, the high degree of factual obligation connected with the conclusion of a MOU may counterweight this possible source of insecurity.[263] While within the European Union the mutuality of exchange of information is ensured by directives, this is not the case in relation to third countries. Here MOUs are important for establishing this mutual obligation.[264]

Within a few years, MOUs have become a standard means for enforcing cooperation in the field of securities regulation.[265] As of January 1999, 46 Memoranda of Understanding and similar agreements were concluded between IOSCO members, including one involving the Commission of the European Communities.[266] The overall number of MOUs amounts to about 200, according to one estimate.[267] At the end of 1997, the SEC had entered into 32 arrangements with foreign counterparts for information sharing and cooperation in the investigation and prosecution of securities law violations.[268] The main source of authorization is the International Securities Enforcement and Cooperation Act of 1990.[269] As an outgrowth of its experience in the enforcement arena, the SEC points out that it has expanded its arrangements to encompass cooperation on regulatory matters.[270]

Germany negotiated ten MOUs between 1996, when the German central supervisory agency, the *Bundesaufsichtsamt für den Wertpapierhandel,* started its full operations, and June 1998.[271] These are based on the authorization in § 7 of the German Securities Trading Act.[272]

Within the European Union, it was commonly assumed that the Directives in the field of securities regulation render MOUs between the supervisory agencies of the Member States mostly superfluous because they oblige national authorities to cooperate and share information.[273] This view obviously changed somehow in 1999 when the 17 European supervisory agencies concluded a *multilateral* MOU aiming at the improvement of cross-border information flows

---

[262] See GREENE 1994, 649.
[263] BERGSTRÄSSER 1998, 376.
[264] BERGSTRÄSSER 1998, 377.
[265] See JORDAAN 1998, 270; see also SCHNYDER 1996, 158–159.
[266] Cf. the list at the homepage of IOSCO at *http://www.iosco.org.*
[267] See BERGSTRÄSSER 1998, 376.
[268] Cf. SEC 1997 Annual Report at *http://www.sec.gov/asec/annrep97/frontm.htm.*
[269] Cf. supra 1.
[270] See SEC 1997 Annual Report, supra note 265.
[271] See ASSMANN AND SCHNEIDER 1999, § 7 at 3.
[272] Wertpapierhandelsgesetz, BGBl. I 1998, 2708.
[273] See BERGSTRÄSSER 1998, 378–379.

and cooperation;[274] however, *bilateral* MOUs between agencies of the Member States have not been concluded so far.

The two most important principles of a MOU are, first, the obligation to grant assistance even if the incriminated behavior does not violate the securities regulations in the state receiving the request, and, second, the obligation to ensure confidential treatment of the information received.[275] In 1991, IOSCO drafted 'Principles for Memoranda of Understanding' that define which issues a MOU should address.[276]

F. Conclusion

Countries should encourage rather than discourage international capital mobility. Accessible international capital markets allow world savings to look for their most productive uses regardless of their location and create possibilities for an international pooling of risks and diversification of investment. They also have a disciplinary function on national policymakers. If capital is allowed to flow, policy failures will be punished.

This pressure is also being felt by national regulators. Globalized markets confront national policymakers with a specific trilemma. A policymaker may likely want to achieve three goals when designing a financial system: continuing national sovereignty; financial markets that are regulated, supervised, and somehow protected; and the advantages of a globalized capital market. Unfortunately, however, these three objectives are incompatible. Any coherent reform cannot avoid favoring two parts of the trinity at the expense of the third. Thus any radical blueprints for reform are unrealistic, rather no more than an improvement of the trade-offs between the the three objectives can be considered a realistic option.

A policymaker has basically three options to address the core question of an internationalized market: Which jurisdiction or jurisdictions are supposed to regulate a given conduct in connection with a cross-border securities transaction? He can pursue non-cooperative, partly cooperative, or truly cooperative strategies. The latter seems to be preferable to both an aggressive and a

---

[274] WITTICH 1999.

[275] See BERGSTRÄSSER, 1998, 377.

[276] Text available at the organization's Internet address at *http://www.iosco.org*. According to the Principles, a MOU idealiter addresses ten issues: (i) MOU's subject matter, (ii) its implementation procedures, (iii) confidentiality, (iv) the rights of the market participants subject to a MOU request, (v) consultation with foreign authorities, (vi) a public policy expectation, (vii) types of assistance, (viii) permitted uses of information obtained, (ix) participation by the requesting authority, and (x) sharing of cost; cf. id. at 3–12; the Principles are discussed and analyzed with JORDAAN 1998, 275–285.

restricted extraterritorial application of securities regulation which, in the long run, can be considered a second-best solution only. Rather, the extraterritorial reach of securities regulation should be curtailed wherever possible.

However, benefits of increased capital mobility will be better realized through regulatory decentralization than greater centralization. This means legal harmonization in the field of international securities regulation should be used only as an exceptional policy instrument and not as a rule because it suppresses regulatory competition.

Contrary to a widespread assumption, regulatory competition has basically positive effects and there is at least no general danger of a regulatory 'race to the bottom' in a globalized capital market. Rather, the potential of regulatory competition as a knowledge-creating (discovery) process should be tapped. Harmonized legislation, in contrast, results in a great loss of regulatory diversity and of valuable adaptations to national conditions.

An effective allocation of regulatory jurisdiction, mutual recognition, and international cooperation in enforcement can be alternatives to harmonization of substantive regulation. Without suppressing regulatory competition they help to lower entry barriers to national securities markets and to reduce transaction costs. Thus, those who advocate substantive harmonization of international securities regulations bear a double burden of proof. First, they have to show convincingly that a substantive market failure exists that calls for regulatory harmonization. Second, they have to prove that the assumed positive results of intervention outweigh the dangers of internationally harmonized government failure.

References

ANDENAS, MADS, 'European Takeover Directive and City,' 18 *The Company Lawyer*, 1997, 101–104.

ANDENAS, MADS, AND STEPHEN KENYON-SLADE, 'E.C. Financial Market Regulation and Company Law.' London 1993.

ASSMANN, HEINZ-DIETER, AND PETRA BUCK, 'Europäisches Kapitalmarktrecht,' *Europäisches Wirtschafts- & Steuerrecht*, 1990, 110–123, 190–226.

ASSMANN, HEINZ-DIETER, AND UWE H. SCHNEIDER, 'Wertpapierhandelsgesetz.' 2. ed., Cologne 1999.

BASEDOW, JÜRGEN, 'Weltkartellrecht – Ausgangslage und Ziele, Methoden und Grenzen der internationalen Vereinheitlichung des Rechts der Wettbewerbsbeschränkungen.' Tübingen 1998.

BASEDOW, JÜRGEN, 'Conflicts of Economic Regulation,' 42 *The American Journal of Comparative Law*, 1994, 423–447.

BASEDOW, JÜRGEN, 'Von der deutschen zur europäischen Wirtschaftsverfassung.' Tübingen 1992.

BAUM, HARALD, 'Börsen- und Kapitalmarktrecht in Japan.' In: K. J. Hopt, B. Rudolph and H. Baum, eds., *Börsenreform – Eine ökonomische, rechtsvergleichende und rechtspolitische Untersuchung*. Stuttgart 1997, 1265–1399.

BAUM, HARALD, 'Faktische und potentielle Eingriffsnormen,' 53 *Rabels Zeitschrift für ausländisches und internationales Privatrecht*, 1989, 146–164.

BAUM, HARALD, AND STEPHAN BREIDENBACH, 'Die wachsende internationale Verflechtung der Wertpapiermärkte und die Regelungspolitik der U. S. Securities and Exchange Commisssion: Neue Entwicklungen in der internationalen Anwendung des amerikanischen Kapitalmarktrechts,' *Wertpapier-Mitteilungen*, 1990, Special Suppl. No. 6/1990.

BAUMS, THEODOR, 'Zur Harmonisierung des Rechts der Unternehmensübernahmen in der EG.' *Arbeitspapier* 3/95. Institut für Handels- und Wirtschaftsrecht, Universität Osnabrück.

BAUMS, THEODOR, 'Anwendungsbereich, Kollision und Abstimmung von Kapitalmarktrechten.' *Arbeitspapier* 5/94. Institut für Handels- und Wirtschaftsrecht, Universität Osnabrück.

BEARD, ELLIOT M., 'A Critical Analysis of the Effects of *Colello v. SEC* on International Securities Law Enforcement Agreements,' 7 *Duke Journal of Comparative & International Law*, 1996, 271–295.

BEDDOES, ZANNY MINTON, 'Time for a Redesign?', *The Economist*, January 30, 1999, Special Supplement, *A Survey of Global Finance*.

BEHRENS, PETER, 'Die Wirtschaftsverfassung der Europäischen Gemeinschaft.' In: G. Brüggemeier, ed., *Verfassungen für ein ziviles Europa*. Baden-Baden 1994, 73–90.

BEHRENS, PETER, 'Elemente eines Begriffs des Internationalen Wirtschaftsrechts,' 50 *Rabels Zeitschrift für ausländisches und internationales Privatrecht*, 1986, 483–507.

BERGSTRÄSSER, SUSANNE, 'Cooperation between Supervisors.' In: Guido Ferrarini, ed., *European Securities Markets – The Investment Services Directive and Beyond*. London 1998, 373–381.

BIANCHERI, CARLO, 'Cooperation among Supervisory Authorities under the ISD.' In: Guido Ferrarini, ed., *European Securities Markets – The Investment Services Directive and Beyond.* London 1998, 363–371.

BÖHLHOFF, KLAUS, 'Kriterien und Methoden einer Regulierung der internationalen Kapital- und Wertpapiermärkte.' In: F. Kübler, H.-J. Mertens and W. Werner, eds., *Festschrift für Theodor Heinsius.* Berlin/New York 1991, 49–59.

BRANDT, GEROLD, 'Symbiose aus De-Regulierung und Re-Regulierung der Finanz-märkte.' In: H. Büttner and P. Hampe, eds., *Die Globalisierung der Finanzmärkte. Auswirkungen auf den Standort Deutschland.* Mainz 1997, 161–170.

BREEDEN, RICHARD C., 'Foreign Companies and U.S. Securities Markets in a Time of Economic Transformation,' 17 *Fordham International Law Journal,* 1994, S. 77.

BROWN, MEREDITH, GISELLE HANTZ, AND SCOTT BUDLONG, 'Protecting US shareholders in UK tender offers,' *International Financial Law Review,* December 1998, 13–17.

BUCK, PETRA, 'Drittländerbehandlung auf dem europäischen Kapitalmarkt.' In: Wolfgang Graf Vitzthum, ed., *Europäische und Internationale Wirtschaftsordnung aus der Sicht der Bundesrepublik Deutschland.* Baden-Baden 1994, 113–136.

BÜTTNER, HANS, AND PETER HAMPE, eds., 'Die Globalisierung der Finanzmärkte. Auswirkungen auf den Standort Deutschland.' Mainz 1997.

BUXBAUM, RICHARD M., AND KLAUS J. HOPT, 'Legal Harmonization and the Business Enterprise—Corporate and Capital Market Law Harmonization Policy in Europe and the U.S.A.' Berlin 1988.

BUXBAUM, RICHARD M., GÉRARD HERTIG, ALAIN HIRSCH AND KLAUS J. HOPT, eds., MARTINA HERTIG, ass. ed., 'European Business Law—Legal and Economic Analyses on Integration and Harmonization.' Berlin 1991.

CARBONE, SERGIO M., AND FRANCESCO MUNARI, 'The Enforcement of the European Regime for Investment Services in the Member States and Its Impact on National Conflict of Laws.' In: Guido Ferrarini, ed., *European Securities Markets – The Investment Services Directive and Beyond.* London 1998, 317–361.

CELLA, JOSEPH J., AND JOHN REED STARK, 'SEC Encorcement and the Internet: Meeting the Challenge of the Next Millenium,' 52 *The Business Lawyer,* 1997, 815–849.

CHEEK III, JAMES, 'Approaches to Market Regulation.' In: Fidelis Oditah, ed., *The Future for the Global Securities Market: Legal and Regulatory Aspects.* Oxford 1996, 243–255.

CHOI, STEPHEN J., AND ANDREW T. GUZMAN, 'Portable Reciprocity: Rethinking the International Reach of Securities Regulation,' 71 *Southern California Law Review,* 1998, 903–951.

CHOI, STEPHEN J., AND ANDREW T. GUZMAN, 'National Laws, International Money: Regulation in a Global Capital Market,' 65 *Fordham Law Review,* 1997, 1855–1908.

CHOI, STEPHEN J., AND ANDREW T. GUZMAN, 'The Dangerous Extraterritoriality of American Securities Law", 17 *Northwestern Journal of International Law & Business,* 1996, 207–241.

COFFEE, JOHN C. JR., 'The Future as History: The Prospects for Global Convergence in Corporate Governance and Its Implications.' *Unpublished paper,* December 1998.

COFFEE, JOHN C. JR., 'Brave New World?: The Impact(s) of the Internet on Modern Securities Regulation,' 52 *The Business Lawyer,* 1997, 1195–1233.

COFFEE, JOHN C. JR., 'Competition Versus Consolidation: The Significance of Organiza-tional Structure in Financial and Securities Regulation,' 50 *The Business Lawyer,* 1995, 447–484.

COMMISSION OF THE EUROPEAN COMMUNITIES, 'Financial Services: Implementing the Framework for Financial Markets: Action Plan.' Com (1999) 232, 11.05.99.

COMMISSION OF THE EUROPEAN COMMUNITIES, 'Completing the Internal Market: White Paper from the Commission to the European Council.' Luxembourg 1985.

COMMITTEE ON GOVERNMENT OPERATIONS, 'Seventieth Report, Problems with the SEC's Enforcement of U. S. Securities Laws in Cases Involving Suspicious Trades Originating from Abroad.' Washington, D.C. 1988.

COX, JAMES D., 'Rethinking U.S. Securities Laws in the Shadow of International Regulatory Competition,' 55 *Law and Contemporary Problems*, 1992, 157–198.

CRUICKSHANK, CRISTOPHER, 'Is there a Need to Harmonise Conduct of Business Rules?" In: Guido Ferrarini, ed., *European Securities Markets – The Investment Services Directive and Beyond*. London 1998, 131–134.

DEUTSCHES AKTIENINSTITUT E.V., ed., 'DAI-Factbook 1997.' Frankfurt/M. 1997.

DODGE, WILLIAM S., 'Extraterritoriality and Conflict-of-Laws Theory: An Argument for Judical Unilateralism,' 39 *Harvard International Law Journal*, 1998, 101–169.

ENGEL, CHRISTOPH, 'Das Internet und der Nationalstaat.' Reprint aus der Max-Planck-Projektgruppe Recht der Gemeinschaftsgüter Bonn. 1999/7 (1999a).

ENGEL, CHRISTOPH, 'Institutionen zwischen Staat und Markt.' Reprint aus der Max-Planck-Projektgruppe Recht der Gemeinschaftsgüter Bonn. 1999/3 (1999b).

ENGEL, CHRISTOPH, 'Legal Experiences of Competition among Institutions.' In: L. Gerken, ed., *Competition among Institutions*. London 1995, 89–118.

FEDDERS, JOHN M., FREDERICK B. WADE, MICHAEL D. MANN, AND MATTHEW BEIZER, 'Waiver by Conduct—A Possible Response to the Internationalization of the Securities Markets,' *Journal of Comparative Business & Capital Markets Law*, 1984, 1–54.

FEENSTRA, ROBERT C., 'Integration of Trade and Disintegration of Production in the Global Economy,' 12 *Journal of Economic Perspectives,* Fall 1988, 31–50.

FERRARINI, GUIDO, ed., 'European Securities Markets: The Investment Services Directive and Beyond.' London 1998.

FERRI, MARCO, 'Securities Regulations as a Limitation on Access to Foreign Securities for the Individual United States Investor: A Proposal for Change,' 11 *Florida Journal of International Law*, 1997, 473–486.

FITCHEW, GEOFFREY, 'Political Choices.' In: R.M. Buxbaum, G. Hertig, A. Hirsch and K. J. Hopt, eds., M. Hertig, ass. ed., *European Business Law—Legal and Economic Analyses on Integration and Harmonization*. Berlin 1991, 1–15.

FORD, CHRIS, AND JOHN KAY, 'Why Regulate Financial Services?". In: Fidelis Oditah, ed., *The Future for the Global Securities Market: Legal and Regulatory Aspects*. Oxford 1996, 145–155.

FOX, MERRITT B., 'The Political Economy of Statutory Reach: U.S. Disclosure Rules in a Globalizing Market for Securities,' *Michigan Law Review*, 1998, 696–822.

FOX, MERRITT B., 'Securities Disclosure in a Globalizing Market: Who Should Regulate Whom?" 95 *Michigan Law Review*, 1997, 2498–2632.

FRANKEL, TAMAR, 'Cross-Border Securitization: Without Law, But Not Lawless,' 8 *Duke Journal of Comparative & International Law*, 1998, 255–282.

FÜLBIER, UWE, 'Regulierung der Ad-hoc-Publizität. Ein Beitrag zur ökonomischen Analyse des Rechts.' Wiesbaden 1998.

FÜRST, OREN, 'A Theoretical Analysis of the Investor Protection Regulations Argument for Global Listing of Stocks.' *Paper*. International Center for Finance at Yale 1998.

GERKEN, LÜDER, ed., 'Competition among Institutions.' London 1995.

GEIGER, URI, 'The Case for Harmonization of Securities Disclosure Rules in the Global Market,' *Columbia Business Law Review*, 1997, 241–317.

GERUM, ELMAR, AND HELMUT WAGNER, 'Economics of Labor Co-Determination in View of Corporate Governance.' In: K. J. Hopt, H. Kanda, M. J. Roe, E. Wymeersch and S. Prigge, eds., *Comparative Corporate Governance – The State of the Art and Emerging Research*. Oxford 1998, 341–357.

GRASSO, RICHARD A., 'Globalization of the Equity Markets,' 20 *Fordham International Law Journal*, 1997, 1108–1128.

GREENE, CAROLINE A. A., 'International Securities Law Enforcement: Recent Advances in Assistance and Cooperation,' 27 *Vanderbilt Journal of Transnational Law*, 1994, 635–672.

GRUNDMANN, STEFAN, 'Europäisches Kapitalmarktrecht,' 115 *Zeitschrift für Schweizerisches Recht*, I/1996, 103–149.

GRUNDMANN, STEFAN, 'Deutsches Anlegerschutzrecht in internationalen Sachverhalten,' 54 *Rabels Zeitschrift für ausländisches und internationales Privatrecht*, 1990, 283–322.

VON HAYEK, FRIEDRICH A., 'Die Verwertung des Wissens in der Gesellschaft.' In: id., *Individualismus und wirtschaftliche Ordnung*. 2. ed., Salzburg 1976, 103–121.

VON HAYEK, FRIEDRICH A., 'Der Wettbewerb als Entdeckungsverfahren.' In: id., *Freiburger Studien. Gesammelte Aufsätze*. Tübingen 1969, 249–265.

HOPT, KLAUS J., 'Europäisches Gesellschaftsrecht – Krise und neue Anläufe,' 19 *Zeitschrift für Wirtschaftsrecht*, 1998, 96–105.

HOPT, KLAUS J., 'Europäisches und deutsches Übernahmerecht,' 161 *Zeitschrift für das gesamte Handelsrecht und Wirtschaftsrecht*, 1997, 368–420.

HOPT, KLAUS J., 'European Takeover Regulation: Barriers to and Problems of Harmonizing Takeover Law in the European Community.' In: K. J. Hopt and E. Wymeersch, eds., *European Takeovers. Law and Practise*. London 1992, 165–191.

HOPT, KLAUS J., AND HARALD BAUM, 'Börsenrechtsreform in Deutschland.' In: K. J. Hopt, B. Rudolph and H. Baum, eds., *Börsenreform – Eine ökonomische, rechtsvergleichende und rechtspolitische Untersuchung*. Stuttgart 1997, 287–467.

HOPT, KLAUS J., BERND RUDOLPH, AND HARALD BAUM, eds., 'Börsenreform – Eine ökonomische, rechtsvergleichende und rechtspolitische Untersuchung.' Stuttgart 1997.

HOPT, KLAUS J., EDDY WYMEERSCH, eds., 'European Insider Dealing.' London 1992.

JORDAAN, HENDRIK F., 'Has IOSCO Advanced International Securities Law Enforcement?: An Analysis in the Light of SEC MOUs with Emerging Markets,' 26 *Securities Regulation Law Journal*, 1998, 269–301.

KAMAR, EHUD, 'A Regulatory Competition Theory in Corporate Law,' 98 *Columbia Law Review*, 1998, 1908.

KAUFFMAN, 'Secrecy and Blocking Laws: a Growing Problem as the Internationalization of the Securities Markets Continues,' 18 *Vanderbilt Journal of Transnational Law*, 1985, 809.

KERBER, WOLFGANG AND VIKTOR VANBERG, 'Competition among Institutions: Evolution within Constraints.' In: L. Gerken, ed., *Competition among Institutions*. London 1995, 35–64.

KITCH, EDMUND W., 'Competition Between Securities Markets: Good or Bad?" In: Fidelis Oditah, ed., *The Future for the Global Securities Market: Legal and Regulatory Aspects*. Oxford 1996, 233–242.

KITCH, EDMUND W., 'Business Organization Law: State or Federal?" In: R. M. Buxbaum, G. Hertig, A. Hirsch and K. J. Hopt, eds., M. Hertig, ass. ed., *European Business Law—Legal and Economic Analyses on Integration and Harmonization*. Berlin 1991, 35–50.

KITCH, EDMUND W., 'Regulation and the American Common Market.' In: D. Tarlock, ed., *Regulation, Federalism, and Interstate Commerce*. Cambridge, Mass. 1981, 7–55.

KIEL, PETER, 'Internationales Kapitalanlegerschutzrecht.' Berlin 1994.

KOMMISSION DER EUROPÄISCHEN GEMEINSCHAFTEN, 'Finanzdienstleistungen: Abstecken eines Aktionsrahmens.' KOM(1998) 626 endg.

KOMMISSION DER EUROPÄISCHEN WIRTSCHAFTSGEMEINSCHAFT, 'Der Aufbau eines europäischen Kapitalmarkts.' Luxemburg 1966.

KÖNDGEN, JOHANNES, 'Rules of Conduct: Further Harmonisation?" In: Guido Ferrarini, ed., *European Securities Markets – The Investment Services Directive and Beyond*. London 1998, 115–130.

KÖTZ, HEIN, 'Alternativen zur legislatorischen Rechtsvereinheitlichung,' 56 *Rabels Zeitschrift für ausländisches und internationales Privatrecht*, 1992, 215–218.

KÖTZ, HEIN, 'Rechtsvereinheitlichung —Nutzen, Kosten, Methoden, Ziele,' 50 *Rabels Zeitschrift für ausländisches und internationales Privatrecht*, 1986, 1–18.

KÜBLER, FRITZ, 'Rechtsbildung durch Gesetzgebungswettbewerb? Überlegungen zur Angleichung und Entwicklung des Gesellschaftsrechts in der Europäischen Gemeinschaft,' 77 *Kritische Vierteljahresschrift*, 1994, 79–89.

KRUGMAN, PAUL, 'Der Mythos vom globalen Wirtschaftskrieg.' Frankfurt/M. 1999.

LICHT, AMIR, 'Regulatory Arbitrage for Real: International Securities Regulation in A World Interacting Securities Markets,' 38 *Virginia Journal of International Law*, 1998, 563–638.

LOMNICKA, EVA, 'The Internal Financial Market and Investment Services.' In: M. Andenas and S. Kenyon-Slade, eds., *E.C. Financial Market Regulation and Company Law*. London 1993, 81–90.

LONG, WILLIAM, 'Legal Principles for Regulating Financial Services on the Internet,' *Butterworths Journal of International Banking and Financial Law*, 1998, 501–507.

LONGSTRETH, BEVIS, 'A Look at the SEC's Adaption to Global Markets Pressures,' 33 *Columbia Journal of Transnational Law*, 1995, 319–336.

MACEY, JONATHAN R., 'Administrative Agency Obsolescence and Interest Group Formation: A Case Study of the SEC at Sixty,' 15 *Cardozo Law Review*, 1994, 909–949.

MAILANDER, CHRISTOPHER J., 'Financial Innovation, Domestic Regulation and the International Marketplace: Lessons to be Drawn from the International Bond Market,' 31 *The George Washington Journal of International Law and Economics*, 1997–1998, 341–392.

MAHONEY, PAUL G., 'The Exchange as Regulator,' 83 *Virginia Law Review*, 1997, 1453–1500.

MANN, MICHAEL D., JOSEPH G. MARI, AND GEORGE LAVDAS, 'Developments in International Securities Law Enforcement and Regulation,' 29 *The International Business Lawyer*, 1995, 729–874.

MANKOWSKI, PETER, 'Das Internet im Internationalen Vertrags- und Deliktsrecht,' 63 *Rabels Zeitschrift für ausländisches und internationales Privatrecht*, 1999, 203–294.

MENG, WERNER, 'Regeln über die Jurisdiktion der Staaten im amerikanischen Restatement (Third) of Foreign Relations Law,' 27 *Archiv des Völkerrechts*, 1989, 156–194.

MERKT, HANNO, 'Das Europäische Gesellschaftsrecht und die Idee des Wettbewerbs der "Gesetzgeber",' 59 *Rabels Zeitschrift für ausländisches und internationales Privatrecht*, 1995, 545–568.

MERTENS, HANS-JOACHIM, 'Nichtlegislatorische Rechtsvereinheitlichung durch transnationales Wirtschaftsrecht und Rechtsbegriff,' 56 *Rabels Zeitschrift für ausländisches und internationales Privatrecht*, 1992, 219–242.

MESTMÄCKER, ERNST-JOACHIM, 'Zur Wirtschaftsverfassung in der Europäischen Union.' In: R. H. Hasse, J. Molsberger, and C.Watrin, eds., *Ordnung in Freiheit. Festgabe für H. Willgerodt.* Stuttgart 1994, 263–292.

MESTMÄCKER, ERNST-JOACHIM, 'Der Kampf ums Recht in der offenen Gesellschaft,' 20 *Rechtstheorie*, 1989, 273–288.

MESTMÄCKER, ERNST-JOACHIM, 'Staatliche Souveränität und offene Märkte. Konflikte bei der extraterritorialen Anwendung von Wirtschaftsrecht,' 52 *Rabels Zeitschrift für ausländisches und internationales Privatrecht*, 1988, 205–255.

MILHAUPT, CURTIS, AND GEOFFREY MILLER, 'A Regulatory Cartel Model of Decisionmaking in Japanese Finance,' 2 *Zeitschrift für japanisches Recht*, No. 4, 1997, 18–29.

MILHAUPT, CURTIS, AND GEOFFREY MILLER, 'Cooperation, Conflict, and Convergence in Japanese Finance: Evidence from the "Jusen" Problem,' 29 *Law and Policy in International Business*, 1997, 1–78.

MOLITOR, BERNHARD, 'Deregulierung in Europa.' Tübingen 1996.

NEYE, HANS-WERNER, 'Der Vorschlag 1997 einer Takeover-Richtlinie,' 18 *Zeitschrift für Wirtschaftsrecht*, 1997, 2172–2177.

NUNNENKAMP, PETER, 'Grenzenloser Handel und Kapitalverkehr?", *Internationale Politik*, 1/1999, 3–10.

OBSTFELD, MAURICE, 'The Global Capital Market: Benefactor or Menace?", 12 *Journal of Economic Perspectives*, Fall 1998, 9–30.

OKRUCH, STEFAN, '"Hindrängen" zur Ordnung und "Entdeckung" des Rechts: Fragen zur kulturellen Evolution.' Reprint aus der Max-Planck-Projektgruppe Recht der Gemeinschaftsgüter Bonn. 1998/4.

RATNER, DAVID L., 'Securities Regulation in a Nutshell.' 5. ed., St. Paul, Minn. 1996.

REMIEN, OLIVER, 'Europäisches Einheitsrecht mit nationaler Abänderungsbefugnis?.' In: D. Martiny and N. Witzleb, eds., *Auf dem Wege zu einem Europäischen Zivilgesetzbuch*, Berlin 1999, 125–139.

ROMANO, ROBERTA, 'Empowering Investors: A Market Approach to Securities Regulation.' In: K. J. Hopt, H. Kanda, M. J. Roe, E. Wymeersch and S. Prigge, eds., *Comparative Corporate Governance – The State of the Art and Emerging Research.* Oxford 1998, 143–217.

ROQUETTE, ANDREAS J., 'New Developments Relating to the Internationalization of the Capital Markets: A Comparison of Legislative Reforms in the United States, the European Community, and Germany,' 14 *University of Pennsylvania Journal of International Business Law*, 1994, 565–622.

RUDOLPH, BERND, AND HEINER RÖHRL, 'Grundfragen der Börsenorganisation aus ökonomischer Sicht.' In: K. J. Hopt, B. Rudolph and H. Baum, eds., *Börsenreform – Eine ökonomische, rechtsvergleichende und rechtspolitische Untersuchung.* Stuttgart 1997, 143–285.

RUTLEDGE, PHILIP, 'The internet, investors and financial markets: recent US developments,' *European Financial Services Law*, 1998, 272–284.

SEALY, L.S., 'The Draft Thirteenth E.C. Directive.' In: M. Andenas and S. Kenyon-Slade, eds., *E.C. Financial Market Regulation and Company Law*. London 1993, 135–147.

SCHLOSSER, PETER, 'Der Justizkonflikt zwischen den USA und Europa.' Berlin 1985.

SCHMIDT, HARTMUT, 'Economic Analysis of the Allocation of Regulatory Competence in the European Communities.' In: R. M. Buxbaum, G. Hertig, A. Hirsch and K. J. Hopt, eds., M. Hertig, ass. ed., *European Business Law—Legal and Economic Analyses on Integration and Harmonization*. Berlin 1991, 51–60 (1991a).

SCHMIDT, HARTMUT, contribution to the discussion. In: R. M. Buxbaum, G. Hertig, A. Hirsch and K. J. Hopt, eds., M. Hertig, ass. ed., *European Business Law—Legal and Economic Analyses on Integration and Harmonization*. Berlin 1991, 91 (1991b).

SCHMIDTCHEN, DIETER, 'Territorialität des Rechts, Internationales Privatrecht und die autonome Regelung internationaler Sachverhalte,' 59 *Rabels Zeitschrift für ausländisches und internationales Privatrecht*, 1995, 56–112.

SCHNEIDER, JOACHIM, 'Kapitalmarktrechtlicher Anlegerschutz und Internationales Privatrecht.' Frankfurt/M. 1998.

SCHNYDER, ANTON K., 'Internationales Kapitalmarktrecht – Fragestellung, Regelungskonflikte, Koordination,' 115 *Zeitschrift für Schweizerisches Recht*, II/1996, 151–167.

SCHNYDER, ANTON K., 'Wirtschaftskollisionsrecht – Sonderanknüpfung und extraterritoriale Anwendung wirtschaftsrechtlicher Normen unter besonderer Berücksichtigung von Marktrecht.' Zürich 1990.

SCHUSTER, GUNNAR, 'Die internationale Anwendung des Börsenrechts.' Berlin et al. 1996.

SCHUSTER, GUNNAR, 'Extraterritoriality of Securities Laws: An Economic Analysis of Jurisdictional Conflicts,' 26 *Law & Policy in International Business*, 1994, 165–202.

SECURITIES AND EXCHANGE COMMISSION, 'Proposed rule: Cross-Border Tender Offerings, Business Combinations and Rights Offerings,' *Release Nos. 33–7611, 34–40678*. November 1998.

SECURITIES AND EXCHANGE COMMISSION, 'Market 2000 – An Examination of Current Equity Market Developments.' Washington, D. C. 1994.

SECURITIES AND EXCHANGE COMMISSION, 'Concept Release on Multinational Tender and Exchange Offers,' *Release Nos. 33–6866, 34–28093*. June 1990.

SECURITIES AND EXCHANGE COMMISSION, 'Policy Statement of the Securities and Exchange Commission on the Regulation of International Securities Markets,' *CCH Federal Securities Law Reporter*, ¶ 84, 341. November 1988.

SECURITIES AND EXCHANGE COMMISSION, 'Staff Report on the Internationalization of the Securities Markets.' Washington, D. C. 1987.

SECURITIES AND EXCHANGE COMMISSION, 'Request for Comments Concerning a Concept to Improve the Commision's Ability to Investigate and Prosecute Persons Who Purchase or Sell Securities in U. S. Markets from Other Countries.' In: *CHH Federal Securities Law Reporter*, ¶ 83, 648, 1984.

SOMMER, A. A., JR., 'IOSCO: Its Mission and Achievement,' 17 *Northwestern Journal of International Law & Business*, 1996, 15–29.

STEIL, BENN, ed., 'The European Equity Markets.' London 1996.

STEINBERG, MARC I., AND DARYL L. LANDSDALE, JR., 'Regulation S and Rule 144A: Creating a Workable Fiction on an Expanding Global Securities Market,' 29 *The International Lawyer*, 1995, 43–63.

STEPHAN, PAUL B., 'The Futility of Unification and Harmonization in International Commercial Law,' 39 *Virginia Journal of International Law*, 1999, 743–797.

STOBER, ROLF, 'Globalisierung der Wirtschaft und Rechtsprinzipien des Weltwirtschaftsrechts.' In: U. Hübner and W. Ebke, eds., *Festschrift für Bernhard Großfeld zum 65. Geburtstag*. Heidelberg 1999, 1173–1199.

STREIT, MANFRED E., 'Systemwettbewerb im europäischen Integrationsprozeß.' In: U. Immenga, W. Möschel, and D. Reuter, eds., *Festschrift für Ernst-Joachim Mestmäcker*. Baden-Baden 1996, 521–535.

STREIT, MANFRED E., AND WERNER MUSSLER, 'Systemwettbewerb im europäischen Integrationsprozeß.' In: Lüder Gerken, *Europa zwischen Ordnungswettbewerb und Harmonisierung*, ed., Heidelberg 1995, 75–107.

SULGER, TODD A., 'Harmonization of Securities Market Regulation in the European Union: Is the Price Tag Too High?,' 29 *California Western International Law Journal*, 1998, 221–241.

SYKES, ALAN O., 'The (Limited) Role of Regulatory Harmonization in the International Goods and Services Markets,' *Journal of International Economic Law*, 1999, 49–70.

TRACHTMAN, JOEL P., 'Trade in Financial Services under GATS, NAFTA and the EC: A Regulatory Jurisdiction Analysis,' 33 *Columbia Journal of Transnational Law*, 1995, 37–122.

TRACHTMAN, JOEL P., 'Unilateralism, Bilateralism, Regionalism, Multilateralism, and Functionalism: A Comparison with Reference to Securities Regulation,' 4 *Transnational Law & Contemporary Problems*, 1994, 69–117.

TRACHTMAN, JOEL P., 'International Regulatory Competition, Externalization, and Jurisdiction,' 34 *Harvard International Law Journal*, 1993, 48–104.

TRUDEL, PIERRE, 'Jurisdiction on the Internet: A Canadian Perspective,' 32 *The International Lawyer*, 1998, 1027–1066.

VAN ZANDT, DAVID E., 'The Regulatory and Institutional Conditions for an International Securities Market,' 32 *Virginia Journal of International Law*, 1991, 47–81.

VEELKEN, WINFRIED, 'Interessenabwägung im Wirtschaftskollisionsrecht.' Baden-Baden 1988.

VERDIER, DANIEL, 'Domestic Responses to Capital Market Internationalization Under the Gold Standard, 1870–1914,' 52 *International Organization*, Winter 1998, 1–34.

WALLMAN, STEVEN M. H., 'Competition, Innovation, and Regulation in the Securities Markets,' 53 *The Business Lawyer*, 1998, 341–371.

WARNER, WAIDE E., '"Mutual Recognition" and Cross-Border Financial Services in the European Community,' 55 *Law and Contemporary Problems*, Autumn 1992, 7–28.

WARREN, MANNING G. III., 'Global Harmonization of Securities Laws: The Achievements of the European Communities,' 31 *Harvard International Law Journal*, 1990, 185–232.

WEBER, STEFAN, 'Kapitalmarktrecht. Eine Untersuchung des österreichischen Rechts und des Europäischen Gemeinschaftsrechts.' Wien 1996.

V. WEIZÄCKER, CARL CHRISTIAN, 'Logik der Globalisierung.' Göttingen 1999.

WHITE, LAWRENCE J., 'Competition versus Harmonization—An Overview of International Regulation of Financial Services.' In: Claude E. Barfield ed., *International Financial Markets: Harmonization versus Competition.* Washington, D.C., 1996, 5–48.

v. WILMOWSKY, PETER, 'Gesellschafts- und Kapitalmarktrecht in einem gemeinsamen Markt,' 56 *Rabels Zeitschrift für ausländisches und internationales Privatrecht,* 1992, 521–546.

WITTICH, GEORG, 'Einheitlicher Europäischer Finanzmarkt.' Speech at the *Zweites Kapitalmarktrechtssymposium der Deutschen Börse AG,* Frankfurt/M., June 9, 1999.

WOLF, CH., JR., 'Markets or Governments: Choosing between Imperfect Alternatives.' 2. ed., Cambridge, Mass. 1993.

WYMEERSCH, EDDY, 'The Implementation of the ISD and CAD in National Legal Systems.' In: Guido Ferrarini, ed., *European Securities Markets – The Investment Services Directive and Beyond.* London 1998, 3–40.

ZARING, DAVID, 'International Law by Other Means: The Twilight Existence of International Financial Regulatory Organizations,' 33 *Texas International Law Journal,* 1998, 281–330.

GLOBALIZATION OF FINANCE: HOW TO DEAL WITH MANDATORY RULES

by Yoshiaki Nomura, Ôsaka[*]

Contents

A. Introduction

As local markets become liberalized worldwide, corporate finance is becoming more and more globalized. Firms seek low-cost financing regardless of where the market is. It was only a few years ago that Japanese firms fled from the Japanese capital market into the Eurobond market.[1] In the first half of 1998, Japanese firms issued 90% of their bonds in Japan, compared with 70% in the same period in 1997. The total amount of yen-denominated straight bonds issued abroad by Japanese firms decreased from ¥170 billion in the first half of 1997 to ¥60 billion yen in the same period in 1998. This ranked third in volume

---

[*] Part of the work in this Article was supported by Science Research Fund of the Japanese Ministry of Education, 1997–99. I am grateful to my colleague, Associate Professor Colin McKenzie, for his help in suggesting many valuable improvements.
[1] 'Eurobonds are traditionally defined as bonds which are issued, and largely sold, outside the domestic market of the currency in which they are denominated.' 'The International Bond Market,' 31 Bank of England Quarterly Bulletin 521 (1991).

following ¥118 billion yen of German mark denominated bonds and ¥388 billion yen of US dollar bonds.[2]

With the start of the Big Bang in Japan,[3] the year 1998 saw a series of legislation aimed at facilitating receivables financing, especially by way of securitization.[4] The legal infrastructure for securitization is now in place. Firms are given more freedom to securitize their assets and manage their balance sheets better.[5] The SPC Act together with the *Saitoku-Hô* will accelerate the trend toward securitization and globalization of corporate finance.[6]

The liberalization of the means of finance has introduced several mechanisms for investor protection. One such mechanism is found in the SPC Act. Article 109 of the Act requires the bond issuer (SPC) to contract with the so-called *Tokutei Shasai-kanri Kaisha* (Commissioned Company for Special Bondholders, hereinafter referred to as the 'Commissioned Company'). The Commissioned Company, acting on behalf of the bondholders, receives payments, protects rights, and does other matters for the management of special bonds.

If an SPC established under the SPC Act issues Euro–Yen bonds, does the mandatory rule of Article109 apply? Does it make a difference if the governing

---

[2]   See 'Foreign Bond Issues by Japanese Corporations,' *Kôshasai Geppô* (Bond Monthly Report), November 1998 at 9.

[3]   The forerunner of the Big Bang was the revised *Gaikoku-kawase oyobi Gaikoku-bôeki Hô* (Foreign Exchange and Foreign Trade Act) implemented in 1 April 1998. The old version of this Act contained the word 'control' in its title.

[4]   In addition to the *Tokutei-mokuteki Kaisha ni yoru Tokutei-shisan ni kansuru Hôritsu* (Act concerning the Enhancement of Liquidity of the Specified Assets by Special Purpose Company), 1998 Act No.105, (hereinafter referred to as the 'SPC Act'), the following two Acts should be noted. *Saiken-Jôto no Taikô-Yôken ni kansuru Minpô no Tokurei-tô ni kansuru Hôritsu* (Act for the Special Rules of the Civil Code concerning the Opposability of Assignment), 1998 Act No.104, (hereinafter referred to as the '*Saitoku-Hô*') and *Saiken-kanri Kaishû-gyô ni kansuru Tokubetsu Sochi Hô* (Act Providing for Special Measures for Servicer Business), 1998 Act No.126.

[5]   For the assignment side of the story, see Yoshiaki Nomura, ' The Law Applicable to the Assignment of Receivables: Japanese Conflict-of-Law Rules in the Age of Securitization' 41 *The Japanese Annual of International Law* 44–60 (1998).

[6]   *Nihon Keizai Shinbun* (Japan Economic Newspaper), 9 July 1999, explains this trend as follows. By using the *Saitoku-Hô*'s assignment-registration system, Japanese trading companies have begun to raise finance by assigning their accounts receivable to the SPC set up within and outside Japan. The amount of proceeds in Japanese yen from the assignment of receivables outstanding at the end of June 1999 is 46 billion for Nisshô Iwai Corp, 25 billion for Marubeni Corp. and 10.5 billion for Itochû Corp. The registration shows that most of their receivables were assigned in December and March, when the financing demand was most acute. It is observed that the financial products serviced by the cash flow of the assigned receivables were purchased by institutional investors, most of which are local banks.

law of these bonds is English or Japanese law? If the same SPC issues Yen denominated bonds in Japan under a foreign law, does Article 109 apply?

This article discusses the scope of the application of the mandatory rules with respect to the Commissioned Company and its counterpart in the Commercial Code. It is suggested that the rules have mandatory effect only if the offering in question is made within the territory of Japan. It follows that companies may not contract out of these rules by choosing a foreign law as the applicable law to the bond offering in Japan. Finally, it is recommended that a legislative effort should be made to clarify the scope of the international application of these mandatory rules since they are taken into account in the calculation of risks and costs associated with a securitized transaction.

B.   The Forum's Mandatory Rules

On 15 June 1998, the SPC Act was enacted.[7] The policy goals of this Act are twofold.[8] The first and most important goal is to facilitate the securitization of assets by issuing securities backed by assigned assets.[9] Second, the Act purports to set up an arrangement that adequately protects investors who acquire the asset-backed securities (hereinafter referred to as 'ABS').[10]

---

[7]   See supra note 4.

[8]   Article 1 of the SPC Act sets forth the two purposes of the Act. See also *Kinyû Seido Chôsa-kai* (The Financial System Research Council) published a report on 13 June 1997, entitled 'Regarding the Reform of the Japanese Financial System— Contributing to the Vitalization of the National Economy—,'(hereinafter referred to as the 'Council Report'). See <http://www.mof.go.jp/english/tosin/e1a602f5.htm>. The Council Report discuses the goals which the possible legislation should adopt. It recommended that a bill should be submitted 'in the next regular Diet session concerning necessary legal measures.'

[9]   See Article 2 (9) for the definition of asset securitization. The Council Report, supra note 8 states: 'Under the current Commercial Law, SPCs are subject to rules for maintaining a minimum capital of 10 million yen and at least three directors, etcetera. These rules create cost burdens in establishing and maintaining SPCs when separate SPCs are established for each individual package of loans that they are trying to securitize. This may eventually cause the decline in the product appeal of ABS. Therefore, it is necessary to discuss legal measures concerning the simplification of the procedures for establishing SPCs, as well as the legal status of SPCs.'

[10] For the investor protection measures, the Council Report, supra note 8 says: 'Additionally, if one considers the unique characteristics of ABS, which are issued based only on the transferred assets as collateral, it is necessary to consider the manner of investor protection at the level of the scheme's structure....b. For example, an SPC has been established for the sole purpose of receiving assets transferred and issuing securities. If an SPC conducts businesses other than those discussed above, there is increased risk that the SPC could go bankrupt. Thus, from the perspective of

cont. ...

In order to implement these policies, this Act sets out to create a legal vehicle for securitization, which is to exist for the sole purpose of issuing securities backed by the assigned assets. In the industry parlance, this type of vehicle is called the 'special purpose vehicle' or the 'SPV.' The SPC Act chose to create a new corporate form, the Special Purpose Company or the SPC, which is distinct from a company under the Commercial Code.[11]

Issuing of Asset Backed Securities by SPC

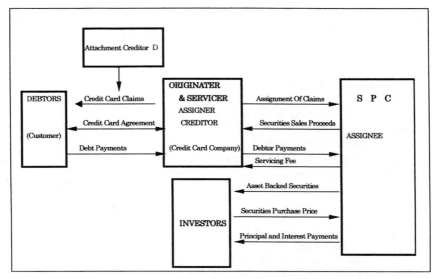

As a result, a vehicle for securitization may take the form of partnerships (*Kumiai*) under the Civil Code,[12] partnerships (*Tokumei Kumiai*) under the

---

ABS investor protection, it is a problem if the SPC conducts other businesses. Also, in situations where the ABS's asset collateral is diverted to purposes other than ABS repayment, there is a potential hindrance in collecting the invested money.'

[11] The reasons for this decision may be found in the Council Report, supra note 8 and 9. It should be noted that a company under the Commercial Code has virtually unlimited capacity to act. According to Supreme Court precedent, the capacity of a company is not limited by the purposes expressly provided in the memorandum of association (see Article 43 of the Civil Code), and includes any activities that are directly and indirectly necessary to carry out its purposes. A contribution to a political party was held to be within the purposes set out in the memorandum of association, 'as far as it is interpreted, in the objective and abstract observation,' to be made to carry out the company's '*shakaiteki Yakuwari*'(social roles). See Supreme Court Judgement (Grand Bench), 24 June 1970, 24 Minshû 625 (1970).

[12] See Articles 667 – 688.

Commercial Code,[13] companies under the Commercial Code, special purpose companies under the SPC Act and other special purpose vehicles set up under foreign laws.

Though not expressly provided in the SPC Act itself, the most urgent need for creating such a legal form in Japanese law was to securitize bad loans secured by immovables and to securitize the immovables, which secure the bad loans.[14] Added to this implied purpose was the expectation that by facilitating the establishment of an SPC, the Act would offer a self-sufficient mechanism for securitization in Japan and it would prevent the vehicles from fleeing into foreign jurisdictions.[15]

The SPC under this Act can tap securities markets by issuing equity or debt securities to investors. First it may issue preference shares (Art. 37). Second, it may issue debt securities or bonds (Art. 108). It is the second type of securities that needs to be managed by a third party company other than the issuer and the bondholders. The bonds that the SPC issues are called '*tokutei shasai*' or '*special bonds*.' They are so named so that they may be distinguished from ordinary bonds issued by a company under the Commercial Code (see Art. 296). Most significantly, the 'special' bonds are always backed by the assets assigned by the originator to the SPC,[16] while bonds issued by ordinary companies are not.[17]

The SPC Act sets up several mechanisms for investor protection. In addition to the requirements for disclosure applicable to equity and debt securities in general,[18] two mechanisms are set up to protect the bondholders. First, Article 112 creates a lien for the bondholders on the general property of the SPC.[19] Second, Article 109 provides, as we have seen above, that when the SPC offers the bonds, it shall appoint the Commissioned Company and authorize it to

---

[13]   See Articles 535 – 542.

[14]   See Satsuki Katayama, *SPC Hô towa Nanika: Shisan no Shôkenka to Ryûdôka ni Mukete* (What is the SPC Act?—To Make Assets Liquid and Securitized), 25–34 (1998). However, there have been few cases in which the SPC Act was utilized for this purpose. See Nomura supra note 5 at note 45. See also infra note 27.

[15]   See Shôichi Royama, 'Shôkenka no Teichaku wo Negatte' (May the Securitization Stay), in Katayama, supra note 14 at 1. Given the regulatory and mandatory nature of the SPC Act, it is submitted that many securitization schemes would continue to take advantage of the differences between countries and markets.

[16]   See Article 2 (9) and Article 110 of the SPC Act. Articles 144,152

[17]   If one disregards the costs and risks inherent in the form of company under the Commercial Code, one can use this company as an SPV, which issues the asset-backed securities.

[18]   See Articles 5, 6, 18, 38, 110, 143, 144 (3) and (4), and *Shôken-torihiki Hô* (Securities Act) Article 2 (1).

[19]   Other than the general charge on the company's property, the SPC may issue bonds secured by specific property. See Article 113 (2).

receive payments, protect rights, and do other matters for the management of bonds on behalf of the bondholders.

We find the predecessor of the latter mechanism in the Commercial Code when ordinary companies issue straight bonds.[20] Article 297 of the Commercial Code makes it mandatory for the bond issuing company to contract with *Shasai-kanri Kaisha* or the commissioned company for the bondholders (hereinafter referred to as the 'commissioned company'). The rule provides two exemptions from this requirement. The first is the private placement exemption,[21] and the second is the professional-investors exemption.[22] The SPC Act strengthened the requirement by removing the private placement exemption.

Article 111 of the SPC Act specifies the powers of the Commissioned Company. The Commissioned Company has the power to carry out all judicial and extrajudicial acts which are necessary to receive payment on behalf of the bondholders or to preserve and protect their rights (Article 111 (1)). On the resolution of the bondholders' meeting, it may defer the repayment of the total amount of bonds, waive or compromise the liability incurred from the default (Article 111 (4)). So far as is necessary to carry out these acts, the Commissioned Company may examine the status of business activities and property of the SPC which issued the bonds (Article 111 (6)). Compared with the commissioned company in the Commercial Code, the Commissioned Company's role is more active.[23]

What if the SPC offers bonds without appointing the Commissioned Company? For the breach of duty under Article 109, Article 183 of the SPC Act imposes a penalty (*karyô*) not exceeding one million yen on the promoters, directors and other officers of the SPC.[24] However, there is no provision to determine the private law effect of the breach. The counterpart provision of the Commercial Code (Article 297) has the same problem. Article 314 of the

---

[20] Before the amendment of 1993, the Commercial Code provided for the voluntary appointment of the bondholder 'trustee.' The 1993 amendment introduced the mandatory appointment of the commissioned company following the Trust Indentures Act of 1939 of the United States. A similar mechanism is found in *Tanpotsuki Shasai Shintaku Hô*, (Secured Bond Trust Act) (Art. 2) .

[21] This is where the face value of each bond is 100 million or more.

[22] This is where the total amount of the bonds divided by the lowest amount specified on the bond is less than 50.

[23] The Commissioned Company needs the permission from the court to exercise its power to examine these matters (Article 309–3 of the Commercial Code). Even this 'limited' power of the MBC is very strong compared with its United States counterpart. The trustee in the Trust Indenture Act of 1939 is a passive recipient of information provided by the issuer.

[24] *Karyô* or *ayamachi-ryô* is admistrative in nature. It should be distinguished from *karyô* or *tôgaryô* which is a criminal punishment (see Criminal Code Article 9). A similar sanction is found in the Commercial Code for the breach of Article 297.

Commercial Code may be applied by analogy.[25] It provides that if after the resignation, removal or liquidation of the commissioned company, the company does not appoint a new commissioned company with the consent of the bondholders meeting (or permission of the court), 'the maturity of the total issuance shall be accelerated.'[26] In the case of the SPC, it will face acceleration if it does not appoint the Commissioned Company after the issuance of the bonds.

The foregoing discussion shows that the Commissioned Company rule backed by its strengthened function as a 'watch-dog' has a mixture of administrative and civil characteristics. Apart from this, the SPC Act attempts to realize its professed purposes by rules backed by regulations rather than remedies.[27] Regulations and mandatory rules mean costs and risks. Therefore, it is a great concern for businesses to know whether they can avoid the regulatory and mandatory aspects of the Act and enjoy the merits of the SPC's.

C. The Applicable Law And Mandatory Rules

Whether the mandatory Commissioned Company rule of Article 109 [backed by other features] of the SPC Act is applicable to a certain case depends on some 'connecting' factors. In the following discussion, we take three such factors as significant. They are the place of issuance, the governing law, and the location of the bondholders as a class.[28] The last factor is identical with the place where a

---

[25] Shûichi Yoshikai, *Heisei 5 nen, 6 nen Kaisei Shôhô* (Revised Commercial Code, Amended in 1993–94) 275–276 (1996).

[26] Article 314 (1) and (2).

[27] First, a *Shisan Ryûdôka Keikaku* (Asset Securitization Plan) supplemented by *Shisan Ryûdôka Jisshi Keikaku* (Implementation Schedule) must be prepared (Articles 5 and 6) and second, together with these documents, the registration of the SPC must be made (Article 7). The registration may be rejected by the Prime Minister (Article 8). For other regulations, see 'Strategies for Reviving the Japanese Economy,' Report to Prime Minister Obuchi, 26 February 1999. See http:/www.kantei.go.jp/foreign/ senryaku/chap3.html. This Report calls for the immediate amendment of the SPC Act, which is inconvenient to use for securitizing good assets. In addition to improving the tax treatment of securitization related transactions, the following revisions are proposed: subscribing the preference shares for a consideration other than cash should be permitted (revision to Article 38); restrictions on out-sourcing of the business (revision to Article 144), borrowing limits (revision to Article 151), restrictions on the disposal of special assets (revision to Article 152), and restrictions regarding the write-off of preference shares (revisions to Articles 48 and 119) should be removed. On these matters, deregulation should be undertaken from the viewpoint of structuring attractive investment instruments.

[28] The 'nationality' or 'domicile' of the issuer is not relevant in our discussion of the SPC Act.

particular issue is targeted. On the other hand, the currency in which the bonds are denominated is not in itself a determinative factor, unless the country of the currency attempts to control the issue.[29] The question of currency would certainly affect those who buy the bonds. In other words, the currency question is not a determinative but a practical factor, which may be considered in the light of the third factor, i.e. the location of the bondholders as a class.

Though the real cases may involve more factors, which may be combined variously, it would be practical to consider the question of application in the following two situations. The first situation is where the company set up under the SPC Act issues bonds outside Japan. This is typical of Eurobonds. The second situation is where the SPC issues bonds within Japan. This is the case of domestic bonds. We will further divide each of these situations into two cases, according to what law governs the case.

I.   Four Cases

1.   Eurobonds

Case 1: The company established under the SPC Act issues Eurobonds (denominated in Yen or in a foreign currency) in London and the legal relationship between the issuer and the bondholder is determined by a foreign law.
Case 2: The same legal relationship between the Japanese SPC and the Eurobond-holder is governed by Japanese law.

In the typical Eurobond issue, the subscription agreement is made between the issuer and the managers (security firms or 'investment banks'). The fiscal agency agreement is made between the issuer and a bank. Sometimes a trust deed is made between the issuer and a financial institution as a trustee, where the trustee is appointed for the bondholders to protect their interests. The relationship between the issuer and bondholder is determined by the terms and conditions of the bond. The bondholders are bound by the terms of the fiscal agency agreement or the trust deed by way of reference.[30]

---

[29] For example, the Foreign Trade and Exchange Act, before the 1997 amendment became effective, required a foreign issuer of Euro-Yen bonds to obtain the permission of the Finance Minister (Articles. 20, 21 and 70).

[30] See Yoshiaki Nomura, 'International Finance' in Hiroshi Matsuoka, *Gendai Kokusai Torihiki Hô Kogi* (The Lectures on Modern Law of International Transactions), 107, 133–135 (1996).

It should be noted that a trustee may (in the United States) or may not (in England) be required by statute.[31] The commissioned company is a 'trustee' required by Japanese law.

2.   Domestic Bonds

Case 1: The Japanese SPC issues bonds in Japan under a foreign law.
Case 2: The Japanese SPC issues bonds in Japan under Japanese law.

In the Commercial Code or the SPC Act, a public offering is the typical method of issuance.[32] In offering bonds, a *shasai keiyaku* (company bond contract) is made between the issuer (borrower) and the individual *shasai kensha* (lender).[33] The original lender subscribes to the issue and the issuer makes the allotment of bonds (subscription agreement). The legal relationship after the issuance between the issuer–borrower and the bondholder–lender is stipulated in the terms and conditions of the bond. In the Commercial Code model, the terms of the commissioned company agreement between the issuer and the bank(s) is to bind the bondholders by reference.[34]

II.   Three Approaches

Does the requirement of the Commissioned Company of Article 109 apply in these cases? In order to consider this question, we will use the following three approaches: first, the *depeçage* approach; second, the governing law approach; and third, the jurisdictional approach.

---

[31]   See Philip R. Wood, *International Loans, Bonds and Securities Regulation* 167 (1995). See also Nomura, supra note 30 at 135–137.

[32]   See Article 301 of the Commercial Code and Article 110 of the SPC Act.

[33]   Compared with the procedure traditionally followed in the Eurobond issue, it must be noted that in the Commercial Code model, the *shasai keiyaku* includes the terms and conditions of the bond. Thus we refer to the governing law of the *shasai keiyaku*. The fact is that there are other methods of issuing bonds (for example, Article 302 of the Commercial Code permits the method similar to the 'bought deal.'). Therefore, the characterization of the legal relationship must be different accordingly. See Tsuneo Ôtori, *Shasai Hô* (Law of Bond),19 (19).

[34]   For example, it is stated on the face of the bond as follows: 'We, the Commissioned Companies for Bondholders, hereby certify that we shall perform our duties and functions set forth in the Conditions of Bonds [on the reverse hereof] in accordance with the Agreement with Commissioned Companies for Bondholders dated ....' It seems that the relationship between the Commissioned Companies and the bondholder is characterized as a contract for the third parties. See Article 537 of the Civil Code.

As we see in the following discussion, these approaches were developed to deal with two different mandatory rules. The *depeçage* approach has the very practical purpose of derogating from the requirement of a court's consent, which is required to make the bondholders' meetings effective (Article 327 of the Commercial Code). The last two approaches are the efforts to explain the commissioned company requirement that we have discussed earlier (Article 297 of the Commercial Code). As we also see later, how we characterize a particular mandatory rule determines which approach we should adopt in a specific case.

1. Depeçage Approach

The *depeçage* approach permits the contracting out of the Commissioned Company requirement if so stipulated in the *shasai keiyaku* or the contract between the issuer and bondholders. This approach is criticized because it permits cherry picking by the parties, which leads to the avoidance of law.[35] However one lawyer cites an agreement on the Euro Yen bond issue in which the mandatory provisions of the Commercial Code relating to the bondholder's meeting were substituted by English law and practice, though the agreement was governed by Japanese law.[36]

By the same argument, this lawyer justified his treatment of the case where KEPCO (Korean Electric Power Company) issued Yen denominated bonds in Japan and afterwards went private. The bondholders' meeting was held in Japan in order to change part of the terms and conditions of the bond. This lawyer took the position that notwithstanding the rule of Article 327 of the Commercial Code, no consent by the court was necessary for the resolution of the bondholders' meeting to be effective against all bondholders. He reasons that though the provision in question is a mandatory rule applicable to bonds issued in Japan by Japanese companies, it is not the kind of public policy which should be applied to samurai bonds ('foreign bonds' issued in Japan by foreign entities).[37] If the Commissioned Company requirement provided for in the SPC

---

[35] Koji Harada, 'Shasai o meguru Hôritsu-kankei to sono Junkyoho' (Legal Relationship concerning Company Bonds and its Governing Law) 1356 *Shôji Hômu* 8, 10, 1358 *Shôji Hômu* 8 (1994). Mr. Harada, who participated in the preparation of the revision of the Commercial Code, adds that the views following the depeçage approach were presented in the process of revision and in the deliberations of the bill. See ibid. at 10 and its note 31.

[36] Kunio Hamada, 'Gaikoku Hokkôtai no Enkasaiken (Samurai-sai) ni kansuru Saikensha Shûkai ni kansuru Shomondai' (Some Problems on the Bondholder's Meeting with respect to Yen-denominated Bonds issued by a Foreign Issuer (Samurai-bond)) 1295 *Shôji Hômu* 28, 1297 *Shôji Hômu* 20, at page 21, Note 6, 1298 *Shôji Hômu* 18 (1992).

[37] See generally, Hamada, supra note 36, especially 1297 *Shôji Hômu* at 20–21.

Act ranks as low in the public policy as the court's consent requirement, it should not be applicable to all cases, Eurobonds Cases 1 and 2, and Domestic Bonds Cases 1 and 2, under this approach.

Aside from the exceptional nature of *depeçage*, this conclusion would negate the very effect of the governing law. We must follow the above critic to say that this approach gives too much discretion to the parties other than the bondholders (or the lawyers of the parties!). Even if one accepts that the rules for the bondholder's meeting express a relatively weak local policy of Japan, one cannot permit the derogation of these rules by depeçage or reference to a foreign law when the issue was made in Japan.

2. Governing Law Approach

The governing law approach is very simple to state. The requirement of the commissioned company (Article 297 of the Commercial Code) is applied to the issuer–bondholder relationship if that relationship is governed by Japanese law.[38] On the other hand, this mandatory rule is not applicable if the governing law to the issuer–bondholder relationship is a foreign law.

If we follow this approach, the requirement of the Commissioned Company under the SPC Act is not applicable to Eurobonds Case 1, which is governed by a foreign law. However, there is a risk that a Japanese court may apply this requirement to Eurobonds Case 1 if it finds the application of the foreign law is incompatible with the public policy of the forum.[39] For the same reason but with more force, a Japanese court may impose the requirement of the Commissioned Company in Domestic Bonds Case 1, excluding the governing foreign law.

The governing law approach follows the general principle of conflict of laws in that when the parties choose the governing law of contract, the reference is to the legal order of the country including the mandatory rules of law.[40] However, there are many rules of law of a mandatory nature, which apply regardless of the governing law. The public policy exception in conflict of laws discussed above is one of the traditional methods to deal with this reality. On the other hand, there are many mandatory rules, which may not apply even if they are part of the legal system to which the governing law belongs. For example, the penalty

---

[38] See Harada, supra note 35, 1358 *Shôji Hômu* at 11–13.

[39] Article 33 of the *Hôrei* states: 'The application of a foreign law designated to govern in accordance with this Act shall be refused if such application is contrary to public order or good morals.'

[40] Article 7 of the *Hôrei* is interpreted as such. It provides as follows:
'The intention of the parties shall determine the law of which country shall govern the existence, validity and effect of a juristic act.
If the intention of the parties is uncertain, the law of the place of acting shall govern the existence, validity and effect of a juristic act.'

or *karyô* for the violation of the commissioned company requirement[41] would not apply to a *shasai keiyaku* which has only a remote connection with Japan.

Furthermore, if we admit that a particular mandatory rule *does not* apply to the contract because the governing law of the contract is foreign, it is as if we determine the nature of that mandatory rule as such. In other words, the policies that the mandatory rule intends to pursue are not so strong as to warrant persistent application. Should we adopt the governing law approach, we must ask, in the process of interpretation, what policies the mandatory rule for the Commissioned Company in the SPC Act intends to realize. On what conditions should the interests of the bondholders be protected?

3. Jurisdictional Approach

The basic tenet of the jurisdictional approach is that the state may apply some mandatory rules to a case because that state has a jurisdictional basis or link with the case, which justifies its application. This tenet resonates with the basic ideas of conflict of laws and with the recent theories of 'special connection.'[42] However, the approach most simply fits in the framework of legislative or prescriptive jurisdiction.[43] Although the jurisdictional approach has a close connection with the tenet of conflict of laws, it admits the application of some mandatory rules independent of the conflict of laws.

In Japan, two views are offered on this approach to explain the requirement of the commissioned company in Article 297 of the Commercial Code. One view characterizes this rule as a 'territorial mandatory rule.'[44] This view suggests that the requirement apply regardless of the governing law when the bonds are offered in Japan.

Another view, while supporting the conclusion of the first view, offers a different explanation.[45] This view characterizes the rule on the commissioned

---

[41] See Article 183 (1) (24) of the SPC Act and Article 498 (1)(22) of the Commercial Code. See also supra note 24.
[42] See Article 7 of the 1980 Rome Convention on the Law Applicable to Contractual Obligations, and the comments in the *Report on the Convention on the Law Applicable to Contractual Obligations* by Mario Giuliano and Paul Lagarde, Official Journal of the European Communities No C 282/34 (1980).
[43] See, e.g. *Restatement (Third) of the Foreign Relations Law of the United States*, Part IV, especially Introductory Note and chapter 1, (1987).
[44] Kenjirô Egashira, 'Shasai Hô no Kaisei,' (Revision of the Bond Law), 1027 Jurist 34, 36 (1993).
[45] Kazuo Ishiguro, 'Shasai Kanri Kaisha no Setchi Kyôsei to Euromarket—Heisei 5-nen Shôhô Kaisei no Kokusaiteki Shatei o Megutte,' (The Commissioned Company Requirement and the Euromarket—On the Scope of the International Application of 1993 Revision of the Commercial Law) in the series of articles entitled 'Borderless
cont. ...

company as a kind of 'absolute mandatory rule.'[46] An absolute mandatory rule is defined as 'the rule of law that has such a strong policy goal as to be applicable in the forum state, regardless of the governing law of the contract or any other relations.'[47] In other words, the scope of the international application of Article 297 and other related provisions is determined in the light of their specific policies, regardless of the governing law of the bonds. This is part of the process that is adopted in the extraterritorial application of state law such as law of securities regulation.[48]

This second view proposes a flexible test of 'close connection' instead of the territorial test of the first view. Let us return to the four Cases above in order to see if these two tests would produce different results in applying Article 109 of the SPC Act. According to the first view, it is surmised that the Commissioned Company rule of the Act applies to Domestic Bonds Cases 1 and 2 because the place of issue (or offering)[49] is Japan. Thus, the rule does not seem to apply to Eurobonds Cases 1 and 2.[50]

In contrast, the second view requires more factors to decide whether Japan has a closer connection with these cases. For example, the mandatory rule concerning the Commissioned Company may apply to Eurobonds Cases 1 and 2 regardless of the governing law, if the issue is targeted at the Japanese investors. In addition, if the currency of denomination is Yen, the likelihood that Japanese investors will subscribe or purchase these bonds is higher. It should be noted, however, that the Yen-denominated bonds, 'issued' outside Japan but intended

---

Economy no Hôteki Shiza,' (Legal Perspectives for the Borderless Economy), Bôeki to Kanzei (Trade and Tariffs), December 1994 issue at 56 and January 1995 issue at 72.

[46] Ishiguro supra note 45 at 79 of the January 1995 issue proposes to treat the same rule as *kainyû kihan* or 'Eingriffsnormen,' being an administrative regulation contrasted with a private contract.

[47] Ishiguro supra note 45 at 63–65 of December 1994 issue. He classifies the rules of law into three categories, first, absolute mandatory, second, relative mandatory, and third, directory or facultative. The 'absolute mandatory rule' is further divided into two subcategories, one relating to the bare exercise of state power, embodied in criminal and administrative sanctions, and the other relating to private contracts.

[48] Ishiguro supra note 45 at 72 of January 1995 issue. See e.g., Nomura supra note 30 at 137.

[49] In a strict sense, 'offering' does not include the case of a bought deal where the securities firm subscribes and pays for the total issue of the bonds in order to resale them (to make a 'secondary offering') to investors. Compare Articles 301 and 302 of the Commercial Code.

[50] Here, we will not deal with the question of whether a similar mandatory rule under the governing foreign law should substitute for the mandatory rule of Article 109 or whether the facultative aspect of the rule may be applied as part of the governing Japanese law .

to be sold to the Japanese investors may be interpreted, under the Territorial Approach, as if they were offered in Japan.

On the other hand, it would seem inappropriate to subject Eurobonds Cases 1 and 2 to the mandatory requirement of the Commissioned Company, regardless of the governing law, if the bonds are to be issued and purchased outside Japan.

D. Conclusion

Article 109 of the SPC Act provides that in offering bonds, the SPC shall appoint the Commissioned Company for the protection of the bondholders.[51] We have seen that this rule backed by a 'watch-dog' provision and *karyô*,[52] coupled with other features of the SPC Act,[53] is more regulatory in nature than its counterpart in the Commercial Code.[54] The policies for bondholder protection underlying this requirement should be limited to those cases that have a close connection with Japan.

Hence, it is suggested that this mandatory requirement should not be considered as part of the private legal system which can be designated by conflict of laws as the governing law. Whether this rule is applicable to a case with one or more international factors cannot be ascertained by means of conflict of laws. It should be determined by interpreting the rule itself.

This means that we should reject both the Depeçage Approach and the Governing Law Approach. The first approach will give the parties too much discretion so that the legal relationships between the issuer and the bondholders would become complicated.[55] The Governing Law Approach disregards the policies underlying the rule for the Commissioned Company. It may result in permitting inconsistent results among the bondholders residing in Japan. Further, there is no guarantee that a Japanese court may resort to the forum's public policy to exclude the governing foreign law.[56]

It is submitted that the Jurisdictional Approach be adopted to interpret the requirement of the Commissioned Company. Of the two views under this approach, the territorial test has the merit of being easy to apply. The most important factor of territoriality is the place of offering. However, when 'Eurobonds' are targeted to Japanese investors located in Japan, the place of offering may be interpreted as being located in Japan.

---

[51] See text accompanying supra note 19.
[52] See supra note19.
[53] See text accompanying supra notes 27.
[54] See text accompanying supra notes 20–22.
[55] See text accompanying supra note.
[56] See text accompanying supra note 39.

In discussing the Jurisdictional Approach, we have stressed that the mandatory rule of Article 109 *does apply* regardless of the governing law. The remaining question is what rule of law should apply if the rule of Article 109 of the SPC Act *does not* apply to a *shasai-keiyaku* governed by Japanese law. First, if the *shasai-keiyaku* 'incorporates' the terms of the rule in the prospectus or in the terms and conditions of the bond, there is no reason to deny the validity of these contract terms. Second, if the *shasai-keiyaku* has no provisions regarding the Commissioned Company, the bondholders may turn to the bondholders meeting or they may resort to the ordinary protective measures with other general creditors of the issuer.

A short note must be added to the mandatory provisions concerning the bondholders meeting.[57] As stated above,[58] this mechanism includes some mandatory provisions such as the consent of the court (Commercial Code Article 325). As the forum's mandatory rules, they should generally be applied to Domestic Bonds, regardless of the governing law of the bond. However, the nature and purpose of these rules are different from the Commissioned Company requirement. The mandatory provisions concerning the bondholders meeting do not intend to regulate the industry or prescribe the conduct of the issuer. Therefore, it is suggested that they be applied as part of the governing Japanese law.[59]

The foregoing argument shows that the Commissioned Company requirement in the SPC Act has such a strong regulatory nature that it should be applied to the issuer-bondholder relationship with an international factor, regardless of the governing law. The same can be said about a similar and milder provision in the Commercial Code. However, there is no clear guidance to ascertain the scope of the international application of these mandatory rules. Considering that corporate finance takes place beyond national borders, it is proposed that the scope of the international application of these rules be provided for in the rules themselves or in the related regulations. This kind of guide is especially important since the mandatory rules with respect to the issuance of securities are taken into account in the calculation of risks and costs associated with a securitized transaction.

Finally, some more fundamental questions should be asked concerning the legislative process of the mandatory rules in question, which have an important effect on private transactions: Does this type of bondholder protection measure really work? Is there any empirical evidence to suggest that the measures are

---

[57] The provisions of the Commercial Code pertaining to the bondholders meeting are made applicable by Article 113 (1) of the SPC Act.

[58] See text accompanying supra note 37.

[59] An equivalent foreign court may be substituted in the requirement of the court's consent.

effective and efficient?[60] It is hoped that future empirical and economic studies will demonstrate that many mandatory rules introduced in the name of investor protection are in reality excessive, costly and unworkable.

---

[60] Even when the law did not require the appointment of the commissioned company (see supra note 20), it was suggested that banks' meddling in the offering as the commissioned company pushed up the cost of issuing and prompted the companies to issue outside Japan. See Misao Tastuta, *Company Law*, note (a) at 270 (1998).

Part 3: International Insolvency and
International Private Law

UNCITRAL MODEL LAW AND THE COMPREHENSIVE REFORM OF JAPANESE INSOLVENCY LAWS

by Junichi Matsushita, Tokyo*

Contents

---

*   I would like to express special thanks to Professor Kôno for his efforts in organizing this symposium and Ms. Stacey Steele for helpful assistance.

A. Introduction

Due to the increasing volume of international trade and investment, we find more and more cross-border insolvency cases than ever. The purposes of insolvency law are equal distribution among creditors, maximization of the value of a debtor's assets, and effective reorganization of a debtor's business in a rehabilitation proceeding. There is no doubt that the law should function to achieve these goals in multinational insolvency cases to the greatest extent possible. Nowadays, it is widely accepted that each country is expected to have a fair and harmonized legal framework for international insolvency cases.

In 1997, UNCITRAL adopted the Model Law on Cross-Border Insolvency after two years of intensive drafting work. In Japan, coincidentally, a project aimed at the comprehensive reform of insolvency laws was begun in 1996, and is still ongoing. In this article, first, I will make a brief overview of UNCITRAL Model Law (B.). Then I will focus on the project of reforming Japanese insolvency laws and legislative discussion concerning cross-border insolvency (C.).

B. UNCITRAL Model Law on Cross-Border Insolvency

I.   Characteristics of the Model Law

In comparison with other bi- or multi-national conventions for cross-border insolvency that are (or have been) in force, I would like to make two preliminary remarks about the character of the Model Law.

First, with respect to the form of instrument used, it is interesting to note that a model law approach, rather than a treaty approach, was chosen. The Model Law is meant to be incorporated into each country's insolvency law, and does not bind any State *per se*. It is true that a few countries insisted on drafting a treaty, especially one with provisions about cooperation between courts, because they thought such matters should be uniformly based on reciprocity. However, a model law approach was favored because it is flexible and 'best suited to induce in the shortest time harmonized modernization of national laws in the area of cross-border insolvency.'[1] Therefore, the fewer changes each State makes in adopting the Model Law, the more harmonization will be achieved. Yet, because the Model Law seems to be flavored with a common law approach in

---

[1]   Paras. 15 and 26 of 'Report of the United Nations Commission on International Trade Law on the work of its thirtieth session (12–30 May 1997), General Assembly Official Records – Fifty-second Session Supplement No. 17 (A/52/17).' UNCITRAL documents in the footnotes in this article can be found in its web site: the URL is 'http://www.un.or.at/uncitral.'

some aspects, civil law countries will scrutinize its legal framework and individual provisions before incorporating it into national laws.

Second, the Model Law does not make an ambitious attempt to unify substantive and procedural insolvency law of each country, but rather modestly confines itself to a few aspects: court access for foreign representatives and creditors, recognition of foreign insolvency proceedings, and judicial cooperation.[2] This is quite a practical step at an early stage of establishing an international legal framework.

II. Overview of the Model Law

The Model Law consists of five chapters and 32 articles. I am going to make a chapter-by-chapter overview, picking up important issues and making comments.

1. Chapter I (General Provisions)

Chapter I consists of general provisions, including the scope of application (article 1) and public policy exceptions (article 6). Article 2 provides a definition of 'foreign main proceeding,' which means a foreign insolvency proceeding commenced in the State where the debtor has the center of interest, and 'foreign non-main proceeding,' which means a foreign insolvency proceeding taking place in the State where the debtor only has an establishment. This distinction is important, mainly with respect to the effects of recognition of foreign proceedings pursuant to articles 20 and 21. It should be noted that a foreign proceeding commenced in a State where the debtor has only assets, and neither the center of interest nor an establishment, is excluded from these definitions. Article 5 provides for the extraterritorial effect of an insolvency proceeding, giving the trustee power to act in foreign countries.

2. Chapter II (Access of Foreign Representatives and Creditors to Local Courts)

Articles 9 through 12 provide for access of foreign representatives to local courts, and articles 13 and 14 provide for access of foreign creditors to local courts. A foreign representative can file for a local insolvency proceeding, even before recognition of the proceeding (articles 9 and 11), or can file an

---

[2]   Paras. 3 and 5 of 'Guide to Enactment of the UNCITRAL Model Law on Cross-Border Insolvency (A/CN. 9/442).' (hereinafter 'Guide to Enactment')

application for recognition of the insolvency proceeding in which the trustee is appointed, without any licenses or consular actions.[3] However, recognition is required when the trustee participates in the domestic insolvency proceeding, for example, when the trustee makes an appeal or an objection to a creditors' claim (article 12).[4]

Article 13 gives 'national treatment' to foreign creditors. In addition, article 14 provides for a sort of 'affirmative action' for foreign creditors. In principle, it requires individual notification[5] to foreign creditors, even when public notification (like publication through an official gazette) would suffice for local creditors, although the court still retains discretion to order publication in another form in an exceptional case.

3.   Chapter III (Recognition of a Foreign Proceeding and Relief)

a)   General Description

In this Model Law, 'recognition' is a key concept that gives intraterritorial effect to foreign insolvency proceedings. Two points should be noted here. First, 'recognition' is a court decision, and the Model Law does not take an automatic recognition approach (such an approach can be found in the EU Convention on Insolvency Proceedings[6]). The Model Law requires this special procedural step to grant relief for a foreign insolvency proceeding, because it can avoid discrepancy regarding whether the proceeding can be recognized, thereby achieving greater legal certainty. Second, the notion of 'recognition' in the Model Law is completely different from that of 'recognition' as in 'recognition of a foreign judgment.' That is, effects of the foreign insolvency proceeding do not flow into the country where the proceeding is recognized as such, and *domestic* insolvency law will determine the scope and contents of relief to be granted upon recognition.[7]

---

[3]   Para. 93 of Guide to Enactment, *supra* note 2.

[4]   Article 12 relates to article 24, which allows a foreign trustee to intervene in any 'individual' proceeding where the debtor is a party upon recognition.

[5]   This is especially important when notification is made regarding commencement of an insolvency proceeding and time limit to file claims. No letters rogatory or other, similar formality is required. Paragraph (2) of article 14.

[6]   Articles 16 (1) and 17 (1) of European Union Convention on Insolvency Proceedings, opened for signature Nov. 23, 1995, 35 I.L.M. 1223 (1996).

[7]   There was controversy during the drafting work of the Model Law over whether the word 'recognition' was appropriate. *See*, the Explanatory comments on article 11 [6] in 'Report of the Working Group on Insolvency Law on the Work of Its Twentieth Session (Vienna, 7–18 October 1996)' (24 October 1996) (A/CN. 9/433).

b) Requirements of Recognition

A foreign proceeding shall be recognized if the proceeding is commenced in a country where the debtor has the center of its main interests or an establishment,[8] and the recognition of the proceeding would not be manifestly contrary to domestic public policy.[9] These rather simple requirements are expected to make the recognition process as efficient as possible. There is no requirement of reciprocity, mainly because inclusion of reciprocity would not only lead to uncertainty due to difficulties in determining the extent to which reciprocity was available, but would also be inconsistent with the basic aim of the Model Law to foster greater international cooperation.[10]

c) Effects of Recognition

A foreign proceeding is recognized as a 'foreign main proceeding' if it takes place in the country where the debtor has the center of its main interests, and as a 'foreign non-main proceeding' if it is commenced in the country where the debtor has only an establishment and no gravity of economic interest.[11]

Recognition of a foreign main proceeding produces certain 'automatic' effects,[12] including a stay of individual proceedings and executions, and suspension of the debtor's right to dispose of its assets (Paragraph (1), (a), (b), and (c) of article 20). These effects are indispensable to ensure an orderly and fair resolution of cross-border insolvency cases.

Moreover, article 21 provides for additional discretionary relief that can be given upon recognition of either a foreign non-main proceeding or a foreign main proceeding. These measures are granted at the discretion of the court, rather than taking effect automatically. Relief includes: extending of the scope of the stay and suspension provided for by article 20 (1); obtaining information and evidence concerning a debtor's assets and business; giving a right to administer and dispose of the debtor's assets to the foreign representative or

---

[8] This is often referred to as 'indirect competence.' Article 16 provides for presumption for this requirement.

[9] In addition to the requirements in the text, article 17 (1) also requires that the foreign representative within the meaning of article 2 (d) file a petition for recognition with a competent court referred to in article 4, submitting documents specified in paragraph (2) of article 15.

[10] Para. 43 of 'Report of the Working Group on Insolvency Law on the Work of Its Eighteenth Session (Vienna, 30 October – 10 November 1995)' (1 December 1995) (A/CN. 9/419).

[11] An insolvency proceeding taking place in a country where the debtor has only assets and no center of main interest or establishment is not eligible for recognition.

[12] These effects could be 'mandatory' in a country where a court decision is required for the stay or suspension and the court is bound to issue such orders. Paras. 32, 142 of Guide to Enactment, *supra* note 2.

another person appointed by the court; and turnover of the debtor's assets to the foreign proceeding.

In addition, article 19 allows a foreign representative to file for urgent relief while an application for recognition is pending. The measures in article 19 are discretionary, as are the measures in article 21. However, the relief under article 19 is a little more limited than the relief under article 21.[13]

Upon recognition, a foreign representative can not only intervene in a proceeding in which the debtor is a party (article 24), but also initiate an avoidance action to set aside fraudulent or preferential transfers (article 23). The Model Law is modest enough not to refer to choice of law rules concerning avoidance.

4. Chapter IV (Cooperation with Foreign Courts and Foreign Representatives)

Articles 25 through 27 establish a somewhat flexible framework for cooperation and direct communication between a local court and a foreign court or foreign representatives, and between a local trustee and foreign courts or foreign representatives. For this cooperation, recognition is not required. Among the forms of cooperation provided for in article 27, approval by courts of agreements (often called 'concordat' or 'protocol') concerning the coordination of concurrent proceedings is important.

5. Chapter V (Concurrent Proceedings)

In contrast to the EU Convention principle that prevents a local proceeding from being commenced or continued after recognition of a foreign main proceeding, especially when the foreign proceeding is a rehabilitation proceeding,[14] the Model Law imposes almost no limits on the availability of local proceedings even after recognition of a foreign main proceeding (article 28). Strict limitations would go beyond the ambit of the project, could give rise to complex issues, and might reduce the acceptability of the Model Law.[15] Therefore, what matters next is the legal framework for coordination between a local proceeding and a foreign proceeding to maximize the value of the debtor's assets or to achieve the most advantageous restructuring of the enterprise. Article 29 deals

---

[13] The court is supposed to take into account adequate protection of local creditors when it grants, denies, or modifies discretionary relief under articles 19 and 21. Article 22 (1).

[14] *See*, articles 3 (3) and 33 of EU Convention, *supra* note 6.

[15] The Explanatory comments on article 16 [18] in 'Report of the Working Group on Insolvency Law on the Work of Its Twentieth Session, *supra* note 7.

with coordination between a local proceeding and a foreign proceeding, establishing flexible primacy of the local proceeding over the recognized foreign proceeding.[16] Article 30 deals with coordination where two or more foreign proceedings seek recognition, basically giving preference to the foreign *main* proceeding. As well, both provisions require the court to cooperate with foreign courts and foreign representatives pursuant to articles 25 through 27.

Article 32 provides for the so-called 'hotchpot rule' to adjust distribution to a certain creditor who has already been paid in part in a foreign proceeding.

C. Comprehensive Reform of Japanese Insolvency Laws and International Insolvency Issues

I. Comprehensive Reform of Japanese Insolvency Laws

In Japan, after we completed the total reform of the Code of Civil Procedure in June 1996, a project for the comprehensive reform of Japanese insolvency laws[17]started in October 1996. The Advisory Committee for the reform of the insolvency laws, consisting of academics, attorneys, judges, and officials from the Ministry of Justice, was set up in the Civil Bureau of the Ministry of Justice. The Committee was at that time expected to submit drafts of bills for new insolvency laws by 2001. In September 1998, however, the Liberal Democratic Party, the ruling party, and Mr. Nakamura, the former Minister of Justice, announced that they had decided to urge the Advisory Committee to finish the drafting work of a new rehabilitation law by June 1999, in consideration of the increasing number of small and mid-size business failures. Thus, the legislative process has been divided into two steps: the first, the enactment of the new rehabilitation law[18] in 1999; and the second, the amendment of the Bankruptcy Law and Corporate Reorganization Law in 2001 according to the original legislative schedule.

II. 'The First Questionnaire'

The Advisory Committee published 'the First Questionnaire' (*'Kentô-jiko'*) for discussion and comments in December 1997. The 'Supplement to the First Questionnaire' (*'Hosoku-setsumei'*) pointed out that, among the many issues to

---

[16] The Model Law does not adopt a rigid hierarchy between the proceedings because that would unnecessarily hinder the ability of the court to cooperate and exercise its discretion under articles 19 and 21. Para. 190 of Guide to Enactment, *supra* note 2.

[17] For a brief overview of the current Japanese insolvency laws, *see* Appendix A.

[18] This new proceeding is tentatively named 'Debt Adjustment Proceeding.'

be discussed in this reform process, there are three major issues: new legal framework to deal with the increasing number of consumer bankruptcies; remodeling of rehabilitation proceedings for small and mid-size business; and a new legal scheme for cross-border insolvency cases. As you may know, Japan has an anachronistic legacy of the strict territoriality. Part 3 of the questionnaire deals with international insolvency,[19] which consists of four subchapters.

Subchapter I deals with the international jurisdiction of insolvency cases. The difference between the two alternatives presented in the 'the First Questionnaire' is whether or not an insolvency proceeding can be commenced based only on assets, that is, without the existence of a debtor's center of the interests of business.

Subchapter II deals with the international effects of Japanese insolvency proceedings and consists of two issues: extraterritorial effects and intraterritorial effects. First, it is unanimously accepted that a Japanese proceeding should have extraterritorial effects when the debtor has the center of its business interest in Japan. One major issue is whether a Japanese 'non-main' proceeding has extraterritorial effects and whether a trustee appointed in the proceeding has a right to administer and dispose of the debtor's assets situated abroad. The hotchpot rule is proposed for cases where a creditor is paid in a foreign country after an insolvency proceeding is commenced in Japan. Some may argue that adjustment of payment should go beyond the hotchpot rule to a rule that requires such creditors to return the amount they received abroad to the Japanese trustee as unjust enrichment. Second, with respect to intraterritorial effects, the proposal is basically modeled after the legal framework for recognition of foreign main proceedings. It is worth noting that a right to administer and dispose of the debtor's assets will be given to the foreign representative as an 'automatic' effect of recognition and that no other additional relief is proposed.

Subchapter III relates to concurrent proceedings. One alternative imposes an absolute limitation on the possibility of commencing an insolvency proceeding in Japan after recognition of a foreign main proceeding, while the other alternative allows a parallel proceeding to be commenced in Japan even after recognition of a foreign main proceeding. The hotchpot rule is also proposed here. It seems to be quite difficult to make detailed rules concerning 'deemed distribution' to be deducted from local distribution, especially in a case where the foreign proceeding is a rehabilitation proceeding and creditors are paid time after time in accordance with the payment plan in the foreign country.

Subchapter IV mainly proposes to abolish the reciprocity principle concerning status of foreigners and foreign companies, and nobody is opposed to this proposal.

---

[19]   For translation of Part 3, *see* Appendix B.

III. Prospects for the Future Japanese Legislative Process

I would like to mention three points with respect to the future legislation: They are, the recognition of a foreign 'non-main' proceeding, judicial cooperation and the future legislative schedule.

First, 'the First Questionnaire' does not refer to recognition of foreign non-main proceedings. However, it is conceivable that there may be cases where a 'main' proceeding for a certain debtor cannot be opened for some reason, but dissipation of the debtor's assets needs to be avoided as soon as possible. Thus, in addition to recognizing main proceedings, foreign non-main proceedings should also be eligible for recognition in order to deal with such cases in a harmonized way by giving discretionary relief.[20]

Second, judicial cooperation is not touched upon in 'the First Questionnaire.' In civil law countries, including Germany and Japan, where the concept of direct communication and cooperation between local courts and foreign courts is quite unfamiliar, it would be difficult to provide for express provision for judicial cooperation between courts. For this reason, cooperation between local representatives and foreign representatives is expected to play an important role instead.

Third, as shown in 'the First Questionnaire,' the Japanese international insolvency laws will be enacted and amended basically in accordance with the essence of the Model Law with some exceptions. However, because the reform schedule has been accelerated with respect to the new rehabilitation law, as I mentioned above (I.), matters that directly cover only the new rehabilitation proceedings will be enacted in the first step of the schedule. I think that international jurisdiction of the proceeding, extraterritorial effects of the proceeding, and status of foreign persons and companies in the proceeding are included in this category.[21] On the other hand, matters that cover not only the new rehabilitation proceedings but all other insolvency proceedings, are likely to be scheduled to be enacted in the second step where all the other proceedings themselves are amended, that is, by the year 2001. Recognition of foreign insolvency proceedings seems to be included in this category.[22] Between 1999 and 2001, Japanese insolvency proceedings will have extraterritorial effects, and foreign insolvency proceedings can be recognized in a limited way, to the extent

---

[20] Discretionary relief may also be needed for a stay of exercise of security interest, depending on the nature of the foreign proceeding for which recognition is applied. *See,* articles 20 (2) and 21 (1)(a).

[21] A right of a foreign trustee to file for a new rehabilitation proceeding and to represent creditors in the foreign proceeding is also probably included in this category. *See,* article 11 of the Model Law.

[22] International jurisdiction of the bankruptcy proceeding and corporate reorganization proceeding, extraterritorial effects of these proceeding, and status of foreigners and foreign companies in these proceeding will also be included in the 2nd step.

the current case law allows. However, this somewhat awkward situation is expected to end in 2001. After 2001, when a new legal framework for recognition of foreign insolvency proceedings is expected to be established, we will have fair and harmonized international insolvency law.

D. Conclusion

Needless to say, insolvency law is one of the most important foundations of the business world. Well-harmonized international insolvency laws will enhance the efficiency of the globalized economy in the long run. However, harmonization will not be achieved if countries become absorbed in securing reciprocity with other countries with respect to the enactment of legislation based on the Model Law.[23] It is a positive decision on the part of UNCITRAL not to put a provision of reciprocity in the Model Law. Although it is almost impossible for Japan to incorporate the Model Law into domestic laws word by word, I hope Japan will show leadership and adopt the sense and overall intent of the Model Law.

E. Appendix A: Current Japanese insolvency proceedings (*see* Table 1 through 4 for overview)

In Japan there are currently five types of judicial insolvency proceedings, two of which can be categorized as liquidation proceedings and the other three as rehabilitation proceedings. The following is a brief chronological description of the legislation.

In 1922, the Bankruptcy Law[24] was enacted, modeled on the German Bankruptcy Law of 1877. Bankruptcy proceedings are the most basic insolvency proceedings from the viewpoint of both theory and practice. In the same year, the Composition Law[25] was enacted, which was basically modeled after the Austrian Composition Law of 1914. These two proceedings are applicable to both natural persons and legal persons.

In 1938, special liquidation proceeding (liquidation proceeding) and corporate arrangement proceeding (rehabilitation proceeding) were provided when the Commercial Law[26] was amended, both of which apply only to stock corporations.

---

[23] Ron Harmer, *The UNCITRAL Model Law on Cross-Border Insolvency*, INTERNATIONAL INSOLVENCY REVIEW, Vol. 6, pp. 145, 152 (1997).

[24] *Hasanhô* [Bankruptcy Law], Law No. 71 of 1922.

[25] *Wagihô* [Composition law], Law No. 72 of 1922.

[26] *Shôhô* [Commercial Law], Law No. 48 of 1899.

After World War II, in 1952, under the great influence of the U.S. Bankruptcy Act, especially old Chapter X, the Corporate Reorganization Law[27] was enacted, although its basic structure is a mixture of German bankruptcy law and US reorganization law.

1. Type of Proceeding and Law

	Bankruptcy	Composition	Corporate Arrangement	Special Liquidation	Corporate Reorganization
Type	Liquidation	Reorganization	Reorganization	Liquidation	Reorganization
Law	Bankruptcy Law	Composition Law	Commercial Law (§§381–403)	Commercial Law (§§431–456)	Corporate Reorganization Law
Enactment	1922 (1952: discharge)	1922	1938	1938	1952
Who may be a debtor	any person	any person	stock corporation	stock corporation	stock corporation

2. Scope of Stay (N: Not Stayed, D: Discretionary Stay, M: Mandatory Stay)

	Bankruptcy	Composition	Corporate Arrangement	Special Liquidation	Corporate Reorganization
Secured Creditor	N	N	D	D	M
(from filing to commencement)	N	N	N	N	D
Set Off	N	N	N	N	N

3. Officers

Bankruptcy	Composition	Corporate Arrangement	Special Liquidation	Corporate Reorganization
Trustee (mandatory)	(DIP under supervision)	(DIP*) *discretionary appointment of examiner or trustee	Special Liquidator	Trustee (mandatory)

[27] *Kaisha kôseihô* [Corporate Reorganization Law], Law No. 172 of 1952.

4. Distribution

Bankruptcy	Composition	Corporate Arrangement	Special Liquidation	Corporate Reorganization
Cash distribution	Plan (special majority of creditor plus court approval*)	Plan (consents of all creditors)	Cash distribution or Plan (*)	Plan (*) (classification of secured and unsecured claims and interests)

F. Appendix B: Excerpt from 'The First Questionnaire' (translated by Junichi Matsushita)

PART 3 INTERNATIONAL INSOLVENCY

I. International jurisdiction of insolvency cases
1.   Are there any points which should be reformed concerning the international jurisdiction of insolvency cases?
2.   What do you think about legislating for the following provisions?
   (1) A Japanese court has jurisdiction over an insolvency case (including both liquidation proceedings and reorganization proceedings) for a debtor who has its center of interests of business in Japan.
   (2) A Japanese court has jurisdiction over an insolvency case not only in the case of a debtor referred to in (1) but also in the case of a debtor who does not have its center of interests of business in Japan but has assets in Japan.

II. International effects of insolvency proceedings
1.   Are there any points which should be reformed concerning the international effects of insolvency proceedings?
2.   Relating to extraterritorial effects of Japanese insolvency proceedings:
   (1)   What do you think about legislating the following provisions?
   A.   The effects of insolvency proceedings commenced in Japan and the powers of a trustee and other administrators who have rights to administer and dispose of a debtor's assets extend to–
      a.   debtor's assets located in foreign countries.
      b.   debtor's assets located in foreign countries in the case of a debtor referred to in *I.* 2 (1), but not to the debtor's assets located in foreign countries in the case of a debtor referred to in *I.* 2 (2).
   B.   If either of the alternatives in A. apply, where a creditor receives payment after the commencement of an insolvency proceeding from the debtor's assets that are located in foreign countries and are subject to the effects of an insolvency proceeding in Japan, the creditor is deemed to receive the same amount of distribution as payment in the insolvency

proceeding, so long as the payment is less than the distribution he would have received in the insolvency proceeding in Japan if he had not receive the payment.

(2) Do you think there are any other points to be discussed?

3. Relating to intraterritorial effects of foreign insolvency proceedings:

(1) What do you think about legislating the following provisions?

A. A trustee or an administrator who was appointed in a foreign insolvency proceeding and has rights to administer and dispose of the debtor's assets (hereinafter, 'foreign trustee') can file an application for recognition of the foreign insolvency proceeding to a Japanese court.

B. An application for recognition of a foreign insolvency proceeding must be filed exclusively to—

a. the District Court which has jurisdiction over the location of the debtor's domicile or debtor's principal place of business, or the location of the debtor's assets which can be levied if the debtor has no domicile or principal place of business.

b. Tokyo District Court or Osaka District Court.

C. From the time of filing an application for recognition until the application is decided, a foreign trustee can apply to the court for any necessary provisional preservative relief.

D. The court shall recognize the foreign insolvency proceeding, if the debtor has its center of interests of business in the country where the insolvency proceeding was commenced, except when recognition of the proceeding contravenes public order in Japan.

E. Upon recognition of a foreign insolvency proceeding, rights to administer and dispose of the debtor's assets shifts from the debtor to the foreign trustee, and individual executions by creditors are stayed.

(2) Do you think there are any other points to be discussed?

III. Concurrent insolvency proceedings

1. Are there any points which should be reformed concerning dealings with concurrent insolvency proceedings?

2. What do you think about legislating for the following provisions?

(1) Regarding whether or not a parallel insolvency proceeding can be commenced in Japan:

A. If a foreign insolvency proceeding that was commenced in a country where the debtor has its center of business is recognized in Japan, an insolvency proceeding for the same debtor cannot be commenced in Japan.

B. Even if a foreign insolvency proceeding that was commenced in a country where the debtor has its center of business is recognized in Japan, an insolvency proceeding for the same debtor can be commenced in Japan.

(2) Regarding adjustment of distribution:

    A.   If insolvency proceedings for the same debtor are commenced in both Japan and a foreign country, and if a creditor receives distribution in respect of its claim in the foreign proceeding, the creditor is deemed to receive the same amount of distribution for the same claim in the insolvency proceeding in Japan as the distribution in the foreign insolvency proceeding, so long as the distribution in the foreign proceeding is less than the distribution he would have received in the insolvency proceeding in Japan if he had not receive the distribution in the foreign proceeding.

3.   Do you think there are any other points to be discussed concerning concurrent proceedings?

IV. Status of a foreigner and a foreign corporation

1.   Are there any points which should be reformed concerning the status of a foreigner or a foreign corporation?

2.   What do you think about legislating the following provisions?

    A foreigner or a foreign corporation has the same status as a Japanese or a Japanese corporation with regard to bankruptcy proceedings. (This means deletion of the proviso found in the article 2 of the current Bankruptcy Law.)

V. Others

   Do you think there are any other points which should be reformed in order to deal with international insolvency cases properly?

INTERNATIONAL BANKRUPTCY FROM THE VIEWPOINT OF PRIVATE INTERNATIONAL LAW AND INTERNATIONAL CIVIL PROCEDURE

by Yoshihisa Hayakawa, Tokyo[*]

Contents

A. Introduction

This paper concerns 'International Bankruptcy Law'. This paper, however, does not aim to directly examine 'International Bankruptcy Law' itself. The main

---

[*]   This paper is generally based upon the author's article in Japanese, Yoshihisa Hayakawa, '*Kokusai Tôsan no Kokusai Shihô Kokusai Minji Tetsuzuki Hô Teki Kôsatsu,*' 46 Rikkyô Hôgaku 155 (1997).

purpose of this paper is to analyze researchers' stances when they examine the topic.

At present, there is no uniform 'International Bankruptcy Law'. Few countries have bilateral conventions on this matter. UNCITRAL's attempt in this field is not to make a multilateral convention but to make a model law. Currently, each country has its own rule for resolving this problem. Among them, this paper focuses upon Japanese 'International Bankruptcy Law'. Japanese 'International Bankruptcy Law' is, of cause, usually examined by Japanese researchers. Therefore, in the part B. of this paper, Japanese researchers' attitudes toward this problem will be analyzed and a particular tendency or style of approach will be revealed.

There is, however, another approach to examine this problem. In the part C. this paper will propose a different approach and will experimentally show some of its consequences. This process itself may become an indirect examination of Japanese rules of international bankruptcy itself.

Finally, in the part D. the approaches will be compared and this paper will propose an appropriate research style in this matter for the future.

B.   Japanese Studies of 'International Bankruptcy Law'

I.   Overview

The first Japanese article focusing upon 'International Bankruptcy Law' was Professor Aoyama's article, *'Tôsan Tetsuzuki ni okeru Zokuchishugi no Saikentô'* in 1979.[1] In this article, inspired by the concept of 'Internationales Konkursrecht' in one German book, Professor Aoyama examined problems on this concept by means of comparative studies. The legal situations of Germany, Austria, Britain and the United States on this matter were surveyed in this article.

After this article, Professor Kaise published the first Japanese book on this matter, *'Kokusai Tôsan Hô Josetsu'* in 1989.[2] This book adopted the same approach as Professor Aoyama's. In addition to the four countries above, it surveyed 'International Bankruptcy Law' in Switzerland, France, Belgium, Italy and Scandinavian countries. Moreover, it reports some conventions and drafts of conventions. After these comparative studies, problems in Japan were examined.

---

[1]   Yoshimitsu Aoyama, *'Tôsan Tetsuzuki ni okeru Zokuchishugi no Saikentô,'* 25 Minji Soshô Hô Zasshi 125 (1979).
[2]   Yukio Kaise, *Kokusai Tôsan Hô Josetsu* (1989).

In 1991, we can find another example of this kind of studies in one book, '*Kokusai Tôsan Hô*', edited by Professor Takeshita.[3] This book adopted the same style in a more sophisticated manner. Each of the co-authors was a specialist of a foreign country. After more detailed comparative studies, reasonable interpretations of existing 'International Bankruptcy Law' in Japan or drafts of new Japanese legislation were proposed.

We can find this type of research quite recently. 'Kokusai Kin'yû Tôsan', edited by Professor Ishiguro in 1995, adopted the same approach in the field of bankruptcy of financial institutions.[4]

On the other hand, practitioners also wrote a lot of papers or articles in this field. Their works usually reflected actual demands for clear rules of international bankruptcy. Among them, '*Kokusai Hasan he no Shiron*' in 1978 is famous.[5] In this article, Mr. Takeuchi, the most famous lawyer in this field, examined Japanese 'International Bankruptcy Law' with the view that the demands for clear rules were increasing due to rapidly rise of international commercial transactions between Japanese companies and foreign companies.

We can say that, until now, the vague sharp of Japanese 'International Bankruptcy Law' has emerged by means of comparative studies or pushed by actual demands.

II. Existing Statutes in Japan

Why has Japanese 'International Bankruptcy Law' appeared in such a manner? Why have Japanese researchers adopted such an approach?

First of all, I will point out the present existing bankruptcy statues in Japan. There are only four articles which deal with international bankruptcy in the Japanese Bankruptcy Act (*Hasan Hô*) and the Japanese Corporate Reorganization Act (*Kaisha Kôsei Ho*).[6]

Article 2 in the Bankruptcy Act and Article 3 in the Corporate Reorganization Act detail the status of foreigners or foreign companies in Japanese bankruptcy or corporate reorganization proceedings. Although these articles are important, they have not been treated as major topics. That is because Article 3 in the Bankruptcy Act and Article 4 in the Corporate Reorganization Act have been the largest source of problems in this field until now. These articles prescribe the territorial principle in Japanese bankruptcy and corporate reorganization proceedings. Under this principle of territoriality, international

---

[3]   Morio Takeshita et al., *Kokusai Tôsan Hô* (1991).
[4]   Kazunori Ishiguro et al., *Kokusai Kin'yû Tôsan* (1995).
[5]   Koji Takeuchi, '*Kokusai Hasan he no Shiron*,' 76–2 Hôgaku Shirin 45 (1978).
[6]   Hasan Hô [Bankruptcy Act], Law No.71 of 1922; Kaisha Kôsei Hô [Corporate Reorganization Act], Law No.172 of 1952.

considerations seem to be difficult in bankruptcy or corporate reorganization proceedings. For this reason, many scholars have devoted themselves to proposing ways of restricting the scope of these articles.

Japan does not have any other statute or article dealing with international bankruptcy. In short, we do not have any positive 'International Bankruptcy Law' with the exception of the four articles above. This leaves too large a blank area on this matter in Japan. As well, half of the existing articles are obstacles for international cooperation.

III. Traditional Approach to Blank Areas or Obstacles

Of course, it would be desirable to make a new legislation immediately. It is, however, unrealistic, especially under the usual law-making process in the Japanese Diet. Due to increasing demands for international considerations, Japanese legal professionals have attempted to make a Japanese 'International Bankruptcy Law' by means of interpreting the large blank areas or interpreting the existing articles to promote international cooperation, in spite of these articles' essential policy. Comparative studies on 'International Bankruptcy Law' were excellent tools for making such 'creative' interpretations.

Such 'creative' interpretations are not curious in Japanese legal fields. Such an approach may be seen as a Japanese legal tradition. We can easily find this type of interpretations in other fields. Under the extremely slow law-making process in the Japanese Diet, in the name of 'interpretation', Japanese scholars sometimes attempt to fill up blank areas with the rules they think reasonable. Even if an area is filled with a statute, when they think that the statute is unreasonable or an obstacle, they sometimes try to limit the scope of the statute—to make a blank and fill it with the rule they think reasonable.

Actual demands and comparative studies are always convenient tools for making 'reasonable' rules or authorizing their 'reasonable' rules.

We can find one typical style of Japanese 'interpretation' of laws here. And we can find such a traditional approach in Japanese researchers' stances when they examine problems of 'International Bankruptcy Law'. That is because, under the concept of 'International bankruptcy Law', this field is filled with blank areas and obstacles.

However, is the concept of 'International bankruptcy Law' a necessary one?

IV. Why is the Concept of 'International Bankruptcy Law' Necessary?

The existence of the concept of 'International bankruptcy Law' leads Japanese researchers to think that this field is filled with blank areas and obstacles and to adopt the above approach with actual demands and comparative studies.

What is 'International Bankruptcy Law', however? Japan does not have any statute on 'International Bankruptcy Law' with the exception of the four articles above. Nevertheless, why should we draw a border like this in the broad legal fields?

There are many various phenomena in civil disputes. Commercial transactions, consumer involved cases, labor problems, environmental pollution, multinational enterprises, secured transactions, etc. These phenomena are not special fields from the viewpoint of private international law or international civil procedure.

Why can we not treat bankruptcy problems as only one phenomenon like them? Why can we not directly examine bankruptcy problems with Japanese private international law and Japanese international civil procedure?

C. International Bankruptcy from the Viewpoint of Private International Law and International Civil Procedure

I. Another Approach

When the effect of bankruptcy cases spread beyond national borders, the cases should be examined, as usual, by means of Japanese private international law and Japanese international civil procedure. This is another approach for examining international bankruptcy problems.

From this approach, choice-of-law problems on bankruptcy are to be decided according to Japanese statutes of private international law—*Hôrei*, for instance.[7] In *Hôrei*, a bankruptcy proceeding is not regarded as a special element to decide an applicable law. Choice-of-law issues in bankruptcy are to be decided as same as choice-of-law issues in other civil cases.

Procedural problems in international bankruptcy are governed by international articles in the Japanese Code of Civil Procedure,[8]—Article 118, for instance. From this approach, a bankruptcy proceeding is regarded only as an aggregation or a cluster of decisions continually issued by a court. Every foreign court decision, which requires recognition in Japan, is examined to decide whether it should be recognized.

This approach does not fit with the theory that international bankruptcy fields are filled with legal blank areas. Under this approach, private international law and international civil procedure govern an international bankruptcy case as same as any other phenomenon.

---

[7] Hôrei [Application of Law (General) Act], Law No.10 of 1898.
[8] Minji Soshô Hô [Code of Civil Procedure], Law No.109 of 1996.

II. International Bankruptcy from the Viewpoint of Private International Law

International bankruptcy from the viewpoint of private international law means that choice-of-law problems on international bankruptcy are to be directly decided by general rules of Japanese private international law because there is no special rule of private international law for international bankruptcy.

Thus, according to this approach, each problem in international bankruptcy cases is to be classified into any of the categories listed in the general rules of Japanese private international law.

Take, for example, the problem of whether a debtor's payment to a third party is to be regarded as a voidable preference. We can classify this problem into the category of 'creditor's avoiding power' in the general rules of private international law.[9] Thus, an applicable law to this problem will be decided according to the direction of general rules for this category.

Or take the question of which assets belong to an estate? In other words, which assets continue to belong to a debtor? We can classify this problem under the category of 'property' in the general rules.[10] We can also classify a recovery of assets from a debtor into this category.[11] An applicable law will be decided according to 'property' rules.

Or take, for example, the question of which applicable law is to govern a foreign corporation itself under Japanese corporate reorganization proceedings? We should classify this problem under the category of 'corporation' in the general rules. Under Japanese private international law, an applicable law in the

---

[9] See, Hayakawa, supra note *, at 167. Most specialists in bankruptcy law might not agree with this view which regards a trustee's avoiding power against a debtor's preference as equivalent to a creditor's avoiding power against a debtor's fraudulent convoyence. See, Katsumi Yamamoto, '*Shôgaisei no aru Naikoku Tôsan Tetsuzuki no Sho Mondai*,' 113-2 Minsho Hô Zasshi 1, at 40 (1995). However, under private international law, both of them have the same character. See, Hayakawa, supra note *, at 177–78.

[10] See, Tadashi Kanzaki, '*Kokusai Tôsan Hô no Saikentô 1—Tôsan Zaidan no Han'i*,' 650 NBL 6, at 13–14 (1998). This series of articles titled as '*Kokusai Tôsan Hô no Saikentô*' is a result of the research activities of one study group. This study group has attempted to examine problems on international bankruptcy not only from the traditional approach but also from the new approach. In this article, Professor Kanzaki examined this problem from the new approach and proposed some options on this problem.

[11] See, Hiroshi Morita, '*Kokusai Tôsan Hô no Saikentô 3—Torimodoshi Ken Tôsan Tanpo ken no Jun'kyo Hô*,' 653 NBL 25, 660 NBL 56, at 653 NBL 26–32 (1998–99).

'corporation' category is the law of the country where the corporation was established.[12]

Resolving choice-of-law problems in this manner is the way of international bankruptcy from the viewpoint of private international law.

III. International Bankruptcy from the Viewpoint of International Civil Procedure

Even under this approach, interpreting Article 3 in the Bankruptcy Act and Article 4 in the Corporate Reorganization Act is important. Several interpreting techniques proposed by several scholars may help to restrict the scopes of these articles.

With the exception of these articles, however, this aforementioned approach does not treat a bankruptcy proceeding as a special field. A bankruptcy proceeding is filled with decisions continually issued by a court. From the viewpoint of international civil procedure, especially from Article 118 as an article for recognition of foreign judgments or decisions, only each decision issued by a foreign court is important. A bankruptcy proceeding's character as a united body is disregard.

Every time a foreign court issues a decision, the necessary conditions listed in Article 118 are examined for recognition of the decision of the foreign court—jurisdiction, notice, due process, public policy and reciprocity.

Rules for resolving problems of international parallel litigation will be applied to problems under the situation of international parallel bankruptcy proceedings.

With the exception of some articles, which deal with international bankruptcy, an international bankruptcy case is to be handled using the regular tools of international civil procedure. This is what international bankruptcy from the viewpoint of international civil procedure means.[13]

D. Conclusion

In this paper, I analyzed the stances which Japanese researchers adopt when they examine international bankruptcy cases. I showed that the Japanese studies

---

[12] See, Yoshihisa Hayakawa, '*Kokusai Tôsan Hô no Saikentô 2 – Tôsan Kigyô Soshiki no Tainai Kankei*,' 651 NBL 13, at 15–17 (1998); Hayakawa, supra note *, at 167–68. See also, Yamamoto, supra note 9, at 23 and at 43. Professor Yamamoto's conclusion is slightly different from mine. About this difference, see, Hayakawa, supra note 12, at 18–20; Hayakawa, supra note *, at 172–74 and at 181–82.

[13] See, Hayakawa, supra note *, at 168–69 and at 178–81.

on this matter are based upon comparative studies and actual demands and are deeply influenced by the concept of 'International Bankruptcy Law'.

On the other hand, I pointed out another approach for deciding international bankruptcy cases that was not based upon the concept of 'International Bankruptcy Law'. This approach aimed to directly examine an international bankruptcy case by means of Japanese private international law and Japanese international civil procedure.

Which approach should researchers adopt when they examine this problem from now on?

To the end, first, we should compare the two approaches by reviewing the treatment of actual cases in Japan.

After WW II, we can find nine Japanese cases dealing with international bankruptcy, including the cases whose judgments did not mention international bankruptcy, despite their inherent international implications. In four of them, the effects of foreign bankruptcy proceedings to foreign trustees' or debtors' standings in Japanese litigation or attachment proceedings were discussed.[14] In one case, the effect of foreign bankruptcy proceedings to interests of financial loans was recognized.[15] In the remainder of the cases, the effects of Japanese bankruptcy proceedings to foreign assets or foreign debts were discussed.[16]

We should pay very close attention to the treatment of actual international bankruptcy cases. An approximate framework or grand design for international bankruptcy, which the traditional approach has sometimes proposed, has not worked well in these cases.

Second, we make note of the fact that there are too many different legal opinions in the traditional approach. That is because the traditional approach has developed around the blank areas where researchers were free to 'interpret'. In contrast, the new approach has statutes or articles on which we can rely.

Third, from the viewpoint of legitimacy, researchers' 'interpretations' that are too free and are not grounded in statutes or articles create many problems.

Considering the circumstances mentioned above, I would propose the adoption of the new approach, international bankruptcy studies from the viewpoint of private international law and international civil procedure.

Of course, comparative studies and analysis of actual demands are important in the drafting of new legislation. In this way, the traditional approach will

---

[14] Tokyo High Court, Decision, 30 January 1981, 994 Hanrei Jihô 53; Ôsaka District Court, Judgment, 30 September 1983, 516 Hanrei Times 139; Tokyo District Court, Judgment, 26 September 1991, 1422 Hanrei Jihô 128; Ôsaka District Court, Judgment, 23 May 1995, 1554 Hanrei Jihô 91.

[15] Tokyo District Court, Judgment, 7 February 1996, 1589 Hanrei Jihô 86.

[16] Tokyo High Court, Decision, 12 January 1959, 180 Hanrei Jihô39; Tokyo District Court, Judgment, 21 December 1976, 352 Hanrei Times 246; Tokyo District Court, Judgment, 16 December 1991, 903 Kin'yû Shoji Hanrei 39; Tokyo District Court, Judgment, 25 May 1993, 1487 Hanrei Jihô134.

contribute to the reform project of bankruptcy law currently conducted by the Advisory Committee in the Civil Bureau of the Ministry of Justice (*Hôsei Shingikai*).[17] Nevertheless, it is expected that the new approach will work well in the next age of the new bankruptcy legislation. That is because it is estimated that the proposed new bankruptcy law will not include a substantial number of articles on international bankruptcy. There may be no provision on choice-of-law in bankruptcy cases. In this case, the new approach will help us to resolve problems on international bankruptcy.

---

[17] See, Hômushô Minjikyoku Sanjikanshitsu, Tôsan Hôsei ni kansuru Kaisei Kentô Kadai (Bessatsu NBL no. 46) (1997).

GERMAN INTERNATIONAL INSOLVENCY LAW UNDER THE NEW INSOLVENCY CODE: CONTINUITY AND EVOLUTION

by Alexander Trunk, Kiel

Contents

A. Introduction

International insolvency law is certainly a more traditional object of analysis than the law of New Media,[1] and it may seem to be less political than questions involved by the introduction of the Euro.[2] Nevertheless, international insolvency law may rightly be quoted as a key example—and major task—of the evolution of international economic law at the brink of the next century.[3] It is not by chance that we have been observing in the last few years a wave of new insolvency laws worldwide, several of which include provisions on international law.[4] Also, on the international level, institutions like UNCITRAL have started to develop unified rules on cross-border insolvencies.[5] One should also mention the European Union's Convention on Cross-Border Insolvency Proceedings of 1995, which has yet to be signed by the United Kingdom and which might eventually create unified rules of international insolvency law within the European Union.[6]

Evidently, the evolution of international insolvency law is driven by economic needs: Economic growth presupposes cross-border economic activity, and this of course is helped—or hampered—by the relevant legal substructure. Well-designed rules on cross-border insolvency contribute to minimize losses when an international business fails, they can further the restructuring of ailing enterprises and they can do justice to creditors damaged by risky or malevolent behaviour of their debtor.

---

[1] As to this topic see the contributions by *Hoeren, Iwamura, Hayakawa* Sh. and *Dogauchi* (in this volume).

[2] Cf. the contribution by *v. Hoffmann* at the conference.

[3] The actuality of this topic is demonstrated by the fact that cross-border insolvency law was on the agenda of at least two international congresses in Japan in the last few years, see *Kôno/Heldrich* (ed.), Herausforderungen des Internationalen Zivilverfahrensrechts (1994) (reports of a symposium at Kyûshû University in 1993), and *Japanese Association of the Law of Civil Procedure* (ed.), The International Symposium on Civil Justice in the Era of Globalization (1993) (congress in Tokyo in 1992).

[4] Most recently, nearly all East European countries passed new insolvency laws, cf. Trunk, Stand und Probleme des Insolvenzrechts in Ost-, Mittelost- und Südosteuropa, Jb.f.OstR 1997/II, pp. 233 et seq.

[5] See the contribution of *Matsushita* (in this volume).

[6] The text of the Convention and of the Explanatory Report by *Virgos* and *Schmit* (German language versions) are published in *Stoll* (ed.), Vorschläge und Gutachten zur Umsetzung des EU-Übereinkommens über Insolvenzverfahren im deutschen Recht (1997), pp. 3 et seq., 32 et seq..

B.   Tendencies of International Insolvency Law

Although there is now a broad international tendency in favour of closer international cooperation in insolvency matters, this tendency is by no means uniform. This is true both for the conceptual approaches to international insolvency law and for the methods and concrete rules in this field.[7] Common law jurisdictions are characterized by a basically liberal approach to cross-border insolvency law, marked by judicial discretion and few, broad rules on cross-border cooperation. Civil law jurisdictions, which at the beginning of this century often imprisoned themselves in dogmatic cages like the so-called universality or territoriality principles of bankruptcy, have mostly softened their positions. In particular in the last 10–15 years theory and jurisprudence in Continental Europe have flourished in evolving differentiated rules of cross-border insolvency law. As a common ground one may say that in Continental Europe domiciliary insolvency proceedings claim extraterritorial application, while non-domiciliary proceedings are usually restrained to property situated in the country of the proceeding. Insolvency proceedings are—with some exceptions—governed by the law of the country where the proceeding is conducted (*lex fori concursus*). In most European countries, foreign insolvency proceedings are now recognized under certain conditions, but these conditions as well as the effects of recognition still differ widely. It will be of great interest how Japan with its peculiar blend of Continental European, American and distinct own legal traditions will position itself in this evolution.[8]

C.   Basic Lines of German International Insolvency Law under the Insolvency Code

German law may serve as an example for the impact of modern tendencies of cross-border insolvency law upon a Civil Law country whose economy is to a considerable degree based on foreign trade. In 1994 the German legislator passed a new law on insolvency, the 'Insolvenzordnung' (or Insolvency Code), which unifies insolvency law in the Western and Eastern parts of Germany.[9] It supersedes the ancient Konkursordnung of 1877 (Bankruptcy Act), the Vergleichsordnung (Composition Act) of 1935 as well as the East German Gesamtvollstreckungsordnung (Collective Execution Act) of 1990. For administrative

---

[7] For a more detailed overview see *Trunk*, Internationales Insolvenzrecht (1998), pp. 45 et seq.

[8] Cf. the contributions of *Hayakawa* Yo. and *Kôno* (in this volume).

[9] Law of 5 Oct. 1994, BGBl. 1994 I pp. 2866 et seq.; Introductory Law of 5 Oct. 1994, BGBl. 1994 I pp. 2911 et seq.; English translation by *Stewart*, Insolvenzordnung—Insolvency Code (1997).

reasons the Insolvenzordnung has been put into force only on 1 January 1999.[10] Court practice under the Insolvenzordnung is therefore still scarce. On the other hand, we have seen a flood of literature on the new Code in the last few months. In the last few years appeared at least three new law journals specialized on insolvency law,[11] and nearly every publisher offers one or more commentaries or other monographs on the new Code.[12] However, as far as cross-border insolvency law is concerned, these new publications have so far not given much of a fresh input to discussion. This is due to the fact that the Insolvenzordnung and its Introductory Law include only few provisions on international insolvency law (namely article 102 of the Introductory Law), and these provisions have been discussed well before 1999.[13] Things would have been different if the Government draft of the Insolvency Code of 1992[14] had been passed into law. This draft included a particular section on international insolvency law (sec. 379–399 of the draft), which would have introduced numerous new conflicts rules and substantive rules on cross-border insolvencies. These rules closely resembled the provisions of the European Insolvency Convention, which was finalized later in 1995. In the last stage of the legislative process, however, the Judiciary Committee of the Bundestag dropped this part of the Government draft. The official reason given was that the German legislator should wait for the European Insolvency Convention to be

---

[10] The new Law applies to insolvency proceedings commenced (in the sense of filing the petition to open a proceeding) on or after 1 January 1999, see art. 103 Introductory Law of the Insolvency Code.

[11] ZInsO (Zeitschrift für das gesamte Insolvenzrecht), Verlag für die Rechts- und Anwaltspraxis, Herne/Berlin; NZI (Neue Zeitschrift für Insolvenz und Sanierung), C.H.Beck, München; InVo (Insolvenz & Vollstreckung), Deutscher Anwalt-Verlag, Bonn. The already-established insolvency law journals (Zeitschrift für Wirtschaftsrecht/ZIP and Zeitschrift für Insolvenzrecht/KTS) continue to appear.

[12] See, e.g. *Eickmann* et al., Heidelberger Kommentar zur Insolvenzordnung (1999); *Kübler/Prütting* (ed.), Kommentar zur Insolvenzordnung, 2 vol. (loose-leaf); *Nerlich/ Römermann*, Insolvenzordnung (loose-leaf); *Smid* (ed.), Insolvenzordnung (1999), *Wimmer*, Frankfurter Kommentar zur Insolvenzordnung (1999). *Bork*, Einführung in das neue Insolvenzrecht, 2d ed. (1998), *Häsemeyer*, Insolvenzrecht, 2d ed. (1998); *Jauernig*, Zwangsvollstreckungs- und Insolvenzrecht, 21.Aufl. (1999); *Smid*, Grundzüge des neuen Insolvenzrechts, 3d ed. (1999); *Arbeitskreis für Insolvenz- und Schiedsgerichtswesen e.V.* (ed.), Kölner Schrift zur Insolvenzordnung (1997).

[13] See, e.g. *Leipold*, Miniatur oder Bagatelle: Das internationale Insolvenzrecht im deutschen Reformwerk 1994, in: Festschrift für Wolfram Henckel (1995), p. 533 et seq.; *Lüer*, Deutsches Internationales Insolvenzrecht nach der Insolvenzordnung, in: Kölner Schrift zur Insolvenzordnung (1997), pp. 1217 et seq.; *Trunk*, Internationales Insolvenzrecht (1998), p. 349 et seq. and passim.

[14] Bundestags-Drucksache 12/2443 of 15 April 1992.

adopted and might decide to apply the Convention also in relation to third countries.[15]

From a scientific point of view the decision of the Judiciary Committee to drop the international part of the Government draft leaves a somewhat mixed impression. On the one hand, many of the draft provisions would have created much-needed clarification. Also, the position of the Committee that the European Insolvency Convention might be—on a national basis—applied to third countries seems quite doubtful.[16] The Convention is based on a particular level of trust between Contracting Parties which may not exist in relation to every third country. National rules on cross-border insolvencies will remain therefore necessary even if the European Convention should step into force some day. However, the Committee was certainly right in arguing that national cross-border rules would have to be consistent with (though not necessarily identical to) the European Convention. It was therefore probably a wise step to provisorily drop the draft provisions, all the more as they were not free from critique.[17]

The result is that German international insolvency law under the new Code remains largely unwritten and is in its major aspects identical to cross-border insolvency law under the Konkursordnung and the Eastern German Gesamtvoll-streckungsordnung. Therefore, as to cross-border insolvency law there is more continuity under the New Law than evolution. Evolution may be seen mainly in five respects:

- international jurisdiction for domiciliary insolvency proceedings is modi-fied (sec. 3 Insolvency Code);
- the same is true, and even to a larger extent, for international jurisdiction in non-domiciliary proceedings (art. 102 subs. 3 Introductory Law);
- there is a new, and highly disputed, conflicts rule on avoidance of trans-actions in insolvency (art. 102 subs. 2 Introductory Law);
- the principle of recognition of foreign insolvency proceedings is now clearly settled in the Act (art. 102 subs. 1 Introductory Law);
- the former rule under the Konkursordnung that singular creditors may continue to levy execution even if the debtor has fallen bankrupt abroad (sec. 237 KO), has finally been abandoned.

German international insolvency law is, of course, not limited to these rather disparate new rules. The following analysis will therefore present German law under the New Code in a more coherent manner. It will start with domestic proceedings—domiciliary and non-domiciliary—, then pass over to recognition

---

[15] BT-Drucksache 12/7302 of 19 April 1994, p. 154.
[16] Cf. *Stoll* (ed.), Vorschläge und Gutachten zur Umsetzung des EU-Übereinkommens über Insolvenzrecht im deutschen Recht (1997), pp. 251 et seq.
[17] Cf. *Trunk*, Zur bevorstehenden Neuregelung des deutschen internationalen Insolvenz-rechts, KTS 1994, pp. 33 et seq. (analyis of the Government draft 1992).

of foreign proceedings. The final part of the analysis will be dedicated to parallel proceedings in Germany and abroad.

D. Domestic Insolvency Proceedings with an International Element

From the point of view of a national legal system one can always distinguish between domestic and foreign insolvency proceedings. Insolvency proceedings are usually conducted at the debtor's individual or corporate domicile, i.e. the country where the debtor's economic activities are centered and where the bulk of his property is situated. Insolvency law is normally focused upon such 'domiciliary' proceedings. However, in order to protect creditors or even the debtor, Germany—like most other Continental European countries—allows also for non-domiciliary insolvency proceedings.

I.   Domiciliary Proceedings

Following the course of an insolvency proceeding, it is of foremost importance to determine which court is competent to open the proceeding. If creditors or the debtor can convince the court that the debtor is insolvent, the court will formally open the proceeding and nominate an insolvency administrator. Insolvency proceedings under the new Code will either lead to liquidation of the debtor's property or to the debtor's financial restructuring. The Insolvenzordnung has introduced a uniform proceeding; it is no longer necessary—or even possible— to choose between bankruptcy (Konkurs) and composition proceedings (Vergleich).

1.   International Competence

As far as domiciliary proceedings are concerned, German international competence—or, if we apply the more ambiguous term: jurisdiction—is only indirectly expressed in the law. According to general rules of German international procedural law, international competence may usually be inferred from the rules on venue, i.e. the local distribution of competence between different German courts.[18] Venue for insolvency proceedings—and therefore international competence as well—has been redefined in sec. 3 of the Insolvenzordnung.

---

[18]   See *Kropholler*, in: Handbuch des Internationalen Zivilverfahrensrechts, Bd.1 (1982), pp. 210 et seq.

Subsection 1 of this provision reads:

The insolvency court in the district of which the debtor is generally amenable to suit shall have exclusive venue. If the center of an independent economic activity of the debtor is located in another place, the insolvency court in the district of which such place is located shall have exclusive venue.

The text establishes two heads of venue: The first is expressed in sentence 1 and refers to the place where the debtor is generally amenable to suit under the rules of civil procedure. According to sec. 12 et seq. of the German Code of Civil procedure this is the place of the debtor's individual or corporate domicile. The second head of venue under sec. 3 of the Insolvency Code refers to the center of the economic activities of the debtor. This is a flexible criterion, which—according to the Code—primes the formal criterion of the first sentence.

What are the parallels—and differences—between the former rules on international competence under the Konkursordnung and the new rules? The first parallel is that sec. 71 of the former Konkursordnung was also only a provision on venue, which had to be applied by analogy to international competence. The second parallel is that the former rule already linked competence in bankruptcy with general jurisdiction under the Code of Civil Procedure. Apart from this, the structure of sec. 3 Insolvenzordnung is completely different from sec. 71 of the Konkursordnung. Under sec. 71 Konkursordnung, the primary head of venue was the main business establishment of the debtor. Only if there was no such establishment (in Germany),[19] domicile applied. Under the Insolvency Code it is the other way round: Domicile is the rule, but subordinate to the new flexible criterion of the debtor's center of economic activities. In most cases both criteria will lead to the same result. Indeed, the wording of the law expresses a presumption that the domicile is also the place of the debtor's main activities. However, in complicated international cases one may well have a dispute of up to three instances over the question whether sentence 1 or sentence 2 of sec. 3 Insolvenzordnung prevails. This can of course be very cumbersome to the conduction of the insolvency proceeding.

I would therefore propose to extend sec. 3 Insolvenzordnung to the cross-border level only in a modified way: German *international* competence can be founded either on sentence 1 or on sentence 2 of sec. 3. This would mean that a German proceeding could be opened if the debtor's domicile were located in Germany, even though his center of activities were situated abroad. True, in such cases there will sometimes be a second 'domiciliary' proceeding abroad.

---

[19] Sec. 71 Konkursordnung did not clearly resolve the question whether German jurisdiction could be based on the debtor's domicile (sec. 71 2nd var.) in cases when the debtor's main business establishment (sec. 71 1st var.) was abroad, cf. *Trunk*, Internationales Insolvenzrecht (1998) p. 100 (in favour of German domiciliary jurisdiction in such cases).

However, concurrent proceedings cannot not be excluded by unilateral rules of international competence anyway, and this need not even be a bad result, for parallel proceedings may well be coordinated with one another.

Another point may be raised briefly: The flexible second criterion of the debtor's center of activities is inspired by art. 2 of the European Insolvency Convention. By this the German legislator intended to harmonize German national rules of competence with the future unified European rules. This purpose has, however, only partly be realized, as art. 2 of the Convention differs in some details from sec. 3 Insolvenzordnung.[20] Yet, the basic idea of creating a flexible criterion of international competence seems to me convincing, as it is a useful tool against negative conflicts of competence[21] and as it furthers international approximation of insolvency laws.

2. Other International Topics at the Preliminary Stage of the Insolvency Proceeding

The competence of the court is of course only one example of international questions that may arise in the preliminary stage of an insolvency proceeding. Other topics are, for example, the right of foreign creditors[22] to apply for an insolvency proceeding or the international reach of provisional measures, e.g. the extraterritorial powers of an interim administrator.[23] In this respect the Insolvency Code does not change the established, largely unwritten rules. As before, foreign creditors enjoy the same rights in the proceeding as German creditors. True enough, sec. 5 of the Konkursordnung, which had expressly stated this principle (and would have—at least theoretically—allowed measures

---

[20] See *Leipold*, Zum künftigen Anwendungsbereich des deutschen Internationalen Insolvenzrechts (Anwendungsbereich, internationale Zuständigkeit, Anerkennung und Vollstreckung), in: *Stoll* (ed.), Vorschläge und Gutachten zur Umsetzung des EU-Übereinkommens über Insolvenzverfahrens im deutschen Recht (1997) p. 190.

[21] If such a criterion does not exist, it may be possible to open a non-domiciliary proceeding (but only with territorial claim of reach).

[22] As to a corporate debtor's application one may ask whether the law of the insolvency proceeding or the 'personal' law of the corporate debtor (*lex societatis*) applies to the *power* of the corporate organs to file for insolvency. Generally, this is left to the *lex societatis*, but particular rules modifying the right to file (e.g. application by individual directors instead of the directors jointly, see sec. 15 Insolvenzordnung) would be characterized as insolvency rules falling under the *lex fori concursus*. Similarly, a *duty* of shareholders or directors to apply for an insolvency proceeding would seem to fall under the *lex fori concursus*, as the legislative purpose of such duties—to initiate insolvency proceedings in time for the protection of creditors— equally applies to foreign corporations, see *Trunk*, Internationales Insolvenzrecht (1998) pp. 103 et seq.

[23] See *Trunk*, Internationales Insolvenzrecht (1998), pp. 112 et seq.

of retorsion against foreign discriminatory practices), has no successor provision in the new Code. However, by dropping sec. 5 Konkursordnung the legislator did not intend to change the law. The provision was just thought unnecessary, as the Insolvency Code is generally based on the principle of equality of all creditors.[24]

Similarly, the Code defines the notion of 'insolvency' without any reference to international elements (cf. sec. 16–19 Insolvenzordnung). It is well established both in theory and in jurisprudence that property or payment behaviour abroad may not be neglected.[25] The same is true, by the way, for German non-domiciliary proceedings.[26]

3. Effects of the Insolvency Proceeding

The insolvency decree, i.e. the judgment formally opening the insolvency proceeding, has a broad range of effects, that may be characterized as procedural and/or substantive. Very often procedural and substantive effects of the insolvency decree can hardly be distinguished or should at least not be submitted to different national laws. For example, restraints on secured creditors may be characterized as substantive as they lower the 'value' of the security, but at the same time they are deeply entrenched in procedure, as the insolvency proceeding may limit lawsuits or execution by such creditors. The new Insolvency Code does not change the established *basic* rule that all effects of the insolvency proceeding, be they procedural or substantive, are governed by the *lex fori concursus*.[27] This rule is justified both by the principle of equal treatment of all creditors and third parties and by the need to have an efficient proceeding.[28]

On the other hand, in the last few years there was an extended discourse about possible exceptions to the *lex fori concursus*. In contrast with the Government draft of 1992, the Insolvency Code is silent about this discussion. Only art. 102 subs. 2 of the Introductory Law, which deals with avoidance of transactions in favour of a *foreign* insolvency proceeding, gives some hints in this direction.

For a very long time, conflict of laws issues in bankruptcy had been somewhat hidden behind the other big topic of cross-border insolvency law: the dispute between the so-called principles of universality and territoriality of

---

[24] See *Geimer*, Internationales Zivilprozeßrecht, 3d ed. (1997), p. 820.
[25] See *Trunk*, Internationales Insolvenzrecht (1998), pp. 106 et seq.
[26] As to these proceedings see infra sub II.
[27] See *Geimer*, Internationales Zivilprozeßrecht, 3d ed. (1997), pp. 818 et seq.
[28] See *Trunk*, Internationales Insolvenzrecht (1998), pp. 88 et seq.

bankruptcy.[29] This was never quite understandable as conflict of laws questions may arise even in 'territorial' bankruptcy proceedings. It is clear, on the other hand, that a 'universalist' approach in cross-border bankruptcy considerably raises the probability of internationally-related disputes.

The basically universalist approach of German insolvency law—in the sense that German domiciliary proceedings claim extraterritorial application both in regard to property and to activities of the debtor or other parties[30]—is today undisputed. The reason is clear: When an insolvency proceeding does not claim extraterritorial application, both liquidation and restructuring cannot adequately fulfil their purposes. Creditors can hardly be kept from seeking individual gain abroad. The debtor need not distribute his foreign property to the creditors. Foreign countries will often feel hindered to recognize a proceeding which itself limits itself to domestic property. German jurisprudence has, in particular since a judgment of the Bundesgerichtshof in 1983,[31] constantly confirmed the extraterritorial claim of German domestic insolvency proceedings. For example, creditors who execute into foreign property have to restitute their gain to the German administrator.[32] Debtors are obliged to lend their support to the administrator in regard of their worldwide property.[33]

All the more it must surprise that the European Insolvency Convention would introduce some elements of territorial self-restraint into domestic insolvency proceedings. As there seems to be a beginning tendency in German jurisprudence and doctrine to adopt elements of the European Convention into national German law,[34] this issue deserves some remarks. After that a few words will be made about the effects of an insolvency proceeding on pending international contracts.

a) Third Party Property and Other Rights in rem

In principle insolvency proceedings cover only property belonging to the debtor. This means that property which is in the possession of the debtor, but is owned by third parties, does not belong to the insolvent estate and has to be handed over to the owner. However in some cases there may be a dispute over the

---

[29] This pair of principles is still greatly emphasized (but seldom clearly defined) by a considerable part of the doctrine, cf. *Häsemeyer*, Insolvenzrecht, 2d ed. (1998), pp. 760 et seq.; *Smid*, Grundzüge des neuen Insolvenzrechts, 3d ed. (1999), pp. 401 et seq., *Zimmermann*, Insolvenzrecht, 3d ed. (1999), p. 151.

[30] See *Trunk*, Internationales Insolvenzrecht (1998), pp. 10, 94 et seq., *Häsemeyer*, Insolvenzrecht 2d ed. (1998), p. 761.

[31] Judgment of 13 July 1983, BGHZ 88, 147.

[32] BGHZ 88, 147. The Court based its judgment on the rules of unjust enrichment, sec. 812 BGB/German Civil Code).

[33] Cf. BVerfG (Federal Constitutional Court), order of 6 June 1986, ZIP 1986, 1336; OLG (Appellate Court) Koblenz, judgment of 30 March 1993, IPRax 1994, 370.

[34] Cf. *Smid*, Insolvenzordnung (1999), Art. 102 EGInsO, p. 1332.

ownership or the insolvency administrator may wish to continue to use such property for a certain time. In such cases insolvency laws often try to find a balance between the interests of the third owner and the insolvency estate. This is particularly true where ownership is used as a means of securing credit to the debtor, as in the case of retention of title agreements or of fiduciary transfers of property. Similar questions arise when the debtor's property is encumbered with security rights *in rem* such as pledges.

Under the old law it was common opinion among writers and courts in Germany that German insolvency rules striking a balance between the insolvency estate and third owners or secured creditors should apply also to property situated abroad.[35] Of course the non-insolvency question if such a right *in rem* exists continues to be determined by common conflict of laws rules, namely the *lex rei sitae*.

The European Insolvency Convention, however, digresses from this position, stipulating that third party security rights in property situated out of the country of bankruptcy are not 'affected' by the insolvency proceeding (see art. 5 and 7 of the Convention). In fact this means a territorial limitation of certain bankruptcy rules.[36] The insolvency administrator has few powers against secured creditors trying to realize their rights immediately and without respect to any restructuring needs of the insolvent debtor.

This would not have to be told in such broadth if there were not a tendency in German jurisprudence to refer to the provisions of the European Insolvency Convention as a tool of further development of German national cross-border insolvency law. For example the Germany Federal Supreme Court only recently changed its jurisprudence on conflict of laws regarding the avoidance of transactions in insolvency, arguing that German autonomous law should not diverge from the European Insolvency Convention.[37] Nevertheless I think this tendency cannot—and should not—be generalized. The cited Supreme Court decision was not exclusively based on the European Convention, but it had also to take account a similar provision in the future (as it then was) German Insolvency Code (art. 102 subs. 2 Introductory Law to the Insolvency Code). As to the effects of an insolvency proceeding upon security rights in property abroad the new Code is silent. I would therefore think that in this respect German law, like before the reform, continues to apply to security rights in property situated abroad. To which degree this extraterritorial claim can be realized depends, of course, to a large degree on the cooperation of the foreign country where the property is situated.

---

[35] See *Trunk*, Internationale Aspekte von Insolvenzverfahren, in: *Gilles* (ed.), Transnationales Prozeßrecht (1995), p. 175.

[36] See *Virgos/Schmit*, Report on the EU Insolvency Convention paras.94–102.

[37] Judgment of 21 November 1996, IPRax 1996, pp. 199 et seq.

b) Pending Contracts

A different, though somewhat related question regards the effects of the insolvency proceeding upon pending contracts of the debtor, i.e. contracts which have not yet been fully performed by both parties at the time the insolvency proceeding is commenced. As always in cross-border insolvency law this involves both a conflict of laws issue and an extraterritoriality issue. Under the old law, the dominant opinion among German writers—which however was largely untested in the courts—was that the law of the bankruptcy forum should apply.[38] I think this opinion is basically justified as it creates equality among the contractors of the debtor and helps the administrator to decide quickly which contracts should be continued or cancelled. However for some types of contracts one may doubt if this solution—the application of the *lex fori concursus*—is adequate. This is especially true for contracts involving elements of enhanced social protection or of political sensitivity, like contracts of employment or contracts of lease of immovables. I would therefore propose to apply to these two types of contract the law of the place where the employment activity is performed (cf. art. 30 subs. 2 of the Introductory Law to the Civil Code: EGBGB) or where the immovable is situated (cf. art. 28 subs. 3 EGBGB).[39] Again this particular rule of cross-border insolvency law applies only to the insolvency issues of the contract, while the rest of the contract is governed by usual rules of conflict of law.

The European Insolvency Convention shares this tendency and provides for a number of particular conflicts rules as to pending contracts. They come quite close to the rules which I just proposed, but are different in detail. For example art. 8 of the Convention calls for application of the *lex situs* not only to immovables leases, but also to contracts to acquire immovables. It is quite probable that German courts will apply these provisions of the Convention by analogy.

On the other hand, the Convention does not limit extraterritorial application of insolvency law in these cases, and German law has no reason to decide differently. Therefore, for example, a contract to purchase goods may be cancelled by the insolvency administrator, even if the goods are situated abroad. Of course this does not hinder the other party to sue the debtor (or the administrator) abroad for performance of the contract. It is an open question whether such a judgment would be disregarded in Germany as violating German public policy.

---

[38] See, e.g., *Kilger/K. Schmidt*, Insolvenzgesetze KO/VglO/GesO, 12th ed. (1997), § 17 KO note 10.
[39] See *Trunk*, Internationales Insolvenzrecht (1998), pp. 170 et seq.

c) Other Questions

International bankruptcies raise further questions, which cannot be dealt here in detail (e.g. the effect of a domestic insolvency proceeding on foreign lawsuits or on a right of set-off under foreign law).[40] According to the jurisprudence of the Federal Supreme Court a creditor who executed into the debtor's foreign property can be sued in Germany by the insolvency administrator to give back what he received abroad.[41] Other topics that have been discussed are the international dimensions of an insolvency plan (composition) or of a discharge in insolvency.[42]

II. (Isolated) Non-Domiciliary Proceedings

Apart from domiciliary proceedings German law provides for a second type of domestic insolvency proceedings, which I will call non-domiciliary proceeding. This is a purely negative definition as—from a comparative perspective—the grounds of jurisdiction for such proceedings vary widely. The focus will at first be set on isolated non-domiciliary proceedings.[43]

1. International Competence

Under sec. 238 of the old Bankruptcy Code (Konkursordnung) jurisdiction for non-domiciliary proceedings could in principle be based only upon a branch establishment of the debtor in Germany. Art. 102 subs. 3 of the Introductory Law to the Insolvenzordnung (Insolvency Code) significantly enlarges juris- diction, which may now be based upon the mere presence of assets of the debtor in Germany.[44] One might say that by this German legislation has aligned itself to Japanese law, which also provides for jurisdiction based on presence of assets (sec. 107 Japanese Bankruptcy Code). True, the German legislator was probably more inspired by the former East German Insolvency Act (Gesamtvoll-

---

[40] For a detailed analysis see *Trunk*, Internationales Insolvenzrecht (1998), pp. 114 et seq., pp. 143 et seq., pp. 179 et seq.

[41] BGHZ 88, 147.

[42] Cf. *Trunk*, Internationales Insolvenzrecht (1998), pp. 227 et seq., p. 347.

[43] Parallel (domiciliary/non-domiciliary) proceedings will be covered infra sub F.

[44] As to the clumsy, even misunderstandable wording of art. 102 subs. 2 EGInsO (Introductory Law to the Insolvency Code) see *Leipold*, Miniatur oder Bagatelle: das internationale Insolvenzrecht im deutschen Reformwerk 1994, in: Festschrift Henckel (1995), pp. 538 et seq. One author reflects about a restrictive interpretation of this provision, *Lüer*, Deutsches Internationales Insolvenzrecht nach der neuen Insolvenzordnung, in: Kölner Schrift zur Insolvenzordnung (1997), p. 1231.

streckungsordnung, literally: Law on General Execution) of 1990, which included a similar provision in sec. 22 subs. 2 Gesamtvollstreckungsordnung.

There was a heated discussion about this extension of German jurisdiction as it seems at first view to run counter a modern tendency to renounce, as far as possible, so-called exorbitant grounds of jurisdiction.[45] Nevertheless I think the legislator rightly considered that both the interests of creditors and of the debtor justify—and even require such an extension of insolvency jurisdiction: Broad jurisdiction makes it possible for creditors to force distribution at least of the debtor's inland property under the principle of creditor equality, even if an insolvency proceeding cannot be opened (or is unfairly administered) at the debtor's foreign domicile. For the debtor, broad non-domiciliary jurisdiction may be a means of quick, effective protection.

Certainly broad non-domiciliary jurisdiction increases the probability of parallel proceedings. However, several parallel proceedings, which may be coordinated, seem less harmful than to admit injustice to creditors or the debtor who cannot get an efficient and fair insolvency proceeding at the debtor's domicile. In any way, creditors or the debtor will commence a non-domiciliary proceeding only when the domestic assets of the debtor are valuable enough to cover the costs of the proceeding.[46]

2.   Territorial Auto-Limitation?

The least clarified aspect of non-domiciliary proceedings concerns the territorial (or extra-territorial) reach of such proceedings. Art. 102 subs. 3 of the Introductory Law to the Insolvenzordnung limits the reach of German non-domicilary proceedings to property of the debtor situated in Germany. The meaning of this limitation, which has been inherited from sec. 238 of the old Bankruptcy Code, leaves much room for interpretation.

As a starting point one may take the wording of art. 102 subs. 3, which says that non-domiciliary proceedings include only the debtor's domestic assets. It is important to note that art. 102 subs. 3 refers to the assets of the debtor, not to his debts.[47] Art. 102 subs. 3 provides for a territorial limitation of the estate, but is

---

[45]   Cf. *Flessner*, Internationales Insolvenzrecht in Deutschland nach der Reform, IPRax 1997, p. 3.

[46]   In some cases creditors or the debtor may be willing to pay the costs of the proceeding from other sources.

[47]   Art. 102 subs. 3 deals only with the effect of the (opened) proceeding. In particular, the provision says nothing about the determination of the notion of insolvency as a precondition for opening the proceeding. Today it is accepted by nearly all authors that in determining insolvency (even in non-domiciliary proceedings) foreign property or activities of the debtor may not be neglected. Indeed, if all debts of a foreign debtor were contrasted with his relatively small domestic assets, this would

cont. ...

silent about the effects of the insolvency proceeding upon the creditors' claims. Correspondingly the impact of the insolvency proceeding upon the creditors' claims is, in principle, to be determined by general rules. For example, not only domestic creditors, but all creditors are entitled to participate in the proceeding. Nevertheless this principle needs some mitigation. For example it would hardly convince to bring all pending contracts of the foreign debtor under the rules of non-domiciliary proceeding. Instead I would propose that non-domiciliary proceedings cover only contracts having a particular link with the country of the proceeding. Following the basic decision of the law that non-domiciliary proceedings are limited to domestic assets, I would propose that in principle German non-domiciliary proceedings cover only pending contracts with partners who are domiciled in Germany. Certainly one may discuss some exceptions to this rule.[48]

Similarly it seems to me that the granting of priorities in non-domiciliary proceedings requires some qualified domestic contact of the priority claim. Therefore in the case of a non-domiciliary proceeding not all the world-wide employees of an insolvent enterprise can claim employees' privileges in the proceeding. Rather, the privilege should be seen as limited to employees whose contracts of employment are most significantly connected with Germany. The relevant criterion is normally the place where the work is performed (cf. art. 30 subs. 2 EGBGB).[49]

E. Recognition of Foreign Insolvency Proceedings

Recognition of foreign insolvency proceedings has in the last few years been intensively explored by German jurisprudence and doctrine. German law of recognition of foreign insolvency proceedings was revolutionized some years ago by a decision of the Federal Supreme Court in 1985.[50] This turnaround focused upon a provision in the old Bankruptcy Code (sec. 237), which stipulated that despite a foreign bankruptcy proceeding creditors were allowed to levy execution into the debtor's German property. Since 1985 this provision has been interpreted by German courts not as a general prohibition to recognize foreign bankruptcies, but as special, execution-related exception to the general

---

lead to the absurd result that even profitable foreign enterprises would have to be regarded as technically insolvent; cf. *Lüer*, Deutsches Internationales Insolvenzrecht nach der Insolvenzordnung, in: Kölner Schrift zur Insolvenzordnung (1997), pp. 41 et seq..

[48] For a more detailed analysis see *Trunk*, Internationales Insolvenzrecht (1998), pp. 248 et seq.

[49] Cf. *Trunk*, Internationales Insolvenzrecht (1998), pp. 255 et seq.

[50] Judgment of 11 July 1985, BGHZ 97, 256.

rule that foreign bankruptcies may be recognized. This landmark decision of the Federal Supreme Court has been overwhelmingly welcomed among authors and was codified first in sec. 22 subs. 1 of the East German Insolvency Law (Gesamtvollstreckungsordnung) of 1990 and now in art. 102 subs. 1 of the Introductory Law to the Insolvency Code. Indeed, both the former East German insolvency law and the new Insolvency Code go one big step further than sec. 237 of the old Bankruptcy Code, as they abolish the broad permission to levy execution in spite of the foreign bankruptcy. The main characteristics of German law on recognition of foreign insolvency proceedings under the new Insolvency Code may be briefly resumed:

I. Prerequisites of recognition

First, it is important to determine exactly the object of recognition. Normally, recognition of foreign insolvency proceedings means recognition of the foreign insolvency decree, which opens the insolvency proceeding with all its effects. However, recognition may also refer to other insolvency decisions, like a judgment in a dispute on avoidance of transactions or a decree confirming a composition or granting discharge in insolvency.[51]

Secondly, the foreign insolvency decision has to comply with certain conditions, which are exposed in art. 102 subs. 1 of the Introductory Law to the Insolvenzordnung: The foreign insolvency proceeding must have been opened by an internationally competent court (competence according to German rules applied by analogy), and recognition may not be contrary to German public policy. Reciprocity is no criterion of recognition in German cross-border insolvency law. This had already been spoken out by the Federal Supreme Court under the old law.[52] Perhaps the Court thought that a reciprocity requirement— derived from the rules on judgment recognition (sec. 328 no. 5 Code of Civil Procedure)—would unduly encumber recognition and thereby harm the interests of the parties of the insolvency proceeding. Maybe it is of some interest that the Russian Federation recently opened its law to recognition of foreign insolvency proceedings on the basis of reciprocity.[53]

Though art. 102 subs. 1 of the Introductory Law to the Insolvency Code does not mention this expressly, it primarily deals with recognition of the foreign insolvency decree opening the proceeding. Only for this decision it makes sense to require the foreign court's international competence to open the proceeding.

---

[51] See *Trunk*, Internationales Insolvenzrecht (1998), pp. 267 et seq.

[52] Judgment of 27 May 1993, IPRax 1993, p. 403.

[53] Art. 7 subs. 7 Russian Insolvency Law of 8 January 1998, commented by *Vitrjanskij*, in: *Vitrjanskij* (ed.), Federal'nyj Zakon 'O nesostojatel'nosti (bankrotstve)', 2d ed. (1999), Art. 1 note 9.

As to other insolvency decisions jurisdiction has to be determined with reference to a corresponding German decision.[54] For example, a foreign judgment on avoidance of transactions will be recognized if the court was competent under rules analogous to German rules. As German law does not attribute such competence to the Insolvency Court, normal rules of international jurisdiction (namely sec. 12 et seq. of the German Code of Civil Procedure) would apply.

II. Effects of recognition

Similarly to the international effects of domestic insolvency proceedings, the effects of recognition of foreign proceedings are to a large degree left open even by the new Insolvency Code.

Art. 102 subs. 1 sentence 1 of the Introductory Law only briefly states that the foreign proceeding also 'includes' property situated in Germany. This formulation is not very exact, as the effects of an insolvency proceeding are not limited to 'property' questions, but the proceeding imposes a broad range of rights, duties and powers on all parties of the proceeding. However there is common consent that art. 102 subs. 1 is not meant to exclude recognition of 'non-property' effects of the proceeding.

Like in domestic proceedings, recognition of foreign proceedings involves both conflict of laws issues and extraterritoriality issues.

1. Conflict of laws

In principle the foreign *lex fori concursus* applies, but this principle is—like in domestic proceedings—not without exceptions. Normally one will develop similar exceptions for domestic proceedings and for recognition, for example as to the effect of bankruptcy upon pending contracts.[55]

Remarkably, art. 102 subs. 2 of the Introductory Law establishes a special conflicts rule for the avoidance of transactions in insolvency. The provision reads:

> A transaction the effects of which are governed by domestic law can be avoided by the foreign insolvency administrator only if the transaction can be avoided under domestic law as well or is not valid under this law for other reasons.

The legal history of this rather isolated provision is rather unclear. Apparently the Judiciary Committee of the Bundestag thought they should introduce at least

---

[54] See *Trunk*, Internationales Insolvenzrecht (1998), pp. 275 et seq., cf. also pp. 121 et seq.

[55] Cf. *Trunk*, Internationales Insolvenzrecht (1998), pp. 284 et seq., 324 et seq.

some provision on the practically important topic of international avoidance of transactions. Doing this they wished to protect the beneficiary of such a transaction who may not have known the circumstances leading to avoidance. They also wanted to align German law on this topic to the European Insolvency Convention, which also provides for a cumulation of the *lex fori concursus* with the *lex causae* of the transaction.[56]

I think such a cumulative application of several laws to one voidable transaction is basically flawed, as it makes avoidance much harder than necessary and leaves nearly unlimited manoeuvering space to the activity of bankruptcy criminals.[57] Before the reform, the clear majority opinion among writers was that avoidance in insolvency was governed by the *lex fori concursus*.[58] One may well have reflected about some exceptions to this rule in certain cases (for example, application of the *lex societatis*, when corporate shareholders receive big dividends in spite of imminent insolvency of the corporation). Even then, one could well determine the center of gravity of such a transaction and need not choose a cumulative solution, which deeply hampers avoidance.[59]

This being as it is, one must nevertheless apply the new provision, but one should not apply it more broadly than necessary. When one reads art. 102 subs. 2 carefully, one remarks that the provision applies only to avoidance by foreign insolvency administrators and to transactions governed by German law. Avoidance by German administrators or avoidance of transactions governed by a foreign law are not covered by art. 102 subs. 2. I would therefore propose to apply to such cases only the *lex fori concursus*,[60] except when the center of gravity of the transaction is clearly situated in another country.

---

[56]   Report of the Judiciary Committee (relating to Art. 106a of the draft version of the IntroductoryCode, which later became Art. 102 EGInsO), BT-Drucksache 12/7303 of 18.4.1994, pp. 117 et seq., reprinted in *Kübler/Prütting* (ed.), Das neue Insolvenz-recht—EGInsO, Bd.II (1994), pp. 309 et seq.

[57]   Same view: *Hanisch*, IPRax 1993, pp. 72 et seq.; *Leipold*, Miniatur oder Bagatelle: das internationale Insolvenzrecht im deutschen Reformwerk 1994, in: Festschrift Henckel (1995), pp. 543 et seq.; *Wenner*, in: *Mohrbutter/Mohrbutter*, Handbuch der Insolvenzverwaltung, 7th ed. (1997), pp. 957 et seq..

[58]   See, e.g. *Lüer*, in: *Kuhn/Uhlenbruck*, Konkursordnung, 11th ed. (1994) §§ 237, 238 note 79; *Wenner*, in: *Mohrbutter/Mohrbutter*, Handbuch der Insolvenzverwaltung, 7th ed. (1997), p. 957, each with references to divergent views.

[59]   Cf. *Trunk*, Internationales Insolvenzrecht (1998), pp. 327 et seq., cf. also pp. 184 et seq.

[60]   Same view: *Kirchhof*, in: *Eickmann* et al. (ed.), Heidelberger Kommentar zur Insolvenzordnung (1999), Art. 102 EGInsO notes 26, 40.

2.   Extraterritoriality

The question of extraterritorial application of insolvency law is not irrelevant to recognition of foreign proceedings, either, though it poses itself in somewhat different terms than in domestic proceedings. Although art. 102 subs. 1 of the Introductory Law to the Insolvency Code seems to put squarely that foreign proceedings 'always' include German property, it is generally accepted that recognition of extraterritorial effect of a foreign proceeding requires that the relevant foreign law makes such a claim at all.[61] It is very doubtful whether German courts would presently recognize effects of a Japanese bankruptcy upon property in Germany, as the Japanese Bankruptcy Code itself pronounces its intention to limit itself to property in Japan.

There is however yet another aspect of extraterritoriality in the recognition context. When a foreign *non-domiciliary* proceeding is recognized, it follows from the legislative purpose of art. 102 subs. 2 of the Introductory Law to the Insolvenzordnung that such a proceeding would not be granted extraterritorial effect upon property of the debtor in Germany.

F.   Coordination of Parallel Insolvency Proceedings

Perhaps yet more intricate than 'simple' recognition of foreign proceedings is the topic of parallel insolvency proceedings. It is important to distinguish between parallel proceedings concerning intertwisted debtors (such as bankruptcies concerning several members of a corporate group) and parallel proceedings in several countries with regard to same debtor.

German cross-border insolvency law at present has no particular provisions on cross-border insolvencies of corporate groups. In particular there is no possibility to consolidate such proceedings. Of course transactions between such corporations may be avoided, pending contracts may be cancelled etc, but all of this happens under the normal rules of each proceeding.

As far as parallel proceedings regarding one debtor are concerned, there is a somewhat rudimentary provision in art. 102 subs. 3 of the Introductory Law, which has already been quoted in the context of isolated non-domiciliary proceedings.[62] From there it follows that recognition of a foreign (domiciliary or non-domiciliary) proceeding does not hinder a secondary insolvency proceeding in Germany. One can deduce from this provision that the effects of the

---

[61]   *Kirchhof,* in: *Eickmann* et al. (ed.), Heidelberger Kommentar zur Insolvenzordnung (1999), Art. 102 EGInsO note 6 with reference to BGH, judgment of 14 November 1996, BGHZ 134, p. 90.

[62]   Supra D.II.1..

secondary German proceeding supersede the effect of the foreign proceeding.[63] In contrast with the Government draft of the Insolvency Code the law presently has no particular provision on cooperation of parallel proceedings. True, it is possible to deduce an obligation to cooperate from general principles of insolvency law, as non-cooperation will often be harmful both to the debtor and to the creditors as a whole. Nevertheless the limits of such cooperation are sometimes difficult to be determined: Should (and may) an insolvency administrator give information about creditors and their claims to the administrator of a parallel proceeding? May the administrator participate in the creditors' assemblies organized in other parallel proceedings? This is a domain where German law poses few prohibitions, but does not give much guidance either. Much depends, therefore, on the willingness of the insolvency administrator, the creditors' committee and of the insolvency court to cooperate. The European Insolvency Convention will introduce a series of provisions supporting such cooperation.[64] One might argue that some of these provisions could be applied in Germany by analogy, even before the Convention steps into force an even in relation to third countries.

G. Resume

German cross-border insolvency law under the new Insolvency Code is characterized more by continuity than by evolution. This is luckily due to the fact that German jurisprudence made its great leap forward towards recognition of foreign insolvency proceedings and mitigation of the territoriality dogma already in the 1980s.

However the Insolvency Code codifies this new and reasonable jurisprudence and even improves it by abolishing the relic of unhindered execution despite a foreign bankruptcy. There are also some other positive developments in the new law: the more flexible definition of international competence for domiciliary proceedings and the broader scope of non-domiciliary proceedings. A major weakness of the new law is the cumulation of laws regarding avoidance of transactions in art. 102 subs. 2 of the Introductory Law to the Insolvency Code. It is to be hoped that this provision will not be interpreted extensively by future jurisprudence.

---

[63] See *Trunk*, Internationales Insolvenzrecht (1998), pp. 345 et seq., cf. also *Spahlinger*, Sekundäre Insolvenzverfahren bei grenzüberschreitenden Insolvenzen (1998), p. 116. It has not yet been decided in German jurisprudence whether in some situations the effects of the foreign (recognized) proceeding and of the domestic non-domiciliary proceeding might coexist.

[64] See *Spahlinger*, Sekundäre Insolvenzverfahren bei grenzüberschreitenden Insolvenzen (1998), pp. 254 et seq., pp. 326 et seq.

The major signal of the new law seems to me that Germany confirms and further develops its policy of international cooperation in insolvency matters, even without an international Convention. Much is left to the organs of the insolvency proceedings, but foreign insolvency administrators or insolvency courts should at any rate try to turn to their German counterparts, if they think cooperation serves the purposes of the parties. German law encourages such cooperation.

CHOICE OF LAW IN INTERNATIONAL INSOLVENCIES
—A PROPOSAL FOR REFORM—

by Peter von Wilmowsky, Hannover

Contents

A. Introduction

Financial distress is not confined to territorial borders. When a firm fails, the economic effects are felt quite frequently not only in the home country, but in other countries as well. This article is devoted to the choice of law issues which arise in international insolvencies. It is divided into two parts: The first part (B.) attempts to summarize the present state of international insolvency law. The second part (C.) seeks to establish a general framework which may guide the development of choice of law provisions for international insolvencies. As this article is written by a German lawyer it will often refer to Germany's international insolvency law.

197

B. Status Quo

In Germany, there is only one statutory provision dealing explicitly with international insolvency law. This provision confines itself to defining some (but not all) effects of foreign insolvency proceedings in Germany.[1] The bulk of German international insolvency law is judge-made law. Two cornerstones merit mentioning with respect to the rules developed by the courts.

I. Universalism

On the one hand, German legal doctrine endorses universalism.[2] This model entails a choice of law rule that refers the legal issues arising in an international insolvency to a single national law—the (insolvency) law of the country in which the insolvency proceeding has been opened.[3] Universalism does not necessarily require a single, unitary proceeding. However, when proceedings in various states have commenced universalism requires that one proceeding take the lead and its substantive insolvency law be applied. Universalism implies that all assets wherever located are administered under a single insolvency law; creditors throughout the world are paid in accordance to the lead state's distribution rules.

A state striving to implement the universalist model needs to take two measures. First it has to give its insolvency law a universal scope of application. This means that in the case of domestic insolvency proceedings all issues of

---

[1]   Einführungsgesetz zur Insolvenzordnung (Statute Introducing the Insolvency Act), Art. 102. This provision reads in part (author's translation): '(1) A foreign insolvency proceeding shall cover the debtor's property in Germany as well. . . . (2) The insolvency trustee of a foreign insolvency proceeding may avoid any legal act which is subject to German law, provided the act could be avoided under German law as well, or, due to other reasons, is void, voidable or unenforceable under German law. (3) The recognition of a foreign insolvency proceeding does not preclude the opening of a domestic insolvency proceeding in Germany. In this case, the domestic proceeding shall cover the debtor's domestic property only; no proof of the debtor's insolvency is required.'

[2]   Bundesgerichtshof (Federal Supreme Court in Matters of Civil Law), 11 July 1985, BGHZ (Entscheidungen des Bundesgerichtshofs in Zivilsachen) 95, 256 (at 273). This decision is regarded as the fountainhead of modern German international insolvency law.

[3]   The general approaches of international insolvency law are outlined by, inter alia: Fletcher, 'The European Union Convention on Insolvency Proceedings: Choice-of-Law Provisions', 33 *Texas International Law Journal* 119 (at 121–124) (1998); Westbrook, 'Choice of Avoidance Law in Global Insolvencies', 17 *Brooklyn Journal of International Law* 499 (at 513–519) (1991); Kayser, 'A Study of the European Convention on Insolvency Proceedings', *Int. Insolv. Rev.* 7 (1998) 95 (at 99–106).

insolvency law are dealt with by domestic insolvency law. Secondly, as regards foreign insolvency proceedings, such state has to refer all questions of insolvency law to the law of the foreign state.

II. Territorialism

On the other hand, German law, like most other international insolvency laws, continues to cling to a territorial understanding of bankruptcy. Under this approach, each country affected by an international insolvency claims power over those assets of the bankrupt which are located within its national borders.

The concept of territoriality can be implemented in various ways. One instrument is the non-recognition of the insolvency proceeding opened in the debtor's home state. This appears to be the starting point of American international insolvency law, which, in principle, does not recognize foreign proceedings opened in the foreign debtor's home state, unless the principles of comity require the court to do so or specific measures of recognition are taken pursuant to § 304 of the Bankruptcy Code. Where neither exception applies, foreign insolvency proceedings do not affect property in the US.[4] On the contrary: If the foreign debtor has any assets in the US, jurisdiction is given to open an insolvency proceeding which will then cover all assets of the debtor wherever located, even those located in the debtor's home state.[5]

As German law does recognize, in principle, foreign insolvency proceedings, it employs another legal device to achieve territorialism. It provides for a specific type of truncated insolvency proceeding, so-called local, or secondary, insolvency proceedings. Most states set up such local proceedings. Jurisdiction is given when the (foreign) debtor has assets within the country. Under German law the property required to be found on German territory does not even need to be substantial.[6] In theory German law permits a local proceeding to be filed in Germany even if the only property situated in Germany is a claim, such as a bank account with a German bank. This will have to be changed, however, once the EU Convention on Insolvency Proceedings enters into force. The Convention requires the domestic assets to amount to an 'establishment', such as an office or factory.[7] Such local proceedings are run like ordinary insolvency

---

[4]   A similar approach is taken by the UNCITRAL Model Law on Cross-border Insolvency (Art. 15 and 17).

[5]   An American insolvency proceeding may be based on the presence of 'a dollar, a dime or a peppercorn' in the United States; see *In re McTague*, 198 B.R. (Bankruptcy Reporter) 428 (1996).

[6]   Einführungsgesetz zur Insolvenzordnung (Statute Introducing the Insolvency Act), Art. 102 (3). The text of this provision is set out in note 1.

[7]   EU Insolvency Convention, Art. 3 (2): ' . . . [T]he courts of another Contracting State shall have jurisdiction to open insolvency proceedings against the debtor only if he

cont. ...

proceedings, except for one difference: As opposed to the home country proceeding, a local proceeding catches only the assets situated within the state.[8] The idea of territorialism implies that the commencement of a local, or secondary, proceeding triggers the application of that country's insolvency law. Any local proceeding trumps the proceeding opened in the home state. The insolvency law of the latter is thus ousted.[9] It is the very purpose of local proceedings to fend off the insolvency law of the debtor's home country.[10]

German insolvency law not only permits local proceedings in Germany, but also recognizes foreign local proceedings. When Germany is the debtor's home country and an insolvency proceeding has been opened here, German law cuts back its extraterritorial reach and no longer claims to apply to foreign assets, once the foreign assets have been made subject to a local proceeding there.[11] At the end of the day national borders will have divided the debtor's assets into various national segments. Each segment will be governed by the respective local insolvency law (provided a local insolvency petition has been filed). Various territorially segregated insolvency proceedings against the same debtor are the result.

The universalist approach is thus relegated to a mere subsidiary rule: Only in cases in which no local proceedings are commenced will the insolvency law of the home country proceeding apply extraterritorially to all assets of the insolvent, wherever located.

---

possesses an establishment within the territory of that other Contracting State. The effects of those proceedings shall be restricted to the assets of the debtor situated in the territory of the latter Contracting State.'

[8] Cf. Art. 28 of the EU Insolvency Convention.—American insolvency law provides the notable exception. An insolvency proceeding opened in the US is not restricted to US assets of the debtor. It always claims to catch all assets wherever located. In other words: American insolvency law does not know local insolvency proceedings. Once a foreign debtor has assets in the US, jurisdiction is given and the US proceeding will cover all assets, even if a proceeding is brought against the debtor in its home state.

[9] Critical of this effect of local proceedings is Trautman, 'Foreign Creditors in American Bankruptcy Proceedings', 29 *Harvard International Law Journal* 49 (at 57) (1988).

[10] In the US, where no local proceedings exist, the general rule is that foreign insolvency proceedings are not automatically recognized. Therefore the opening of an insolvency proceeding is not necessary to fend off the legal effects of a proceeding opened elsewhere. If a foreign insolvency proceeding is to have legal effects in the US the foreign trustee has to resort to an American court which will then decide whether or not ancillary measures pursuant to § 304 B.C. will be taken.

[11] This rule can be found in the EU Insolvency Convention, Art. 17: '(1) The judgment opening the proceedings ... shall ... produce the same effects in any other Contracting State as under the law of the State of the opening of proceedings, unless the Convention provides otherwise and as long as no proceedings referred to in Art. 3 (2) are opened in that other Contracting State.'

III. Cooperation

The main thrust of the legislative endeavors to improve international insolvency law is on establishing international cooperation. A prominent example of this type of endeavor is § 304 of the U.S. Bankruptcy Code of 1978.[12] In cases where an insolvency proceeding was opened in a foreign country, the foreign trustee may apply for a so-called ancillary proceeding in the US. This is *not* an insolvency proceeding, but a vehicle to navigate and control the recognition of foreign insolvency proceedings in the United States.[13] The US bankruptcy judge has broad discretionary powers to assist the foreign proceeding. Although § 304 B.C. is silent on the applicable law, it seems that the measures taken are those of the law of the state of the foreign proceeding.[14] Once an insolvency proceeding is opened in the US (which is always a 'primary' one), § 304 B.C. is no longer applicable. Conflicts arise in cases in which a foreign debtor having assets in the United States is subject to insolvency proceedings both in its home state and in the US, each claiming worldwide application. Once this occurs only informal means are available to coordinate the American proceeding with the foreign proceeding. Such informal coordination was employed in famous cases like Maxwell Communication[15] and Maruko,[16] where the American bankruptcy

---

[12] The provision reads in part: '(a) A case ancillary to a foreign proceeding is commenced by the filing with the bankruptcy court of a petition under this section by a foreign representative. (b) . . . [T]he court may (1) enjoin the commencement or continuation of (A) any action against (i) a debtor with respect to property involved in such foreign proceeding, or (ii) such property, or (B) the enforcement of any judgment against the debtor with respect to such property, . . . ; (2) order turnover of the property of such estate, or the proceeds of such property, to such foreign representative; or (3) order other appropriate relief.'

[13] § 304 B.C. has received considerable attention from academic and practitioner commentators. See, e.g., Westbrook, 'Theory and Pragmatism in Global Insolvencies: Choice of Law and Choice of Forum', 65 *American Bankruptcy Law Journal* 457 (at 471–473) (1991); Krause, Janovski and Lebowitz, 'Relief Under Section 304 of the Bankruptcy Code', 64 *Fordham Law Review* 2591 (1996). Less enthusiastic are Nadelmann, 'The Bankruptcy Reform Act and Conflict of Laws: Trial-and-Error', 29 *Harvard International Law Journal* 27 (1988), and Boshkoff, 'Some Gloomy Thoughts Concerning Cross-Border Insolvencies', 72 *Washington University Law Quarterly* 931 (1994). German publications on § 304 B.C. include: Reinhart, *Sanierungsverfahren im internationalen Insolvenzrecht*, 1995, 110–120; E. Habscheid, *Grenzüberschreitendes (internationales) Insolvenzrecht der Vereinigten Staaten von Amerika und der Bundesrepublik Deutschland*, 1998, 216–262. The UNCITRAL Model Act also requires an 'exequatur' for the recognition of a foreign insolvency proceeding, see Art. 15 and 17.

[14] See Trautman (supra note 9), 29 *Harvard International Law Journal* 49 (at 56).

[15] See *Maxwell Communication Corp. v. Société Generale*, 93 F.3d 1036 (2d Cir. 1996).

administration cooperated with the home country administration in England and Japan, respectively.

In Great Britain § 426 (4) of the Insolvency Act of 1986 makes assistance to foreign primary proceedings mandatory, but restricts it to a list of countries contained in a Schedule to the Act.[17] As opposed to the American counterpart this provision also applies in cases in which a local insolvency proceeding was opened in the United Kingdom. It may thus serve to coordinate a British local proceeding with the foreign primary proceeding. Again, choice of law questions did not receive considerable legislative attention. According to the rather vague language of subsection 5 of § 426 IA, the English court seems to enjoy broad discretion in choosing the applicable law.[18]

The EU Insolvency Convention attempts to coordinate the primary insolvency proceeding with any local proceeding, provided that both types of proceedings are opened within the EU.[19] German insolvency law, at present, does not give any guidance on how a local proceeding brought in Germany shall cooperate with a foreign home country proceeding.

---

[16] The case *In re Maruko* concerned a Japanese corporation headquartered in Tokyo which was engaged in developing commercial properties worldwide. It divided these properties into co-ownership interests which were sold to Japanese nationals. The buyers would then lease back their co-ownership interests to Maruko. These leasebacks guaranteed fixed monthly payments to the co-owners. In 1991, Maruko filed for bankruptcy both in Japan and the United States. In the US proceeding a plan of reorganization was approved in 1994. See the facts stated in 200 B.R. (Bankruptcy Reporter) 876 (Southern District of California, 1996).

[17] The provision reads: 'The courts having jurisdiction in relation to insolvency law in any part of the United Kingdom shall assist the courts having the corresponding jurisdiction in any other part of the United Kingdom or any relevant country or territory.' At present the countries on the list (§ 426 (11) (b) IA) are: Canada, Australia, New Zealand, Ireland, and a collection of present or former colonies such as the Cayman Islands and Bermuda. In German legal literature see Florian, *Das englische internationale Insolvenzrecht*, 1989, 102–112.

[18] § 426 (5) IA reads in part: ' . . . [a] request made to a court in any part of the United Kingdom by a court . . . in a relevant country or territory is authority for the court . . . to apply, in relation to any matters specified in the request, the insolvency law which is applicable by either court in relation to comparable matters falling within its jurisdiciton. In exercising its discretion under this subsection, a court shall have regard in particular to the rules of private international law.'

[19] See EU Insolvency Convention, Art. 33. How secondary proceedings will operate under the EU Insolvency Convention is described by Fletcher, 'The European Union Convention on Insolvency Proceedings: An Overview and Comment, With U.S. Interest in Mind', 23 *Brooklyn Journal of International Law* 25 (at 42–45) (1997), and Wimmer, 'Die Besonderheiten von Sekundärinsolvenzverfahren unter besonderer Berücksichtigung des Europäischen Insolvenzübereinkommens', ZIP (*Zeitschrift für Wirtschaftsrecht*) 1998, 982 (at 987–989).

C. Analytical Framework

A critical review of both concepts (the universalist and the territorialist model) reveals that they promise more than they are able to keep. There is one feature in both models which seems to be seriously flawed. Both approaches (and their accompanying choice of law rules) attempt to cover *all* legal issues which are raised by the insolvency. The universalist theory refers all issues to the law of the state of the primary proceedings. Under the territorial approach the estate is divided, and all insolvency issues for each geographical subpart are referred to the national law of the country of the respective local proceeding. In my opinion these are vain endeavors; it seems to be impossible to refer all legal questions raised by an insolvency to a single national law. Rather, the subject matter should be divided into two groups of legal issues, according to a distinction which seems to play a pivotal role in insolvency law in general—and may offer a better understanding of choice of law issues in particular.

I.   Distinction Between Asset Deployment and Asset Distribution

The distinction I want to emphasize is best understood by looking at the balance sheet of a business enterprise. A balance sheet states the financial situation of a business enterprise. On its left column, the assets are listed; these are the investments the corporation made. They include: Real estate, houses, machinery, office equipment, tools, intangible assets such as stock, patents, bank deposits, and cash. The *first* decision that needs to be taken in an insolvency concerns the asset side of the balance sheet: What shall be done with the debtor's assets? How should they be used? This is the asset deployment decision. In business insolvencies (where the debtor's assets make up a business enterprise) two options are available. One option is to continue the debtor's business. In this case the debtor's assets will stay assembled as a business enterprise; they continue to be devoted to the enterprise. Technically this can be achieved by either selling the whole enterprise to a new owner who will replace the debtor, or leaving the enterprise in the ownership of the debtor, thereby requiring a financial reorganization of the debtor. The alternative is to terminate the debtor's business enterprise. In this case the enterprise will be dissolved, and its assets will be sold piecemeal.

The legal system in general and insolvency law in particular should stay neutral as regards the future use of the debtor's assets. Insolvency law has to ensure that both options are on an equal footing. Neither continuation nor termination should be favored; the legal system should not bias the decision. The decision whether to continue or to dissolve should turn exclusively on the economic prospects of the debtor's enterprise: If continuation promises the higher yield, the debtor's business ought to be continued. If termination promises a higher return, this option ought to be chosen.

Let us turn to the other column of the balance sheet, the liabilities and shareholders' equity. On this side the sources of money are identified, which were tapped in order to finance the debtor's investments. Among those funds are bank loans, bonds the debtor issued, credit extended by suppliers, and the various forms of shareholders' equity. The *second* decision that needs to be taken in an insolvency affects the liabilities side of the balance sheet. One has to decide how the proceeds generated by the asset deployment decision are to be distributed among the people who provided the funding of the debtor's enterprise. This is called the decision on asset distribution. Since in an insolvency it is, by definition, impossible for all claims against the debtor to be met completely, the distribution of proceeds comes down to a distribution of losses. By deciding on asset distribution one determines at the same time which claims remain totally or partially unsatisfied. Therefore, instead of asset distribution one may as well speak of loss distribution. Where the debtor's assets are sold (either as a going enterprise or piece by piece upon termination) cash will be distributed; where the business is continued in the ownership of the debtor, new equity or debt titles will be distributed.

The distinction between asset deployment and asset distribution has proved an extraordinary powerful analytical tool of insolvency law doctrine.[20] Vexing legal problems posed by security interests, setoffs, executory contracts, avoidance powers, and ecological cleanup orders are much better understood when analyzed through the lenses of this distinction. If one analyzes *solvent* enterprises, the distinction between assets and liabilities or, synonymously, between investment and financing is the universally accepted method used by business administration. It would be very difficult to explain why the legal system should ignore this distinction, especially when a business corporation fails.

With this distinction in mind, let us approach the conflict of laws rules. The thesis of my paper is that international insolvency law make use of this distinction and divide the subject matter accordingly. Two sets of questions need to be put forward. First: What national law should govern the asset deployment decision? Secondly: What national law should govern asset, or loss, distribution?[21]

---

[20]   This distinction was pioneered by Jackson, *The Logic and Limits of Bankruptcy Law*, 1986, 22–27, 57–67, and Baird, 'Loss Distribution, Forum Shopping, and Bankruptcy', 54 *The University of Chicago Law Review* 815 (at 819–820) (1987).

[21]   I derive my optimism that changes in the choice of law rules will improve the functioning of insolvency law in international cases in part from the words of Honsberger, 'The Canadian Experience', in: *Cross-Border Insolvency: Comparative Dimensions* (The Aberystwyth Insolvency Papers), 1990, 27 (at 39): 'The solution that would seem to offer the most hope at the present time is through the courts and by the modification and introduction of new conflict of laws rules. . . . It may be that

cont. ...

II. The Law Governing Asset Deployment

As regards asset deployment, conflict of laws has to determine which country's law should apply to the decision whether the bankrupt's enterprise will be terminated and dissolved or whether it will be continued as a going concern (under the control of the debtor or some other entity).

The *territorial model* is ill suited to guide the drafting of an appropriate choice of law rule. If the law applicable to the deployment of the debtor's assets were to be determined according to the territorial model, conflicts law would seriously distort the asset deployment decision. The option to continue the debtor's business would be greatly disadvantaged against the option to liquidate the business. In fact, the option to continue would hardly be available at all. Under the territorial approach the debtor's multinational business enterprise loses its central management in an insolvency. The central management is replaced by various insolvency trustees each of which is in charge of only a part of the enterprise. Each one has to look for the best deployment of the assets situated within the respective national borders. What happens in other countries can neither be foreseen nor influenced. In consequence, it is not unlikely that conflicting decisions will be rendered.

The option to rescue the debtor's enterprise as a going concern is not available to any of the trustees. Neither of them has the power and means to do so. This holds true of both forms of continuation: transfer to a new owner and reorganization of the debtor. With the management of the debtor's business scattered across various countries it will be very difficult to *sell* the entire enterprise. A potential buyer would have to deal with numerous trustees instead of one. It would be extremely difficult to fix values to single parts of the enterprise. A *reorganization* of the enterprise would face considerable obstacles, too. If the enterprise is to be continued in the ownership of the debtor, the debtor's liabilities need to be reduced. This is all but impossible if various national insolvency laws apply. Since the claims of the creditors are directed against the same person, they cannot be split up territorially. It is not possible to reduce the debtor's liabilities in one State by, say, 20%, in another State by 10%, and in a third State by 30%. A reduction of the debtor's liabilities can only be decreed by a single insolvency proceeding.[22] To sum up, the division of the debtor's assets along national borders advocated by the territorial model may prevent the debtor's business to be put to the economically most desirable use. Instead the decision is skewed towards the dissolution of the enterprise. In matters of asset deployment the territorial model with its local territorial insolvency proceedings seems profoundly misplaced.

---

the solutions to many of the problems of international insolvency are closer to hand than one may think.'

[22] Reinhart (supra note 13) 146–148 and 299–323.

If the option to stay in business shall be as readily available as the option to quit, only one national insolvency law must apply. Here, in matters of asset deployment, is the realm of the *universalist approach*. The decision how the debtor's assets shall be used in future, shall be made under the umbrella of a single insolvency law. One insolvency law should govern all issues of asset deployment.

There are two immediate consequences: First, the rules of the *lex fori concursus* should claim worldwide application. Secondly, the other states in which property of the debtor is situated should recognize the extraterritorial reach of the state of the primary proceeding by referring all issues of asset deployment to that country's law. This implies that local, secondary proceedings ought to be barred, or, at least, should apply the asset deployment law of the primary proceeding.[23]

This leaves the question *which* national law should have the sole authority in matters of asset deployment. Most states and international conventions vest the debtor's home state with jurisdiction to conduct the primary insolvency proceeding. 'Home state' is defined by the EU Insolvency Convention as the 'centre of the debtor's main interests' (EU Insolvency Convention, Art. 3 [1]), which is usually the place where the debtor corporation's management is located. However, this is not the only jurisdictional rule one can conceive of. Modern insolvency theorists advocate party autonomy in international insolvency law.[24] They believe that the owners of the firm are better positioned than governments to select the insolvency rule that maximizes firm value. This approach would extend the freedom of choice, which is the accepted choice of law rule for contractual obligations, to insolvency matters. It would be implemented by adding a provision to the corporate charter stating that the firm would file for bankruptcy only in a certain jurisdiction, which would then handle the bankruptcy proceeding according to its law. This choice would first be made at incorporation, and could be amended, subject to certain restrictions, as the structure of the firm changes. This proposal merits approval, provided it is confined to issues of asset deployment.

III. The Laws Governing Asset Distribution

We now shift focus to the second branch of insolvency law: the rules on asset, or loss, distribution. When a debtor becomes insolvent, it is, by definition, no longer able to pay off its entire debt. In this situation the relationship among

---

[23] Cf. the similar conclusion reached by Trautman (supra note 9), 29 *Harvard International Law Journal* 49 (at 57).

[24] Rasmussen, 'A New Approach to Transnational Insolvencies', 19 *Michigan Journal of International Law* 1 (at 4 et seq.) (1997).

creditors determines which creditor will be paid and to what extent. The distribution of the proceeds yielded by the deployment of the debtor's assets turns on the priority status a creditor has as against the other creditors. It is important to identify the legal sources that determine the rank of a creditor in relation to the other creditors. They lie outside insolvency law.[25] Let me give a few examples. That secured creditors enjoy priority to the debtor's assets, up to the value of their collateral, is a rule based in property law and not in insolvency law. That holders of subordinated bonds rank below ordinary unsecured creditors is the consequence of the loan agreement and not of insolvency law. That loans extended by shareholders to their corporation will under certain conditions be subordinated, is a rule developed in corporation law and not by insolvency law. That shareholders bear the residual risk and will get their investment back only after all creditors will have been paid completely, is (also) the subject matter of corporation law and not of insolvency law. It is non-insolvency law which determines the relative priorities among the debtor's financiers.

The relative priorities established under non-insolvency law continue to exist in insolvency. In international cases the relative priorities with which the creditors arrive at the bankruptcy proceeding should continue to be governed by the law under which they were established. Picture the following example: Debtor is a German corporation. It owns real estate in England which is mortgaged to an English bank. The priority the English bank enjoys when the value of the real estate is distributed in the German insolvency proceeding is, first of all, a matter of English law as this law governs the mortgage and the rights pertaining to it.

Of course, insolvency law may intervene and change the relative priorities established under non-insolvency law. One of the prominent changes ordered by bankruptcy law is the pro-rata-rule. It requires that those creditors whose claims are neither secured nor subordninated be paid pro rata in bankruptcy. The non-bankruptcy rule that the creditor who is first in initiating individual debt collection procedures has priority is superseded in bankruptcy. In international cases the question to be asked is: Which country's law should decide whether and, if yes, in which manner the creditors' relative priorities acquired under non-insolvency law should be altered due to the insolvency of the debtor. In other words, on the asset, or loss, distribution side of bankruptcy international insolvency law ought to determine the national law which should govern insolvency-related *interventions* into the priority system established before the debtor went bankrupt.

---

[25] See Jackson (supra note 20) 27–67; Baird (supra note 20), 54 *The University of Chicago Law Review* 815 (at 822–833); von Wilmowsky, *Europäisches Kreditsicherungsrecht*, 1996, 285–292 and 319–322.

1. Universalist Model

Again, let us consider the two general theories. The *universalist* model points to the law of the state where the (primary) insolvency proceeding has been commenced. Under this approach it is the *lex fori concursus* which decides whether and how the relative priorities (established under non-insolvency law) will be changed due to the insolvency of the debtor. The worldwide application of the rules on asset distribution is the rule in virtually all countries.[26]

Interventions on the part of the debtor's employees are a case in point. Under the universalist approach the insolvency law of the *lex fori concursus* decides whether or not employees get a better priority status in insolvency than outside insolvency. The place of employment does not matter. In a German insolvency proceeding any privileges accorded to employees extend to employees working in the debtor's plants in France, Spain, or Malaysia.[27]

The idea of universalism is entirely misplaced when it comes to loss distribution resulting from business failure.[28] The flaw of this approach is obvious: It is not the home state's business to care for all workers, all consumers, all tort victims of the debtor around the world. It is unwise to allow the *lex fori concursus* to monopolize the rules of asset, or loss, distribution. In fact most legislators share this critique. That the universalist model claims to apply not only to matters of asset deployment, but also to matters of asset distribution is the very reason why it failed in practice. Local insolvency

---

[26] No distinction is made between primary and secondary insolvency proceedings. If in a cross-border insolvency various insolvency proceedings have been commenced, each state applies its rules on asset distribution to those assets which happen to be on its territory. Although each proceeding seizes in-state assets only, it distributes the value of those assets to all creditors wherever located. See Bundesregierung, Begründung zum Entwurf einer Insolvenzordnung, Bundesrats-Drucksache 1/92, 237; Kuhn and Uhlenbruck (Lüer), *Konkursordnung*, 11th ed. 1994, §§ 237, 238 ¶ 104; cf. Reinhart (supra note 13) 282–285.—The same holds true of French international insolvency law; see Witz and Zierau, 'Französisches internationales Konkursrecht—Neue Tendenzen und Entwicklungen in der Rechtsprechung der Cour de cassation', *RIW (Recht der Internationalen Wirtschaft)* 1989, 929 (at 931).

[27] Cf. Bundesarbeitsgericht (Federal Supreme Court in Matters of Labor Law), 24 March 1992, *ZIP (Zeitschrift für Wirtschaftsrecht)* 1992, 1158. The Court applied German labor law to the agent of a German corporation, who was permanently working in France. A brief comment on this decision is made by Hanisch, *EWiR (Entscheidungen zum Wirtschaftsrecht)* 1992, 1011.

[28] As yet only few German legal authors reject universalism when it comes to loss distribution. Among them are Baur and Stürner, *Zwangsvollstreckungs-, Konkurs- und Vergleichsrecht, Band II: Insolvenzrecht*, 12th ed. 1990, ¶ 37.12; Trunk, *Internationales Insolvenzrecht*, 1998, 217–218, 394–397; Trunk, 'Arbeitnehmer im Niederlassungskonkurs: international-insolvenzrechtliche Aspekte', *ZIP (Zeitschrift für Wirtschaftsrecht)* 1994, 1586 (at 1589–1590)

proceedings or, in the case of the US, the denial of recognition of foreign proceedings in principle, are the means to fend off the distribution rules of a foreign *lex fori concursus*. It is not the asset deployment decision taken by the primary insolvency proceeding which other states are concerned about. They fear rather that the rules of the *lex fori concursus* on asset distribution will not comport with their own notions of distributive justice.[29] It is against this background that states resort to local, or secondary, insolvency proceedings: They grab the assets they can get (which are those situated within the national borders) and require them to be distributed according to their own rules.

2. Territorial Model

At this stage of the analysis one may be tempted to consider the following separation of functions: The universalist theory applies to all issues of asset deployment, whereas the *territorialist* model might direct us to the laws applicable to asset, or loss, distribution. There are indeed both court cases and academic writing which suggest that proceeds should be distributed according to the law of the country in which the funds originated.[30] If one takes workers as an example, their claims on outstanding wages would not be elevated to priority status as far as the distribution of assets located in Germany is concerned. (With the entry into force of the German Insolvency Act in 1999 workers in Germany no longer receive any priority treatment, but rather remain ordinary unsecured creditors.) The same claims would be privileged, however, when it comes to the distribution of the assets the debtor has in France. The Istanbul Insolvency Treaty of the Council of Europe embraces a somewhat similar approach by providing that creditors entitled to priority in distribution under local law should be paid from local assets, and what remains should be returned to the main proceeding, where the priorities of the main jurisdiction's law will prevail.[31]

---

[29] See, e.g., Hoffmann, 'Cross-Border Insolvency: A British Perspective', 64 *Fordham Law Review* 2507 (at 2510) (1996) (concerning less developed countries)

[30] In *Re Sefel Geophysical Ltd.*, 54 D.L.R. (4th) (Dominion Law Reports) 117 (1988), the (Canadian) Alberta Court of Queen's Bench had to decide on the distribution of the assets of a Canadian business enterprise which was subject to a Canadian insolvency proceeding. A major part of the debtor's assets was situated in the USA. The Court determined the share of the debtor's property which could be attributed to the US assets. This share was then distributed according to American law (instead of Canadian law). See Smart, *Cross-Border Insolvency*, 1991, 207–208, 248; Westbrook (supra note 3), 17 *Brooklyn Journal of International Law* 499 (at 512 n. 53) (1991) ('very interesting and creative approach to international insolvencies'). A similar proposal has been submitted by Reinhart (supra note 13) 318–321.

[31] See Westbrook, 'Developments in Transnational Bankruptcy', 39 *Saint Louis University Law Journal* 745 (at 756) (1995).

Of course, it is perfectly feasible to distribute each national part of the debtor's property pursuant to the rules of the respective *situs* state. Quite another question is why one would want to do so. The common explanation is that this is a way to protect domestic creditors. However, this defense does not withstand close scrutiny.[32] Most legal systems accord nondiscriminatory treatment to foreign creditors, not only in primary proceedings, but in local secondary proceedings as well. *All* creditors may file their claims in the local proceeding. Therefore local proceedings cannot be said to protect local creditors.

The territorial model is ill-suited to determine the national laws which decide on asset, or loss, distribution. One cannot perceive of any reason why the states in which assets of the insolvent debtor happen to be situated should decide on their distribution. When extending credit creditors do not rely on the debtor's domestic assets only. Rather, they place their confidence that the debtor will meet its obligations on its entire property and future earnings. There is no relationship between the liabilities a debtor has incurred and the place where it keeps its assets. Correspondingly, the local assets are not earmarked for local creditors only. Moreover, it is a myth to believe that the state in which assets of the debtor are located is responsible for those creditors who need and deserve help. Again, workers' claims may serve to clarify this point. The debtor's employees do not expect that it is the state in which assets of their employer are situated, which offers them protection in an insolvency proceeding. A worker employed at the (German) debtor's French production site will not expect that the insolvency law of Greece will offer him or her special protection in the case of an insolvency, merely because the employer sports a yacht in the Aegean sea or happens to have a mansion on a Greek island. The territorial approach is based on nothing else but naked power: The location of the debtor's assets is taken as a connecting factor (to determine the law applicable to asset distribution) solely because this state has the immediate power to grab those assets.

3.   Proposed Approach

Having discarded both the universalist model and the territorial model in matters of asset, or loss, distribution, we are left with the query for a more appropriate choice of law rule. The proposal I want to submit draws on the interventionist function of the loss distribution rules. Whenever insolvency law intervenes in order to change the relative priorities established under non-insolvency law, it does so in order to protect certain groups of creditors whom it considers to need and deserve protection. If this structure is mirrored in the conflict of laws, the

---

[32]   Westbrook, 'The Lessons of Maxwell Communication', 64 *Fordham Law Review* 2531 (at 2532) (1996); Westbrook (supra note 3), 17 *Brooklyn Journal of International Law* 499 (at 513–514) (1991).

groups of creditors on behalf of which insolvency law intervenes ought to be taken as points of reference (connecting factors). This leads to the following choice of law rule: The question whether or not such changes ought to be made should be addressed to the insolvency laws of those countries which are in charge of protecting the creditor group in question.[33]

Again, the employees of the debtor may serve as an example. Whether their claims to outstanding wages should be elevated in their priority status is for the insolvency law of that state to decide in which the workers are employed. The debtor's employees working in Germany should be treated according to the distribution rules of German insolvency law, irrespective of the state in which the assets to be distributed are located. The debtor's employees working in France, however, enjoy the priority status accorded them by French law; and this priority should extend not only to the debtor's assets in France, but to all assets wherever located.

Let me give some further examples: Figure a state which has a place in its heart for tort victims and therefore amends its insolvency statute by a provision stating that in the insolvency of the tortfeasor the victims shall enjoy priority over all other unsecured creditors (or even over the secured creditors as well). According to the model submitted here, this provision applies irrespective of the country in which the tortfeasor becomes subject to an insolvency proceeding. And it extends to all assets of the tortfeasor. The personal scope of application should be restricted, however: The provision should apply only where the tort was committed within the state or where the victim is a person the intervening state may legitimately claim to protect. All other tort victims of the tortfeasor should not fall within the provision's international scope of application.

Let us assume a (politically radical) country that harbors strong reservations against security interests. It therefore decides that in an insolvency the secured creditors should lose the privileges accorded them by non-insolvency law; rather all liabilities, including the secured, should be treated equally. Again, this provision may claim to apply extraterritorially to all assets of the debtor, be they within or beyond the national borders. The personal scope of application, however, has to be restricted to those unsecured creditors whom this state may protect. Thus, only those unsecured creditors residing within the state are covered. Distributions on their claims have to take account of the described intervention. They get the pro-rata-share of the entire property of the debtor including the assets pledged as collateral to secured creditors. Another example are the privileges which the insolvency statutes of virtually all countries accord to the expenses incurred in the (insolvency) administration of the debtor's property. This issue should be decided by the *lex fori concursus*.

Under the approach submitted here a variety of insolvency (distribution) laws may be applicable to interventions into the relationship among the debtor's

---

[33] For a more detailed treatment see von Wilmowsky (supra note 25) 318–338.

creditors which had been established under non-insolvency law. The application of interventions of various national laws may lead to conflicting demands. For example, one state may intervene on the part of the employees employed within its borders and require that their claims be accorded priority, whereas another state may make the same request for the product liability claims resulting from sales of the debtor's product within the country. In cases like this the *lex fori concursus* should supply the applicable law to decide the conflicts between irreconcilable distributive interventions. With respect to the substance of such rules, the insolvency (distribution) law of the *lex fori concursus* should place the applicable interventions on the same footing (which would entail that the beneficiaries of the colliding interventions share pro rata where the debtor's property even does not suffice for their claims).

D. Conclusions

The distinction between asset deployment and asset distribution should inform the choice of law rules for international insolvencies. This additive will boost their performance.

As regards issues of asset deployment only a single national law should apply. This is the asset deployment law of the country where the insolvency proceeding is opened (*lex fori concursus*). Its asset deployment law should claim worldwide application. Other states in which assets of the debtor are situated and secondary proceedings opened should refer all issues of asset deployment to the law of the primary proceeding. With respect to international jurisdiction, the debtor should be given the power to select, in its corporate charter, the state of the (primary) proceeding and, by implication, the applicable insolvency asset deployment law. In the absence of such choice jurisdiction shall be vested in the state where the debtor's seat is located.

Issues of asset distribution call for completely different conflict rules. As far as substantive insolvency law is concerned with asset distribution it intervenes into the priority system established among the debtor's creditors by non-insolvency law, and changes it according to its own notions of distributive justice. In international cases, neither the place of the insolvency proceeding nor the place of the debtor's assets should serve as the connecting factor, but rather the group of persons for whose benefit insolvency law intervenes. The personal scope of such measures has to be restricted: Each state may intervene for the benefit of those creditors only who it may legitimately claim to protect. The assets affected by such measures, on the other hand, need not be restricted: The distribution rules may claim to apply to the entire property of the debtor, not only the assets located within the country. Under the choice of law rules suggested here secondary proceedings are no longer necessary to safeguard the interests of other states. Their rules on asset distribution will be applied, within the proper personal scope of application, no matter where the insolvency proceeding has been opened.

THE RECOGNITION OF FOREIGN INSOLVENCY PROCEEDINGS AND PRIVATE INTERNATIONAL LAW

– An Analysis of the UNCITRAL Model Law on Cross-Border Insolvency from the Perspective of Private International Law –

by Toshiyuki Kono, Fukuoka

Contents

A.   Introduction

The Japanese Bankruptcy Law of 1922 (§ 3) and the Corporate Reorganization Law of 1952 (§ 4) adopt a strict principle of territoriality. Neither a Japanese bankruptcy (or reorganization) proceeding has effect in other countries, nor can a foreign proceeding be effective in Japan. Since this rigid position has become outdated in today's legal world, it has been criticized[1] and it is expected that this old-fashioned principle will be amended through the comprehensive reform work of the entire insolvency law system in Japan.[2]

In this reform process the UNCITRAL Model Law on Cross-Border Insolvency (the Model Law) will play an important role. The First Questionnaire on Insolvency, which was published by the Ministry of Justice in 1997,[3] seems to be partially based on the Model Law. Furthermore, since the deadline of the reform work is set for 2001, to adopt the Model Law would be the most effective way to change the current system in the present situation. The Model Law contains 32 provisions and its core is the Chapter 3, Recognition of A Foreign Proceeding and Relief.[4] Under the Model Law foreign insolvency proceedings are divided into main proceedings and non-main ones. Both types of foreign insolvency proceedings could be recognized in Japan (§ § 20 and 21). The Model Law admits concurrent proceedings and coordinates the effects of those proceedings (§ § 28 and 29). If Japan adopts this Model Law and foreign proceedings can be recognized, one result would be that already existing substantive legal relationships in Japan would be affected by the recognized foreign insolvency proceedings. Since the substantive legal relationships in an international context should be regulated by private international law such as the *Hôrei*, the code of private international law in Japan, it must be determined which rule of private international law would be applicable.

In order to do this, however, the effects of the recognition of the foreign proceeding should be confirmed; when a foreign insolvency proceeding is recognized, the following effects occur either automatically or by discretion of the court under § § 20 and 21 of the Model Law:[5] 1) staying of commencement or continuation of individual actions or individual proceedings or executions; 2) suspending of the right to transfer, encumber or otherwise dispose of debtor's assets; 3) providing for the examination of witness, the taking of evidence or the delivery of information concerning the debtor's assets, affairs, rights, obliga-

---

[1] See Katsumi Yamamoto, Japanisches internationales Insolvenzrecht, in Heldrich/ Kono (Hrsg.) Herausforderungen des Internationalen Zivilverfahrensrechts (cited below as Herausforderung) (1994) pp.137–162.

[2] This reform intends to modernize the whole insolvency law system in Japan which is, at present, divided into five different laws. One important point is the reform of provisions on international insolvency. See the contribution of Matsushita's in this volume.

[3] See appendix B of Matsushita's paper.

[4] For the text of the UNCITRAL Model Law on Cross-Border Insolvency (1997) with Guide to Enactment, see the web-site, http://www.uncitral.org/english/texts/index. htm.

[5] See Appendix.

tions or liabilities; 4) entrusting the administration or realization of all or part of the debtor's assets located in the enacting state to foreign representative; 5) extending relief of a provisional nature (§ 19 (1)); and 6) granting any additional relief. Also the right of avoidance should be included in this list, but only the standing to initiate actions to avoid acts detrimental to creditors is stipulated in § 23.

These provisions include some rules of private international law;

- § 20 (2) says that 'The scope, and the modification or termination, of the stay and suspension referred to in paragraph (1) of this article are subject to [refer to any provisions of law of the enacting State relating to insolvency that apply to exceptions, limitations, modifications or termination in respect of the stay and suspension referred to in paragraph (1) of this article]'. It means that upon recognition of main proceedings, the law of the enacting state is applicable to the scope, the modification or termination of the above mentioned effects 1) and 2). Although a contrary view to apply lex fori concursus was expressed in the legislative process of the Model Law, the law of the enacting state, in other words the law of the country of the court applied to was finally chosen.[6]

- According to § 21 (1) (g), upon recognition of a foreign proceeding, whether main or non-main, where necessary to protect the assets of the debtor or the interests of the creditors, the court may, at the request of the foreign representative, grant any appropriate relief, including granting any additional relief that may be available to [insert the title of a person or body administering a reorganization or liquidation under the law of the enacting State] under the laws of this State. Also here the law of the enacting state is the applicable law chosen by the Model Law.

- The applicable law to the above mentioned effects from 1) to 5) in § 21 is not stipulated in the Model Law. However it would be natural to interpret that, like § 21 (1) (g), the law of the enacting state governs also the effects from 1) to 5).

From this we can conclude that the Model Law chose the law of the enacting state, in other words the law of the court applied to as the applicable law to the effect of the recognition of foreign insolvency proceedings. The question for us is whether this choice is appropriate?

These effects are only a part of the effects brought about by the recognition of a foreign insolvency and the Model Law does not contain private international law rules for other important effects such as the right of avoidance. For these effects, the applicable law must be found. The second question for us, therefore, is which law should be applicable?

---

[6]   Kazuhiko Yamamoto, UNCITRAL *Kokusai Moderu Hô no Kaisetsu* (Commentary to the UNCITRAL Model Law on Cross-Border Insolvency), NBL No. 628, 629, 630, 634, 636, 637, and 638 (1998); No. 636, p. 54. See Appendix below.

These two questions will be answered in the section C.. Before going into section C., it might be helpful to reflect the discussion thus far on this topic in Japan.

B. International Private Law in the Context of Insolvency in Japan

The prevailing opinion in Japan has taken the position that *lex fori concursus* is the applicable law to major important issues in insolvency proceedings.[7] As its reasoning it is often suggested that the insolvency proceeding has the nature of a 'collective' procedure and that the law closely related to this proceeding should be therefore applicable. *Lex fori concursus* has the closest connection with the insolvency proceeding and should be applicable.[8] This reasoning is based on procedural considerations. However as long as the applicable law governs substantial legal relationships, the application of *lex fori concursus* should be justified also from the viewpoint of substantive laws.

A possible explanation for the choice of *lex fori concursus* would be rather that the interests of most creditors and other parties are usually concentrated in this forum and that various interests of many parties can be balanced well and fairly through applying *lex fori concursus*. The goal of insolvency proceedings, to collect the assets of an adjudicated bankrupt and to satisfy all creditors, can be achieved through *lex fori concursus* in the best form. Although some recent opinions suggest that the application of *lex fori concursus* should be avoided and that the general conflict of law rules should be applied also to the issues in insolvency cases,[9] the traditional approach should be adopted. *Lex fori concursus* does not have statutory background in Japanese law, but as long as it has a reasonably clear theoretical background, it should be acknowledged as the general rule of private international law in insolvency cases.

On the other hand, *lex fori concursus* is not the only applicable law. It should not be forgotten that there are certain people whose interests must be protected

---

[7] Kaichi Yamato, *Hasan* (Bankruptcy), in Japanese Association of International Law (ed.), Kokusaihô Kôza (Essays on International Law) ((1963) Vol. 3, S. 893.

[8] Katsumi Yamamoto, *Shôgaisei no aru Naikoku Tôsan Tetsuzuki no Shomondai* (Several Issues of Domestic Insolvency Proceedings with International Aspects), Minshôhô Zasshi (Journal of Civil and Commercial Law), Vol. 113 (1995), pp. 167–212; Shoichi Tagashira, *Gaikoku Hasan Tetsuzuki no Tainai teki Kôryoku to Gaikoku Kanzai'nin niyoru Hi'ninken no Kôshi* (The Effects of Foreign Bankruptcy Proceedings in Japan and Exercise of the Right of Avoidance by Foreign Trustee in Bankruptcy), in Okayama Daigaku Hôgaku Zasshi (Law Journal of Okayama University), Vol.44, No.1 (1994), p. 111.

[9] For example see Y. Hayakawa's paper in this volume.

separately from the collective insolvency proceeding and therefore some special rule of private international law ought to be created.

From this stance, the Model law should be examined.

C. The Effects Regulated under the Model Law and the Law of the Country of the Court Applied to

It is to be examined whether the law of the country of the court applied to is an appropriate applicable law to the above mentioned effects of 1) and 2).

I. Stay of Individual Action or Procedure

According to the Model Law, individual actions or executions would be stayed either automatically or by discretion of the court. The purpose of the stay is to protect the bankrupt's assets thereby serving the interests of all creditors. *Lex fori concursus* would therefore be suitable as the applicable law, since this law would represent the interests of the most parties. Moreover, since the scope and the modification or the termination of the stay are closely related to the stay itself, they should be governed by *lex fori concursus*. However, the Model Law chose the law of the country of the court applied to (§ 20 (2)). A possible explanation for this choice would be that this law could better protect the interests of parties in the action: the law of the country of the court applied to gives the trustee a better chance to react quickly and the estate can be better protected through such a speedy reaction. Thus the law of the country of the court applied to could be justified.

However even if a foreign insolvency proceeding can serve for both reorganization and liquidation such as the new German Insolvenzordnung and it cannot be confirmed at the beginning of the proceeding which function the foreign insolvency proceeding plays , according to the Model Law the Japanese court must apply the Japanese law. This means the Japanese court must choose one of the insolvency related laws[10] in Japan, either the Bankruptcy Law or the Arrangement Law. But it would not be easy. If the court should compare *lex fori concursus* and the laws in Japan to confirm which law in Japan would have the most similar function to that of *lex fori concursus*, the advantage of speedy reaction would be lost.

The law applicable to the scope of the stay should theoretically be *lex fori concursus*, since 'if' an action should be stayed and 'how wide' the scope of the stay would be are closely connected.

---

[10] See Katsumi Yamamoto, in Herausforderung p. 137.

Therefore the choice of the Model Law seems to me not perfectly persuasive. The law of the country of the court applied to is however reasonable only to govern the protection of the parties' trust to the judicial system, i.e. only in the case where the stay based on *lex fori concursus* is too foreign to the parties and their trust to the judicial system would be lost. In other words, the law of the country of the court applied to should be applicable only in such an exceptional case.

II.   Suspension of the Right to Transfer Assets of the Debtor

Transactions made by the bankrupt must be stopped to collect and administer the assets of the bankrupt. In a case where the assets are located in different places in the world, the effect of this stop should be uniformly determined. This consideration leads to the application of *lex fori concursus*. On the other hand, as long as there is no procedure to give notice that insolvency proceedings were commenced abroad, it must be taken into consideration how the other party of transactions could be protected. Since the system to protect the party in good faith varies from country to country, a uniform connecting point would not be practical. The law applicable to each transaction *(lex causae)* should therefore govern the protection of the party in good faith. The law of the habitual residence of this party could be another possibility to protect the party in good faith. However the protection here is different from that for consumers. As far as the party enters into a legal relationship with a foreign party, they should know in which circumstances they could be protected according to the applicable law to the transaction.

Instead of applying *lex fori concursus* and *lex causae* the Model Law chose the law of the country of the court applied to (§ 20 (2)). This can be justified only with the reasoning that this law, in fact, serves the better protection of the party in good faith than *lex causae* does. If the stay of a transaction is sought for in Japan, this transaction should usually have the center of gravity in Japan and therefore the applicable law would mostly be the Japanese law. *Lex causae* would be practically identical in most cases to the law of the country of the court applied to. The choice of the Model Law is therefore acceptable.

III.   The Scope of the Bankrupt's Estate

From the viewpoint of substantive legal relationships it is very crucial which properties of the bankrupt belong to the bankrupt's estate. In other words, it is the issue how wide the scope of the bankrupt's estate is. What would be the most suitable applicable law to the scope of the bankrupt's estate? Generally speaking it should be *lex fori concursus*. Since the scope of the estate is one of the most important matters in which all creditors would be interested and therefore the connecting point to this issue must represent the interests of all creditors. As far as the main proceeding is concerned, the scope of the bankrupt's estate should be governed by *lex fori concursus*. This should have been declared in the Model Law.

However, the purpose of collecting assets for all creditors does not apply to the non-main proceeding, since the non-main proceeding can only be admitted on the basis of the request from the insolvency practice and it usually focuses on the interests of local creditors.[11] Therefore, *lex fori concursus* could be less appropriate to non-main proceedings. According to the Model Law under § 21 (3) the court must be satisfied that the relief relates to assets that, under the law of this State, should be administered in the foreign non-main proceeding.... Assets administered in a foreign non-main proceeding must mean that the assets fall into the scope of this proceeding. Therefore, this provision is concerned with the issue of the scope of the estate. Since no provision in the Model Law clarifies how far the scope of non-main proceedings reaches, except the case in which a non-main proceeding in the enacting country is commenced after the recognition of a foreign main proceeding (§ 28[12]), it can be said that the Model Law presupposes in § 21 (3) that the scope of foreign non-main proceeding should be determined by applying the law of the country of the court applied to.

Since *lex fori concursus* is less appropriate in this case, the point is whether the law of the country of the court applied to is reasonable or not. I see no theoretical reason from the viewpoint of substantive law, but only practical reasons, i.e. to give convenience to the court. However, when the issue of the scope of a foreign proceeding comes up, it is most likely to be in cases where other proceedings are also pending. Since the Model Law has provisions to coordinate concurrent proceedings (§ § 29, 30[13]), the conflicts between different scopes of several proceedings can be adjusted with these provisions and the necessity to determine the scope of a foreign non-main proceeding would be very small. Therefore, the law of the country of the court applied to is acceptable.

IV. The Modification of Existing Contractual Relationships

The existing contractual relationships must be cancelled or terminated under certain circumstances upon recognition of a foreign proceeding. Under the Model Law the law of the country of the court applied to is applicable ('additional relief', § 21 (1) g). Two interests are conflicting here: to maintain the bankrupt's assets for all creditors and to protect the party to the contract.

---

[11] Kazuhiko Yamamoto, op.cit. NBL, No.629, p. 42.
[12] See Appendix below.
[13] See Appendix below.

Especially in certain types of contracts the parties need special protection. Therefore, this should be examined here according to the type of contract.

1.   Labor Contract

The interest to maintain the bankrupt's estate for all creditors would lead to the application of *lex fori concursus*. But it should not lead to an unexpected reduction of the protection of the employee. Therefore, a special rule should be created. Which law then is appropriate to protect the interests of the employee? The applicable law to the labor contract could govern the modification of the existing labor contract. However, this law could be the law chosen by the employer, because this law is more beneficial to the employer. Instead, the law of the place in which the employee effects his performance should be applicable, since this law reflects the expectation of the employee. In many cases where the modification or the termination of labor contracts comes up as an issue in Japan upon recognition of foreign proceedings, Japan would often be the place of the performance. Therefore, the law of the country of the court applied to under the Model Law would, in fact, be the most appropriate applicable law.

2.   Lease of Immovable Property

Also here the protection of the tenant must be taken into consideration. For this purpose *lex rei sitae* should be the applicable law. In addition to that, if *lex rei sitae* is not applied, the assets cannot be practically collected. In most cases where the modification of leases is sought by trustees in Japan, Japan would be the place where the objects of the leases are located. Therefore, the law of the country of the court applied to under the Model Law would practically be the appropriate applicable law.

3.   Agency

Bankruptcy of the agent or the principal may terminate the contract of agency or allow the trustee to cancel the contract. If the contract between the agent and the third party could be modified easily, the interests of the third party would be ignored. As long as no procedure for notification of the commencement of bankruptcy in other countries exists, the third party must be preferentially protected. For this purpose the most appropriate governing law would be the applicable law to the contract between the agent and the third party. This law is theoretically different from the law of the place of the agent's office or the law of the place in which the agent fulfills his obligation to the principal. However, they can often be identical. If the modification of the agency contract comes up as an issue in Japan upon recognition of a foreign proceeding, the agent would often have his office in Japan or effects his performance in Japan. Or the applicable law to the contract between the agent and the third party would often be Japanese law. Therefore, the law of the country of the court applied to under the Model Law would, in fact, be appropriate.

D. Other Effects and Applicable Laws:

I. The Separation of Property and Preferential Satisfaction

The separation of property belonging to a third party from the bankrupt's estate has the function to draw a line between creditors' interests and non-creditors' interests. *Lex fori concursus* would be an appropriate applicable law, since this issue is related to the interests of all creditors and this law represents the whole interests of the creditors. On the other hand, however, the separation from the bankrupt's estate is often based on rights *in rem* and these rights must be protected, since these rights are the basis of long term credit. Therefore, *lex rei sitae* is the more appropriate applicable law.

The function of preferential satisfaction is to distinguish certain creditors with preferential status from regular creditors. Since the issue here is how to adjust interests among all creditors, the applicable law to this issue could be *lex fori concursus*, as this represents the interests of all creditors. However, the preferential status is based on security rights and these rights are often the basis of long-term credit. If this preferential status were denied or changed by *lex fori concursus*, it would destroy the financial order of the country where the objects of the security right is located. Therefore, *lex rei sitae* should be applicable.

The Model Law does not contain any provision on the applicable law for the separation of property or to preferential satisfaction. The law of the country of the court applied to which is the favorite of the Model Law can, in fact, be an appropriate applicable law, when it is identical to *lex rei sitae*. It could be often confirmed, since the objects of the right must be located in Japan in many cases, when the separation or the preferential satisfaction comes up as an issue upon recognition of a foreign proceeding.

II. Set-off

Set-off has many functions such as a simple method of payment or saving of procedural energy and costs. However, the most important function from the viewpoint of private international law is the preferential payment. The point here is therefore to distinguish certain creditors from other creditors. Since it is an issue how to adjust the interests among all creditors, *lex fori concursus* would be an appropriate applicable law. On the other hand, the creditor who owes the bankrupt must be able to trust that his obligation is paid off with the obligation imposed on the bankrupt. This trust is protected differently in various countries and the change of this rule in each country would affect the financial order. Therefore, the applicable law to the obligation imposed on the creditor should be the applicable law instead *of lex fori concursus*.

The Model Law does not contain any rules for set-off. Would the law of the country of the court applied to, the favorite of the Model Law, be applicable? The country of the court applied to does not always have the closest connection with the obligation imposed on the creditor. Therefore it would not be appropriate for the case of set-off. A special provision, which governs the set-off issues in the case of bankruptcy, should be created; it should be the law applicable to the obligation imposed on the creditor.

III. The Right of Avoidance

The Model Law contains only a rule on the standing of the trustee for the action to avoid acts detrimental to creditors. No rule is stipulated to determine the governing law. The purpose of the right of avoidance is to protect and maintain the bankrupt's estate. The applicable law must reflect the interests of all creditors. In addition, the applicable law should be thus determined that the connecting point cannot be easily changed. The estate could be otherwise lost through the manipulation of the connecting point. Due to these reasons *lex fori concursus* should be the appropriate governing law of the right of avoidance. However, since the effect of avoidance could be drastic and the third party may be unexpectedly damaged by avoidance, the interests of the third party should be taken into consideration as well. This will be examined in the following three cases.

1.   Transaction of Immovable Property

The demand to protect the parties' interests under the contract concerning immovable is strong, especially when the parties entered into the contractual relationship before the commencement of the foreign proceeding. The trust that they had at the conclusion of the contract should not be ignored. Otherwise nobody would give credit based on immovable. *Lex rei sitae* should therefore be the governing law of the avoidance for the transactions of immovable. When the avoidance of an act concerning a real property is sought in Japan, this property will often be located in Japan. Therefore, the law of the country of the court applied to would, in fact, be appropriate.

2.   Procedural Acts

Can an action or an execution in Japan be avoided? Since the Model Law stipulates only the provisional stay of actions and executions, the applicable law should be determined to answer this question. The first consideration would be if avoidance could give rise to the violation of sovereignty. If Japan follows the principle of the Model Law and recognizes foreign proceedings, it could be interpreted that Japan takes the standpoint that sovereignty will not be an issue concerning foreign insolvency. What should be protected here is rather the trust of the parties in the judicial system. Avoidance would affect the parties' trust in the judicial system much more than any stay. This trust could be better protected *by lex fori* or *lex executionis* than *lex fori concursus* would do. These laws would often be identical to the law of the country of the court applied to.

3.   Acts between Third Parties

Whether a detrimental act for the bankrupt's estate committed by the third party can be avoided depends upon to what extent the trust of the third party should be protected. The best solution would be that the law applicable to the transaction, which may be avoided, governs the avoidance. However, it would allow the parties to choose a law which restricts the avoidance and then it would reduce the bankrupt's assets. Therefore, an applicable law that would not allow the manipulation should be chosen. The law of the country of the court applied to is perhaps less inappropriate than *lex fori concursus*, since this law is often closer to the parties than *lex fori concursus*. The better solution would be, however, a general clause, which allows avoidance in the case where the very close connection between the transaction and the country of the court applied to is proved through taking various elements of the individual case into consideration. The rationale is that it gives flexibility to the court and does not allow the manipulation of the connecting point.

E.   Conclusion

The Model Law contains private international law rules for certain effects of foreign insolvency proceedings. These rules refer to the law of the country of the court applied to. This is not always appropriate from the viewpoint of substantive law, especially when the applicable law must be determined for the issues which are related to the entire interests of all creditors. On the other hand, this law would, in fact, be appropriate for the protection of the interests of a third party or the financial order. However it does not apply only to set-off and the avoidance of acts done by a third party, since these acts have no close connection with a specific place.

Even if Japan adopts the Model Law, the significance of *lex fori concursus* should be confirmed and some special provisions should be created, although the law of the country of the court applied to will work well in many situations.

F. Appendix: UNCITRAL Model Law on Cross-Border Insolvency

§ 20. Effects of recognition of a foreign main proceeding:

(1) Upon recognition of a foreign proceeding that is a foreign main proceeding,

(a) commencement or continuation of individual actions or individual proceedings concerning the debtor's assets, rights, obligations or liabilities is stayed;

(b) execution against the debtor's assets is stayed; and

(c) the right to transfer, encumber or otherwise dispose of any assets of the debtor is suspended.

(2) The scope, and the modification or termination, of the stay and suspension referred to in paragraph (1) of this article are subject to [refer to any provisions of law of the enacting State relating to insolvency that apply to exceptions, limitations, modifications or termination in respect of the stay and suspension referred to in paragraph (1) of this article].

(3) Paragraph (1)(a) of this article does not affect the right to commence individual actions or proceedings to the extent necessary to preserve a claim against the debtor.

(4) Paragraph (1) of this article does not affect the right to request the commencement of a proceeding under [identify laws of the enacting State relating to insolvency] or the right to file claims in such a proceeding.

§ 21. Relief that may be granted upon recognition of a foreign proceeding

(1) Upon recognition of a foreign proceeding, whether main or non-main, where necessary to protect the assets of the debtor or the interests of the creditors, the court may, at the request of the foreign representative, grant any appropriate relief, including:

(a) staying the commencement or continuation of individual actions or individual proceedings concerning the debtor's assets, rights, obligations or liabilities, to the extent they have not been stayed under article 20 (1) (a);

(b) staying execution against the debtor's assets to the extent it has not been stayed under article 20 (1)(b);

(c) suspending the right to transfer, encumber or otherwise dispose of any assets of the debtor to the extent this right has not been suspended under article 20 (1)(c);

(d) providing for the examination of witness, the taking of evidence or the delivery of information concerning the debtor's assets, affairs, rights, obligations or liabilities;

(e) entrusting the administration or realization of all or part of the debtor's assets located in this State to the foreign representative or another person designated by the court;

(f) extending relief granted under article 19 (1);

(g) granting any additional relief may be available to [insert the title of a person or body administering a reorganization or liquidation under the law of the enacting State] under the laws of this State.

(2) Upon recognition of a foreign proceeding, whether main or non-main, the court may, at the request of the foreign representative, entrust the distribution of all or part of the debtor's assets located in this State to the foreign reprensentative or another person designated by the court, provided that the court is satisfied that the interests of creditors in this State are adequately protected.

(3) In granting relief under this article to a reprensentative of a foreign non-main proceeding, the court must be satisfied that the relief relates to assets that, under the law of this State should be administered in the foreign non-main proceeding or concerns information required in that proceeding.

§ 23. Actions to avoid acts detrimental to creditors

(1) Upon recognition of a foreign proceeding, the foreign representative has standing to initiate [refer to the types of actions to avoid or otherwise render ineffective acts detrimental to creditors that are available in this State to a person or body administering a reorganization or liquidation].

(2) When the foreign proceeding is a foreign non-main proceeding, the court must be satisfied that the action relates to assets that, under the law of this State, should be administered in the foreign non-main proceeding.

§ 28. Commencement of a proceeding under [identify laws of the enacting State relating to insolvency] after recognition of a foreign main proceeding

After recognition of a foreign main proceeding, a proceeding under [identify laws of the enacting State relating to insolvency] may be commenced only if the debtor has assets in this State; the effects of that proceeding shall be restricted to the assets of the debtor that are located in this State and, to the extent necessary to implement cooperation and coordination under articles 25, 26 and 27, to other assets of the debtor that, under the law of this State, should be administered in that proceeding.

§ 29. Coordination of a proceeding under [identify laws of the enacting State relating to insolvency] and a foreign proceeding

Where a foreign proceeding and a proceeding under [identify laws of the enacting State relating to insolvency] are taking place concurrently regarding the same debtor, the court shall seek cooperation and coordination under articles 25, 26 and 27, and the following shall apply:

(a) When the proceeding in this State is taking place at the time the application for recognition of the foreign proceeding is filed,

(i) Any relief granted under article 19 or 21 must be consistent with the proceeding in this State; and

(ii) If the foreign proceeding is recognized in this State as a foreign main proceeding, article 20 does not apply;

(b) When the proceeding in this State commences after recognition, or after the filing of the application for recognition, of the foreign proceeding,

(i) Any relief in effect under article 19 or 21 shall be reviewed by the court and shall be modified or terminate if inconsistent with the proceeding in this State; and

(ii) If the foreign proceeding is a foreign main proceeding, the stay and suspension referred to in paragraph 1 of article 20 shall be modified or terminated pursuant to paragraph 2 of article 20 if inconsistent with the proceeding in this State;

(c) In granting, extending or modifying relief granted to a representative of a foreign non-main proceeding, the court must be satisfied that the relief relates to assets that, under the law of this State, should be administered in the foreign non-main proceeding or concerns information required in that proceeding.

§ 30. *Coordination of more than one foreign proceeding*

In matters referred to in article 1, in respect of more than one foreign proceeding regarding the same debtor, the court shall seek cooperation and coordination under articles 25, 26 and 27, and the following shall apply:

(a) Any relief granted under article 19 or 21 to a representative of a foreign non-main proceeding after recognition of a foreign main proceeding must be consistent with the foreign main proceeding;

(b) If a foreign main proceeding is recognized after recognition, or after the filing of an application for recognition, of a foreign non-main proceeding, any relief in effect under article 19 or 21 shall be reviewed by the court and shall be modified or terminated if inconsistent with the foreign main proceeding;

(c) If, after recognition of a foreign non-main proceeding, another foreign non-main proceeding is recognized, the court shall grant, modify or terminate relief for the purpose of facilitating coordination of the proceedings.

INDEX

asset deployment 203–206, 208, 209, 212
asset distribution (→loss distribution)
avoidance of law 142
avoidance of transactions 156, 179, 183, 185, 190–192, 194, 204, 215, 222, 223

banking crisis (Japan) 70, 71, 76
bankruptcy 159, 160–162, 164–173, 177, 180, 181, 183, 185, 186, 188, 189, 191–194, 199, 201, 202, 206, 207, 214, 220, 222
bankruptcy law 157, 160, 161, 164–170, 172, 173, 207, 213, 217
basic laws (Japanese) 74, 76
Berne Convention (on copyright infringement) 57–59, 61, 63, 65
Big Bang 25, 70, 71, 73–76, 134
bond(s) 23, 82, 133–135, 137–142, 144–147, 204, 207
bondholders meeting 139, 147
borderless enterprise 20
bureaucracy 74, 75

capital market(s) 3, 21, 79, 80, 85, 86, 88–91, 93, 94, 100, 106–109, 112–114, 122, 123, 133
choice of law 5, 8, 9, 31, 50–52, 58, 59, 61, 63, 64, 90, 156, 169, 170, 171, 173, 197, 198, 202–206, 210, 212
commercialism 29, 30–32

Commissioned Company(ies) 134, 135, 137–139, 141–147
communication(s) 3, 6, 17–21, 24, 25, 26, 28, 42, 45, 50, 58, 59, 62, 63, 83, 91, 156, 159
competition 2, 10, 40, 43, 78, 85, 86, 88, 90, 100–102, 104, 106–109, 111, 114, 115, 123
competition law 10, 40, 43, 90
conflict of laws 4, 6, 8, 10, 57, 97, 143, 144, 146, 183, 185, 186, 191, 204, 205, 210
Convention on Insolvency Proceedings 154, 198, 199, 202
cooperation 25, 32, 78, 92, 99, 100, 107, 115–123, 152, 153, 155, 156, 159, 168, 177, 185, 194, 195, 201, 225, 226
copyright 40, 41, 44, 49, 50, 57–59, 61–65
corporate finance 133, 134, 147
corporate reorganization 152, 159, 161, 162, 167, 168, 170, 202, 203, 205, 214, 215, 217, 225
Corporate Reorganization Act 157, 161, 167, 171, 213
Corporate Reorganization Law 157, 161, 213
credit card(s) 14, 16
criminal law 40
cross-border insolvency 152, 155, 158, 176, 177, 179, 183, 185, 186, 190, 193, 194, 208
cross-border torts 52

DATE DUE FOR RETURN